The Enthusiasts' Guide to
Buying a Classic British Sports Car

The Major Manufacturers' Models launched between 1945 and the early 1980s

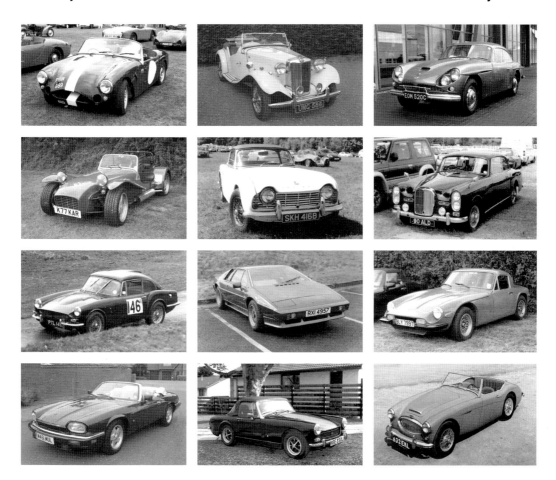

Researched & Written by Peter Hingston

With assistance from Philip Gundy

Front Cover (left to right):
Sunbeam Alpine; Jowett Jupiter; MGB Roadster;
Lotus Elan Sprint; Daimler SP250 Dart; Triumph TR3A;
Jaguar E-Type S2; TVR 3000M; Gilbern Genie;
Aston Martin V8; Morgan Plus 8; Austin-Healey 3000.

Above (left to right):
Fairthorpe Electron Minor; MG TD; Jensen C-V8;
Caterham 7; Triumph TR4; Alvis TE21;
Reliant Sabre 6; Lotus Turbo Esprit; TVR Taimar;
Jaguar XJS Convertible; MG Midget; Austin-Healey 3000.

This book is dedicated to the many classic sports car owners, enthusiasts, clubs and specialists, who all help to keep these wonderful cars alive today and for tomorrow, preserving this important aspect of our motoring heritage.

Copyright © 2007 by Peter Hingston.

Peter Hingston has asserted his right to be identified as the author of this work.

All rights reserved worldwide. No copying permitted. With the exception of quoting brief passages for the purposes of review, no part of this publication may be reproduced without prior written permission from the publisher.

Published by Hingston Publishing Co., Honeymoor Lodge, Eaton Bishop, Hereford HR2 9QT, England.
Website: www.hingston-publishing.co.uk
E-mail: Hingston@btinternet.com

Printed by Craft Print Ltd, Singapore.

ISBN: 978-0-906555-25-5

I would first like to thank several key people who helped me to create this book. First, a big thanks to my wife, Charlotte, who together with our children, Daniel and Corrie, have had to put normal life on hold for several years, especially during the closing months of the book. Charlotte also proofread the text with great care and suggested many useful improvements. In addition, her design background has proved invaluable with the page layouts and cover design. Over the many years it has taken me to research and write this book, her support and encouragement has been vital to the success of the project.

Next, a special thanks to Philip Gundy who helped guide me regarding the book's scope and content, read my drafts and commented both critically and knowledgeably, helped with car photo shoots and often liaised with the clubs on my behalf. Philip has an amazing archive of classic car material to which he kindly allowed me full access.

Finally, a special thanks too to Fiona Madison who helped with initial research, and scanned and worked skilfully with the many photos in this book (a big task in itself). Fiona also assisted with the typesetting, proofreading and the 101 other jobs that crop up in a large book project.

The production of this book has drawn on the expertise of a large number of people who have kindly helped in small or large measure. Attempting to get the huge number of facts correct in this book has been an enormous task but I have been heartened by the kind and often enthusiastic help of many individuals, classic sports car owners and clubs (as listed below). Their assistance with providing information, answering my questions, reading draft texts and making suggestions have all improved my original text immeasurably. My heartfelt thanks to you all. I must add that responsibility for the final text remains entirely with myself. (Listed here alphabetically, by marque, club, then name).

AC	John Goose, Andy Shepherd, Mike Smith, Bryan Spooner, Robin Stainer, Simon Taylor of the AC Owners' Club.
Allard	David Hooper and Jim Tiller of the Allard Owners' Club.
Alvis	David Culshaw (author of *Alvis Three Litre In Detail*); David Larkin of the Alvis Owner Club; Alex & Nick Simpson of Earley Engineering Ltd, Alvis Specialists of Abergavenny, UK.
Arkley	Fleur Britten; Terry Horler of the Midget & Sprite Club (and author of *Original Sprite & Midget*).
Aston Martin	Terry Dutton; Neil Murray of the Aston Martin Heritage Trust.
Austin	Tony Eades of the Austin Counties Car Club.
Austin-Healey	John Harper and Mell Ward of the Austin-Healey Club; Bill Cummings of the Healey Drivers' Club; Terry Horler of the Midget & Sprite Club (and author of *Original Sprite & Midget*).
Berkeley	Ray Bell, Nigel Halliday and Michael Rounsville-Smith of the Berkeley Enthusiasts' Club; Ray Powell.
Bond	Bob Buckby and Pat Taylor of the Bond Owners' Club; Les Gore of The Bug Club.
Bristol	Michael Barton, Geoffrey Herdman, Kevin Jones and Christopher Smithies of the Bristol Owners' Club, and a special thanks to the club for permitting me to use information from their website.
Buckler	Chris Johns of the Buckler Car Register.
Caterham	Adrian Elkin, Andrew Walker and Steve Winterberg of the Lotus Seven Club.
Clan	Jim McEwan and Dave & Joan Williamson of the Clan Owners' Club; Bob Allan of the Imp Club; Fred Brooks.
Daimler	David Nancekievill and Wilf Stephens of the Daimler SP250 Owners' Club.
Davrian	John Rawlins of the New Davrian Register; Bob Allan of the Imp Club.
Dellow	David Haley of the Dellow Register.
DeLorean	Chris Parnham of the DeLorean Owners' Club.
Elva	Roger Dunbar of the Elva Owners' Club.
Fairthorpe	The late John Allan (author of *Fairthorpe Cars*), Charles Armstrong-Wilson and Willie Simpson of the Fairthorpe Sports Car Club.
Frazer Nash	James Trigwell of the Frazer Nash Car Club.
Gilbern	Philip Ivimey of the Gilbern Owners' Club.
Ginetta	Dennis Featherstone and Trevor Pyman (Ginetta author) of the Ginetta Owners Club; Spadge Hopkins of Cottage Classics Ltd; Bob Allan of the Imp Club.
Gordon-Keeble	Charles Giles, Paul Marshall and David Yeomans of the Gordon-Keeble Owners' Club.
Healey	Roger Crouch and John Jaap of the Association of Healey Owners.
HRG	Ian Dussek and Peter Mitchell of The HRG Association.
Innocenti	Terry Horler of the Midget & Sprite Club (and author of *Original Sprite & Midget*).
Jaguar	John Burton, Mick Duffy and Roger Whalley of the Jaguar Drivers' Club; Norman Hicks and Paul Sinnott of the Jaguar Enthusiasts' Club; Philip Porter of the Jaguar XK Club.
Jensen (& J-Healey)	Dave Barnett, David Booth, Richard Calver, Richard Lovell-Butt, Tony Marshall, David Newby, Alan Smith, Dave Turnage, Peter Wallis, Chris Walton and Mike Williams of the Jensen Owners' Club.
Jowett	John Blaze, Eric Firth and Edmund Nankivell of the Jupiter Owners' Auto Club.
Lea-Francis	Jim Jenkins, Ron Robinson and Robin Sawers of the Lea-Francis Owners' Club.
Lenham	Terry Horler of the Midget & Sprite Club (and author of *Original Sprite & Midget*).

ACKNOWLEDGEMENTS

Lotus	Malcolm Ricketts of Club Elite;
	Alan Morgan of Club Lotus (also Brian Buckland for Elan production figures);
	Mike Marsden of the Historic Lotus Register;
	John Bulley, Arthur Clarke, Steve Jarvis and Mike Stripe of the Lotus Drivers' Club;
	Adrian Elkin, John W. Watson (Lotus Seven Register) and Steve Winterberg of the Lotus Seven Club.
Marcos	Isobel Chivers of Club Marcos International;
	Rory MacMath of Marcos Heritage;
	Richard Partridge and Roger Young of the Marcos Owners' Club;
	Maurice Williams and John Webster (Marcos Mantis & Mirage).
MG	Barrie Jones and Stewart Penfound of the MG Car Club's T Register; Frank Burry, George Dutton and Andy Sargent of the MGA Register; Nigel Pratt of the Midget Register; Bernard Rengger of the MGB Register; Victor Smith of the V8 Register; Ginny Cartmell of the MGC Register; also MGC GT owner, Barrie Sharples; Harry Crutchley of the MG Octagon Car Club;
	John Gill, Jonathan Kimber, Richard Ladds, Richard Monk, Roger Parker of the MG Owners' Club;
	Terry Horler of the Midget & Sprite Club (and author of *Original Sprite & Midget*).
Mini Jem	Richard Porter of the Mini Marcos Owners' Club; Rob Statham.
Mini Marcos	Roger Garland of the Mini Marcos Owners' Club.
Morgan	Charles Morgan of the Morgan Motor Co Ltd;
	Brian Downing, Neil Moorcraft, Charles Ritchie, Gordon Stemp, Roger Tatton of the Morgan Sports Car Club.
Panther	Terry Borton, Roger Burn and Graham Milligan of the Panther Car Club;
	George Newell of the Panther Enthusiasts' Club.
Peerless	Nigel Cluley of the Peerless and Warwick Owners' Register.
Piper	Barry Miller of The Piper Sports and Racing Car Club.
Reliant	Phil Howard, Allan Inwood, Jim King and Jerry Ree of the Reliant Sabre & Scimitar Owners' Club;
	David Womack of DWR Norfolk.
Riley	Nigel Trotman of the Riley RM Club.
Rochdale	Derek Bentley of the Rochdale Owners' Club.
Singer	Bill Haverly and Barry Paine of the Association of Singer Car Owners;
	David Freeth and Martin Wray of the Singer Owners' Club.
Sunbeam	Simon Edwards, Keith Hampson and Roy Winters of the Sunbeam Alpine Owners' Club;
	John Badger of the Sunbeam Talbot Alpine Register;
	Graham Vickery of the Sunbeam Tiger Owners' Club.
Swallow	Ken Yankee of the Swallow Doretti Register.
Tornado	Dave Malins of the Tornado Register; Rob Statham.
Trident	David Rowlinson of the Trident Car Club.
Triumph	Derek Pollock of Club Triumph;
	John Craddock of the Stag Owners' Club;
	Chris Cunnington, Mike Ellis, Roger Ferris, Derek Graham, Jon Marshall, Malcolm Paris of the TR Register;
	Belinda Gilby and Karl Wetherell (Triumph Italia);
	Bob Fitsall of the Triumph Roadster Club;
	Richard Briscoe, Nigel Clark, Colin Lindsay, Guy Singleton & Suzie Singleton of the Triumph Sports Six Club.
Turner	Russell Filby of the Turner Register and Peter Tutthill (author of *Turner Sports Cars*).
TVR	Stewart Halstead and Martin Lilley of TVR Engineering Ltd (1978 interviews);
	Ralph Dodds of the TVR Car Club.
Warwick	Nigel Cluley of the Peerless and Warwick Owners' Register.

General

I would also like to thank the following people and organisations for their help (in alphabetical order): Richard Brotherton at the British Motor Industry Heritage Trust Archives; Anders Clausager at the Jaguar Daimler Heritage Trust Archives; John Hingston for last-minute suggestions and help with checking sample sports cars; Mike Horne for help with UK car registration suffix and prefix letters; Bryan Meredith for allowing us to subject his MGB GT to our 100-point Checklist; Tim Sutton at the Rootes Archive Centre Trust; Elizabeth Woolfall for early research and finally the staff at the Birmingham Central Library and the National Library of Wales, Aberystwyth.

Photographs

Over half the photos in this book were taken by myself between the mid-1970s and 2007. I am very grateful to the many individuals and organisations that have provided all the remaining photos. The photos selected for this book are a mix of period and more recent shots – the cars don't change, only the fashions! Most of the photos have not been published before. A detailed list of Photo Credits appears on page 182, but I would like to thank the many photo contributors here (listed by marque then model): **AC:** Buckland from Mike Smith; period Cobra photos from the Ford Motor Co.; 428 and 3000ME from Graham Murrell; 428DHC from Linzi Smart. **Allard:** Palm Beach from Jim Tiller. **Alvis:** many photos on p23-24 are reproduced by permission of Earley Engineering Ltd, Alvis Specialists of Abergavenny, UK; Alvis on p166 from David Culshaw. **Aston Martin:** Many photos were supplied by the Aston Martin Heritage Trust. **Austin-Healey:** Sprite H-AN9 from Stuart Watson. **Berkeley:** Berkeley Enthusiasts' Club. **Bond:** Some Equipe photos supplied by the Bond Owners' Club, reproduced with kind permission of the British Motor Industry Heritage Trust; Bond Bug from Dave Bosworth. **Bristol:** 400 from Ashley James; 404 and 405 from the Bristol Owners' Club. **Caterham:** Caterham Cars and Nigel Riches. **Clan:** Clover from the Clan Owners' Club. **Daimler:** Some photos from Chris Dalton and David Nancekievill. **Dellow:** The Dellow Register. **DeLorean:** Crathes Castle photo from Jim Henderson AMPA. **Elva:** Fred Talmadge. **Fairthorpe:** Charles Armstrong-Wilson. **Frazer-Nash:** James Trigwell. **Gilbern:** Estate from the Gilbern Owners' Club. **Gordon-Keeble:** Charles Giles and Paul Marshall. **Healey:** G Series by Peter Galea, from David Culshaw. **HRG:** Peter Mitchell. **Jaguar:** Some XJS photos from Norman Hicks, Paul Sinnott and Roger Whalley. **Jensen:** Many of the photos from Nic Cooper Photographer; one historic 541 photo supplied by the Jensen Owners' Club. **Lea-Francis:** Rear cover photo by Michel Zumbrum (copyright Andre Wallimann). **Lenham:** From David Matthews of World Wide Austin-Healeys. **Lotus:** MkVI by AE (Nobby) Burch, supplied by the Historic Lotus Register; Type 47 from Martin Ricketts; Plus 2, Eclat & Esprit photos from Lotus Cars; Eclat from Malcolm Cowle; many of the Lotus Elite photos from Mike Stripe; Excel from Kate Ramsden. **MG:** Arnolt from Stewart Penfound; MGA 1500 Coupé from the MG Car Club; MGB Mk1 from Brian Pamment; MGC GT Downton from Barrie Sharples. **Panther:** Later J72 and S1 Lima photos from the Panther Car Club. **Reliant:** Most photos from Jerry Ree at www.magpiemicros.co.uk **Riley:** RMD from Gwyn Morris. **Sunbeam:** Alpine SV rear from Simon Edwards; Harrington from Derek Hewitson; two Tiger photos from Graham Vickery of the Sunbeam Tiger Owners' Club; Tiger rear from the National Motor Museum/MPL. **Trident:** Venturer from David Rowlinson. **Triumph:** TR6 rear from Derek Graham (TR Register); Grinnall from Phil Horsley (Grinnall Register). **Tornado:** Typhoon from Roberto Vespa. **Turner:** 950 Sports from Russell Filby (Turner Register). **TVR:** Many photos from Ralph Dodds of the TVR Car Club; 1600M from Joan Marsh.

In addition, my grateful thanks to Richard Monk of the MG Owners' Club for supplying a number of splendid MG images in attractive settings. Also thanks to Ted Walker (Ferret Fotographics), who has supplied some historic photos of various models and a big thanks to Philip Gundy who has kindly supplied over 20 carefully taken photos for this book. A major provider of superb, period, photos has been the British Motor Industry Heritage Trust at Gaydon, and a special thanks to the Picture Library Manager, Lynda Clark, for her conscientious help.

I would also like to thank the many car owners who most kindly and patiently helped us to photograph their cars. Many also contributed to our knowledge base by answering our many technical questions. I have listed their names here by marque then model: AC Greyhound (Nigel Price); AC Cobra (John Norris); AC 3000ME (John Spencer); Aston Martin V8 (Terry Dutton); Austin-Healey 100 BN1 (AA Laferla); Austin-Healey 100-Six (John Chiplin); Austin-Healey 3000s (Mike Hewitt, Chris Kettel, Derek Wilkinson); Austin-Healey Sprite MkIV (Andy Chatwin); Bond Bug (Les Gore); Bond Equipe GT (WR Pounds); Bond Equipe GT4S (Pat Taylor); Bond Equipe 2-Litres (David Abbitt, Cleo Laine, Ron Winstanley); Clan Crusader (Steve Fenner); Daimler Dart (Chris Dalton, Wilf Stephens); Gilberns (Stephen Arnold, Tony Bull, Stephen Szyplinski); Ginetta G15 (Nykola Taylor); Jaguar XK150S (John Davenport); Jaguar E-Types (Paul Cogdon, Jim Griffiths, Ray Searles); Jaguar XJ-S (Geoff Griffiths); Jaguar XJS (John Roach); Jensen Interceptor (Alan Smith); Jensen FF (Dave Perkins); Jowett Jupiters (Eric Firth, David Kennedy); Lea-Francis (Jim Jenkins, Ron Robinson); Lotus 7 S4 (Mal Hill); Lotus Elan (John Bulley, John King); Lotus Plus 2 (Arthur & Barbara Clarke); Lotus Europa (Steve Jarvis); Lotus Eclat Riviera (Paul Howarth); Lotus Excel (Mark Aston, Paul Fry); Marcos Mantis (John Webster); MGA (John Gill); MG Midget (E. Tedstone); MGB (Graham Gatenby, Philip Gundy); MGB GT Costello (Roger Key); Morgan 4-4 (Percy Powell); Morgan Plus 4 (Gordon Stemp); Morgan 4/4 (William Cuthbert); Morgan Plus 8s (Neil Moorcraft, Charles Ritchie); Panther Lima (Graham & Catherine Milligan); Panther Kallista (Terry Borton); Reliant Scimitar GTE SE5A (Christopher Marsh); Singer Roadsters (Richard Batchelor, Ray Webster); Sunbeam Alpine (John Badger); Sunbeam Alpines (Marie Loxston; Ian Merryweather, Fred Openshaw); Sunbeam Tiger (Paul Clayson); Swallow Dorettis (Roger Giles, Graham Weare); Triumph Roadster (Martin Newman); Triumph GTR4 (Gary Scott); Triumph TR6 cockpit (Rob Wilsher); Triumph Spitfire MkIV (Mrs Hutchinson); Triumph Stags (Michael Ford, Paul Wright); TVR Vixen S2 (Mike Rayment); TVR 2500M (Craig Polly); TVR3000M (Ian Boddington). As I took my photos over a 30-year period, I regret I have either forgotten the name or perhaps never knew the name of every owner who helped me.

Books: Part of my research has involved reading a large number of books (or parts thereof) on specific marques or models. There are some excellent books available and these are often mentioned on club websites or are well known to club members. I recommend these books to you if you want to get to know more about a specific marque or model. Some books are now out-of-print but you may still be able to get a second-hand copy through the club or try: www.amazon.co.uk
If you want to read contemporary road tests, www.Brooklands-Books.com publish compilations of road tests for most models.

Magazines: Another useful source of information is the motoring magazines that cater for classic sports cars, in particular: *Classic & Sports Car, Classic Car, Classic Car Mart, Classic Car Weekly, Classic Motor Monthly* and *Practical Classics.*

Apology: I hope I have remembered to include everybody but if for some reason I have omitted anyone who ought to be mentioned, or if I have misspelled anyone's name, first my sincere apologies and second, do please let me know so I can correct that error in any future edition. Thank you.

This book is a sequel to one I wrote and published myself over 25 years ago. Its title was "Guide to Buying a Used Sports Car" and though it was only a modest booklet, it received good reviews. With the passage of time, the cars I wrote about have become "classics" and I decided to write this rather more ambitious guide.

The purpose of this book is to provide a reasonably comprehensive buyer's guide to classic British sports cars from the major manufacturers since 1945.

This book is not simply a compilation of previously published information but includes much new material, generously provided by well over two hundred enthusiasts. This new information includes revised production figures for some models, estimates of numbers of survivors for many models and a wealth of suggestions as to what to look for when checking cars.

My photography for this new book has been done intermittently since the late 1970s, while the final research and writing has taken me well over three years full-time, but I have greatly enjoyed the task. What has added to this pleasure is the help and encouragement I have received from hundreds of classic sports car enthusiasts. I am indebted to them all.

Which Sports Cars Are Included?

The Cassell Concise English Dictionary defines a **sports car** as a "low, usually two-seater, car built for high speed performance". This is a good starting point, but I have tried to cast the net wider to include as many models as sensibly possible, including cars that could be classed as "sports tourers". However, any selection will inevitably include some cars that a reader may not consider to be "sports cars" and exclude others that a reader might feel should be included. Any selection is therefore bound to be in part subjective, but I hope the models covered will meet with general approval.

In terms of what constitutes a "classic car", I have simply taken the usually accepted 25-year figure as the basis for inclusion, the relevant date being when a model was launched. Hence I include cars launched prior to 1982, (plus a few appropriate later models).

As this book covers principally the major British production sports car manufacturers, to be included a manufacturer must generally have built at least one model which had sales of more than 500 vehicles. I have made some exceptions for completeness.

Excluded from this book are prototypes, replicas, sports-racers, kit cars, beach buggies and tuned versions of standard saloon cars, but the exclusion list is not set in stone and again for completeness I have included a few models that breach these "rules".

This book has been written principally for a British reader, however as a huge number of the cars referred to in this book were exported, information regarding modifications made to such export cars has been included.

Accuracy of Data

When researching this book, my colleague Philip Gundy and I found a surprising number of errors and conflicts of information in published sources (books, magazines and websites). With the help of many classic sports car owners, the car owners' clubs, manufacturers, libraries and car Heritage centres we have tried to sort out the facts, but try as we might, doubtless some errors will have crept into this book too. There are many thousands of discrete pieces of information in this book, so even if we are correct for 99.9% of the time, it means we still have errors somewhere, so I beg readers' forbearance.

In future editions I am keen to eliminate any errors, so if you think you have spotted one, do please write or e-mail me, but please provide the appropriate evidence to substantiate your suggestion. Ideally this should be from primary sources, such as your own first-hand experience, manufacturer's literature or accurately dated photographs.

My contact address is given at the foot of page 2. I will endeavour to reply to all letters and e-mails, but please accept there may be a delay before you hear from me.

Owning sports cars has given me much pleasure over the years and I hope this book may encourage others to purchase their first classic British sports car (or perhaps add to their existing car collection).

Peter Hingston

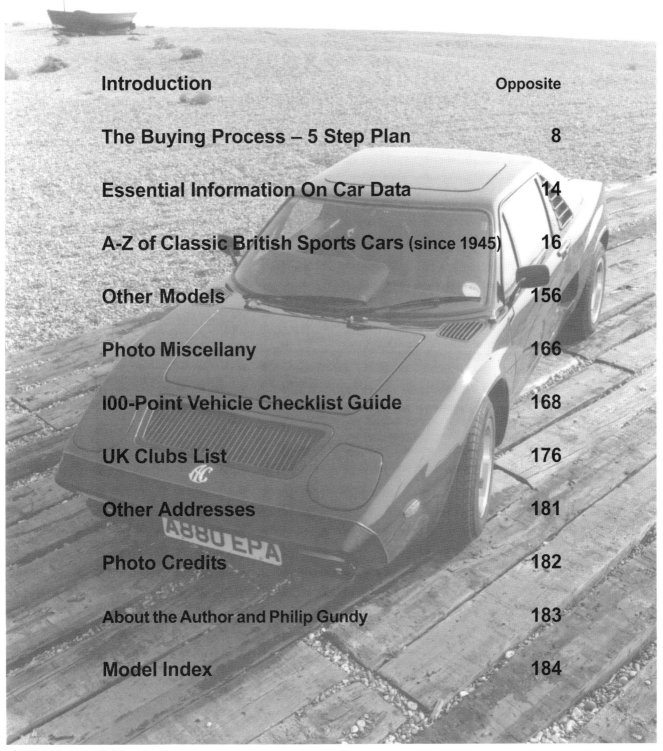

AC 3000ME. Photograph by Graham Murrell.

The buying process with a classic sports car typically has five steps: (1) choosing which model to buy; (2) searching for suitable examples; (3) checking likely cars; (4) buying a car, and (5) the finale. It sounds a deceptively simple process, but of course, it usually is not, particularly if you are going to do it properly.

This chapter on the buying process and the 100-point Vehicle Checklist (which comes later in the book) has been written assuming the buyer has little prior technical knowledge of cars. Experienced enthusiasts may therefore choose to use this chapter and the Checklist as useful aide-memoires.

STEP 1: CHOOSING WHICH MODEL TO BUY

From the following A-Z of sports cars, make a wish list. To learn more about specific models go to classic car shows to see the cars, quiz the owners and make contact with the appropriate clubs. In addition to the obvious criteria, such as whether you want a 2 or 4-seater, a fixed-head or a drophead, here are some other points to consider:

Insurance: It is advisable to check the likely insurance cost of your dream car before you buy one, especially if you are young, have a record of recent claims or you do not have a "clean" driving licence. Contact specialist insurance brokers who know these types of vehicle. You will find their advertisements in the classic car magazines, or ask club members for their recommendations.

Clubs: It is useful to choose a model that has an active owners' club. These clubs can be founts of knowledge. They usually know of cars for sale and can advise on current values. With some rare models the clubs can be the main source of cars for sale and may even know the background of individual cars (which can be very useful). Some clubs also produce a buyer's guide.

A key function of most clubs is to provide help with spares, which might be critical to keeping your classic on the road. They can also keep you up-to-date on safety issues (and there can be significant safety issues). The clubs also offer the comradeship of like-minded enthusiasts. Remember the best time to contact a club (or clubs) is *before* you purchase your classic car.

Left: **An array of MGs at a local club meeting (the MG Owners' Club, near Dundee).**

Condition: Do you want to buy a car in concours condition, or in good running order, or perhaps a restoration project? Consider your budget, your skills, the time you have and your garage space. If considering a restortion project, take particular care if you are

Left: **A "Big Healey" under restoration. A major back-to-bare-metal project in this case.**

offered an unfinished restoration; the project may have stopped due to having run into troublesome, even insurmountable, difficulties. The greatest risk is where a car is partly dismantled with some bits in boxes. Almost inevitably you will find the car is incomplete!

Many people derive great pleasure from taking a car in poor condition and returning it, lovingly, to an as-new state. One sees such delights at every classic car show and the people who do these restorations are to be congratulated for saving a car which otherwise might simply perish. Carrying out a restoration allows the expense of the project to be spread over many months (or years). It also gives one the opportunity to upgrade aspects. But not everyone has the time, knowledge or facilities to undertake a restoration.

Left: **Upgraded brakes and suspension on an MGB under restoration.**

It is worth noting that sometimes it will cost you less to buy a recently restored vehicle than to carry out the restoration yourself.

Servicing & Spares: Before searching for a specific model, it is useful to find out if there is a specialist for it in your area. You may need help with the servicing or any repairs, unless you propose to do that all yourself. Furthermore, the status regarding spares needs to be established, ie the availability of: (1) consumables for routine servicing; (2) replacement mechanical/electrical items and (3) body/chassis parts.

Note that the quality of some reproduction or re-manufactured parts can be poor. Ideally, use only reputable suppliers. The clubs are usually the best sources of advice regarding these issues.

Reliability: Readers who are unfamiliar with classic cars should bear in mind that the majority of these vehicles, even when new, were not as reliable as today's cars, and they require more frequent servicing. A consolation is that much of the servicing can be done by a keen enthusiast.

Security: Like all other cars, classic sports cars can be broken into or stolen. Some models are highly targeted. Open top cars are particularly vulnerable, especially the older models, some of which do not have door locks or any lockable compartment. The level of security offered by most classic cars is much less than we expect from modern cars. Insurers may stipulate that the car has to be garaged or have specified security devices fitted.

Safety: During the period covered by this book (from the mid-1940s to the 1980s) there were tremendous improvements in safety features incorporated into cars. These included collapsible steering columns, rocker switches (rather than protruding toggle switches), split braking systems, seat belts and side intrusion bars. Some of the most recent cars in this book will even boast airbags, but in general terms, safety features will not match today's production models. Please be warned.

Left: **By the 1970s, cars were crash-tested as shown in this impressive result with an MGB GT (probably a V8 model, judging by the wheels).**

Financial Implications: There are some useful financial benefits from owning a classic car. First, they have low depreciation, possibly even appreciation! Compare that with typical modern cars that can lose 40-60% of their value in just three years. Ouch! A second benefit is that insurance on a classic car can be remarkably reasonable provided it is a second car with restricted mileage. There are specialist insurers for classic cars. Remember to have an "agreed value" with your insurer. Yet another benefit applies to cars constructed before 1st January 1973 as they are classed as "historic" and usually exempt from annual road tax. Finally, many models can be serviced by the owner, which can be a major saving.

There can be some financial downsides too, especially if you buy a car with a hidden fault which turns out to be expensive (or very expensive) to fix.

Conclusion: When thinking of which model to buy, remember you want lots of pleasure from this vehicle, not lots of pain!

STEP 2: SEARCHING FOR SUITABLE EXAMPLES

Once you have chosen which model, or models, you would like and can afford to buy, the next step is to find the best possible example for your money. At this stage it is wise to keep your options as open as possible.

The extent of the search, the distances you will have to travel and the time you will have to wait before a suitable example appears depend upon where you live and the rarity of the model you seek.

You will usually find cars advertised by both private sellers and car dealers and you will probably view examples from both, so it is important to remember the significant differences between the two:

Private Sellers: Buying a car privately may save you money, but it can also involve: (a) experiencing inconvenience in arranging to see cars; (b) having limited facilities for inspecting the vehicle and (c) buying a car without any warranty.

Arrange to see the car at the seller's home, ideally in daylight (to see the car better), though an initial meeting could be somewhere else more convenient to you. When you finally meet at the seller's home, check their identity and that the address is the same as shown on the car's V5C Registration Certificate. If you do not correctly identify the seller and confirm their address, any subsequent legal action is likely to fail.

Car Dealers: The alternative, buying from a car dealer, does not eliminate all your problems and there are, sadly, a number of unscrupulous operators. If in doubt, a safer bet may be to buy from a *reputable* specialist car dealer who has been established a long time and is well thought of by the appropriate car owners' clubs.

Where To Look? A good start is to look at the clubs' websites as some advertise cars for sale. Other clubs carry such adverts in their magazines rather than on their websites. As these are cars that are often well-known to the clubs, they may be able to give you additional information about individual cars for sale.

Left: **A classic car show at Alexandra Palace, London.**

Another good place to find classic cars for sale is at classic car shows. Many such shows are held around the country, usually from early spring to late autumn (though there are some notable winter shows too). They range in size from shows that attract a few dozen cars to those major events attracting thousands of classic cars. There are also "one club" events which are usually open to the public and are advertised on a club's website. At all these events one can usually find cars for sale, indicated by "For Sale" signs on the cars. Particularly at the larger car shows, remember to walk around the visitors' car park too, as you will often find a lot of classics parked there and some will be for sale.

Specialist classic car magazines and newspapers (at WH Smith and other newsagents) carry advertisements for classic sports cars for sale. A quick browse will indicate which of these publications are carrying adverts relevant to your search.

Interpreting Adverts: Read the wording carefully. What is being missed out? Try to read between the lines. Note the word "restoration" is often used in adverts but is almost meaningless unless the scope of the restoration work done is specified. Assume nothing and ask questions!

Beware of car dealers who use only a phone number and pretend to be a private seller. This is unlawful.

Classic Car Auctions: There are many classic car auctions and these can be useful as you can see a range of vehicles in one place at one time, and you may possibly purchase a car at a lower price than otherwise.

Below: **Note that letter suffix registrations only became universal from January 1965, ie during 1963-64 some areas continued without them.**

UK CAR REGISTRATION SUFFIX LETTERS

A	Feb 1963 to Dec 1963	**M**	Aug 1973 to July 1974
B	Jan 1964 to Dec 1964	**N**	Aug 1974 to July 1975
C	Jan 1965 to Dec 1965	**P**	Aug 1975 to July 1976
D	Jan 1966 to Dec 1966	**R**	Aug 1976 to July 1977
E	Jan 1967 to July 1967	**S**	Aug 1977 to July 1978
F	Aug 1967 to July 1968	**T**	Aug 1978 to July 1979
G	Aug 1968 to July 1969	**V**	Aug 1979 to July 1980
H	Aug 1969 to July 1970	**W**	Aug 1980 to July 1981
J	Aug 1970 to July 1971	**X**	Aug 1981 to July 1982
K	Aug 1971 to July 1972	**Y**	Aug 1982 to July 1983
L	Aug 1972 to July 1973		

UK CAR REGISTRATION PREFIX LETTERS

A	Aug 1983 to July 1984	**M**	Aug 1994 to July 1995
B	Aug 1984 to July 1985	**N**	Aug 1995 to July 1996
C	Aug 1985 to July 1986	**P**	Aug 1996 to July 1997
D	Aug 1986 to July 1987	**R**	Aug 1997 to July 1998
E	Aug 1987 to July 1988	**S**	Aug 1998 to Feb 1999
F	Aug 1988 to July 1989	**T**	Mar 1999 to Aug 1999
G	Aug 1989 to July 1990	**V**	Sep 1999 to Feb 2000
H	Aug 1990 to July 1991	**W**	Mar 2000 to Aug 2000
J	Aug 1991 to July 1992	**X**	Sep 2000 to Feb 2001
K	Aug 1992 to July 1993	**Y**	Mar 2001 to Aug 2001
L	Aug 1993 to July 1994		

There are, however, some significant cautions. Firstly, the vehicles are often indoors which makes assessing their bodywork much more difficult (bright natural light is more revealing). Secondly, you usually cannot start the engine or test drive the car or put it up on ramps to check the underside. This significantly reduces your ability to assess the condition of the vehicle. Thirdly, the owner may not be available to answer any questions you have. Finally, as with a private seller, there will usually be no warranty and it is then a case of *caveat emptor* ("buyer beware").

If you are an expert or you are knowledgeable about the car that you are bidding for, then an auction may be a suitable way to purchase a classic sports car.

To find out more about these auctions, go to at least one *without* your wallet to see how it works. Admission may be by advance catalogue and this gives you a chance to do some prior research. On the day, allow plenty of time to look over the vehicle(s). Check the paperwork carefully as this is your main safeguard that the car is genuine and its servicing record will give an indication of its condition. Ideally, any restoration work should be fully documented and have a photographic build record.

When you finally go to buy, have a budget and stick to it (remember to allow for the buyer's premium on the hammer price). When bidding starts, don't assume every time the auctioneer calls a bid that it is genuine. There are tricks of the trade. You will be bidding against dealers and if they avoid a particular car, then perhaps you should avoid it too. If the bids go over your preset budget, let it go. There is always another example you could buy and, who knows, it may be a better car!

On-line Auctions: If you consider using an internet auction, all the cautions mentioned above apply and you will also have to make the effort to travel to inspect the vehicle. Tread warily!

STEP 3: CHECKING LIKELY CARS

First, go and take a brief initial look at the car. Remember to take protective gloves, overalls, a torch to see the underside of the car (and into other dark recesses), an old rug to lie on and a magnet to check for body filler. Also, a camera might prove helpful. If it seems promising, complete the "Car Particulars" (on page 168). Also, with the seller's permission, take a full set of photos.

At this point it is probably best not to get too drawn in, but instead to withdraw. This will allow you time to: (a) think coolly about the car, (b) contact the club(s), (c) where relevant, contact the appropriate Heritage centre to verify the car's authenticity and (d) compare the car with others you have seen.

Next, when you are ready, revisit the best car you have seen to date.

With a modern second-hand car, you might first check the car and then check the paperwork. With a classic car it is probably better to start with the paperwork and then, only if that is in order, move on to check the car. This can ultimately save you time and save you from getting keen on a car that turns out to have suspect paperwork.

Examine the paperwork very carefully, ie the Form V5C Vehicle Registration Certificate, MoT Test Certificate, service record (including supporting invoices and receipts), restoration log (where applicable) and SORN paperwork where the car has been off the road for some time. Crosscheck the information and ensure all details match the car. Note that the body/chassis plates were usually riveted to the car and can be readily changed. There have also been instances of forged documents, so hold the V5C up to the light and look for the watermark "DVL", which is repeated across the document. *Never buy a car that does not have a Form V5C.*

A car's provenance may be demonstrated by an unbroken documentary trail back to the original purchase document, proving the car's authenticity (but such a continuous record is unlikely and hence the need for skill in interpreting the documents available).

But Who Owns The Car? You can only make a proper purchase if the would-be seller owns the car in the first place. Unfortunately the car's Form V5C Registration Certificate records only the "registered keeper" who may not be the legal owner. The car may be owned by a finance company. If you bought the car and it later turned out to be owned by a finance company or stolen, then you could lose the car (and what you paid for it).

Normally you should not have these problems if buying from a reputable car dealer, but otherwise you

Left: **With the bonnet up, one can check aspects of the engine and ancillaries. Other things are also revealed, such as corrosion, accident damage and the important engine and body/chassis numbers. (The car shown is an Austin-Healey 3000 MkII 2+2).**

are vulnerable. One company, called HPI (part of Norwich Union Insurance) compiles information on stolen cars and those subject to a finance agreement, and a search can be made, for a fee. Their website is: www.hpicheck.com A similar service is offered by the AA and RAC.

MoT Test Certificate: If the car is allegedly road legal, but has no current MoT Certificate, try to get the seller to have the car tested before you part with any money. Probably any *bona fide* seller would do this anyway. Remember the MoT Certificate is not a guarantee of the car's overall condition – it only checks certain aspects and is only a reflection of the condition of those tested items on that particular day, but it is much better than having nothing tested. Ask to see the mechanic's check sheet for the current MoT as you may learn more.

Heritage Certificate: If the classic sports car you are checking is an Aston Martin, Austin, Austin-Healey, Daimler, Jaguar, MG, Singer, Sunbeam or Triumph, then the seller may hold a Heritage Certificate for the car. This will help to confirm the vehicle's authenticity. If no certificate is available you can contact the relevant archivists (refer to the addresses given later in this book). A sample certificate is illustrated left. If in doubt as to the authenticity of a certificate, contact the relevant issuer.

Discrepancies: If the Vehicle Body VIN*/Chassis/Frame number (sometimes called something different, just to completely confuse you) and the engine number do not match the Form V5C Vehicle Registration Certificate, ask the seller why there is a discrepancy. A change of body colour or engine may perhaps make sense, but a vehicle body/chassis number that does not match the Vehicle Registration Certificate would be an entirely different

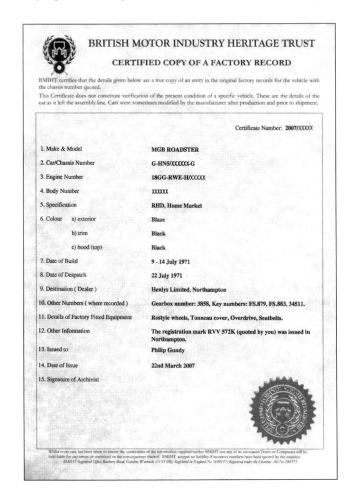

BRITISH MOTOR INDUSTRY HERITAGE TRUST

CERTIFIED COPY OF A FACTORY RECORD

BMIHT certifies that the details given below are a true copy of an entry in the original factory records for the vehicle with the chassis number quoted.

This Certificate does not constitute verification of the present condition of a specific vehicle. These are the details of the car as it left the assembly line. Cars were sometimes modified by the manufacturer after production and prior to shipment.

Certificate Number: 2007/XXXXX

1. Make & Model	MGB ROADSTER
2. Car/Chassis Number	G-HN5/XXXXXX-G
3. Engine Number	18GG-RWE-H/XXXXX
4. Body Number	XXXXXX
5. Specification	RHD, Home Market
6. Colour a) exterior	Blaze
b) trim	Black
c) hood (top)	Black
7. Date of Build	9 - 14 July 1971
8. Date of Despatch	22 July 1971
9. Destination (Dealer)	Henlys Limited, Northampton
10. Other Numbers (where recorded)	Gearbox number: 3858, Key numbers: FS.879, FS.883, 34511.
11. Details of Factory Fitted Equipment	Rostyle wheels, Tonneau cover, Overdrive, Seatbelts.
12. Other Information	The registration mark RVV 572K (quoted by you) was issued in Northampton.
13. Issued to	Philip Gundy
14. Date of Issue	22nd March 2007
15. Signature of Archivist	

Whilst every care has been taken to ensure the correctness of the information supplied neither BMIHT nor any of its associated Trusts or Companies will be held liable for any errors or omissions or the consequences thereof. BMIHT accept no liability if incorrect numbers have been quoted by the enquirer. *BMIHT Registered Office, Banbury Road, Gaydon, Warwick, CV35 0BJ, Registered in England No 1690117; Registered under the Charities Act 266573.*

*VIN = Vehicle Indentification Number

matter. Contact the club and the Heritage organisations (where applicable) for advice.

Restoration Log: If it is claimed that the car has had a restoration, then there should be a "restoration log" which will usually comprise a ring binder with photos taken at key stages of the work, together with invoices and other relevant documents. *Caution:* Do not assume the photos or invoices necessarily relate to the vehicle you are checking!

The Physical Check: If you think you have found a suitable example at an appropriate price, beware of two car buyer's weaknesses: (1) the strong tendency to buy the first car you look at and (2) being so impressed by the car's exterior that you are blind to its mechanical condition. Using the 100-point Vehicle Checklist in this book will, hopefully, overcome this problem. Working through the various checks will take at least 2 hours including the test drive, so you may wish to split the task into two sessions. It will pay you to take the time needed to do the job properly. Take a knowledgeable friend to help you. Stop if you realise the car is not suitable.

If you are not used to driving high performance vehicles, two cautions would not be out of order. First, be careful on your test drive not to let the power get you into trouble, ie drive within your limits (as well as the car's). Second, do not let the thrill, excitement and adrenalin rush of driving a car with rapid acceleration blind you to its potential (and expensive) faults.

After you have finished checking the car and you are sitting back trying to assess your findings, do remember that many components in a car may appear to function satisfactorily even though they are nearing the end of their useful life. This is one reason that it is useful to see a servicing record and the receipts for parts which have been replaced recently.

If buying from a private seller, ask how long they have owned the car and why they are selling it. Short ownership or an unconvincing reason for selling should make you wary. In every case insist on seeing the purchase document from when they bought the car.

If buying from a dealer, enquire as to what warranty they are offering (a minimum of 90 days should be offered). Read the small print of any warranty carefully, particularly the exclusion clauses. Take your time – do not be rushed. If the dealer is some distance from your home, consider how you are going to get repairs done under that warranty. If there is no warranty, it is probably imprudent to buy the car, however temptingly low the selling price, as it will be low for a good reason, and one of the reasons for buying from a dealer is to have the comfort of a warranty, even a short (90 day) one.

Always remember to ask which removable items (eg radio, mats, tools etc) are remaining with the car.

Mileage: If a low mileage is claimed for a classic car, one must treat this claim with caution. First, is the mileage actually low or is it that the speedometer has been replaced at some point in the car's long life or has the reading been tampered with (which is illegal). If the

Left: **The Aston Martin is an example of a marque that ideally requires a qualified expert to check a car before purchase.**

mileage is indeed low, has the car been in storage, undergoing a long restoration or been off the road due to a bad accident? Remember that cars deteriorate if unused and generally prefer to be driven regularly. Good documentation will help answer these questions.

Look through the old MoT certificates to check the indicated mileages.

Corrosion: Assessing the severity of corrosion (ie rust or aluminium oxidisation) can be difficult, but is vital. Corrosion is like an iceberg: what you can see will be only a small part of what is actually there, as usually most of it is hidden. Sometimes filler, paint or underseal is used to conceal rust and that can make it difficult to detect, but a sure test on steel is to use a magnet.

A Caution: Remember that unless the car has had a total restoration, not only may the bodywork be rusty and the engine and gearbox worn out, but every single mechanical and electrical component and trim piece will also be worn. Furthermore, over the years, some unsympathetic owners may have "bodged" repairs or made inappropriate, even dangerous, modifications. Sadly, some sellers cheat by falsifying a car's past, its true identity or its condition.

A Second Opinion: When you are completely happy with the car's paperwork and condition, consider getting an unbiased second opinion. Depending on your level of expertise, it may be wise to have a professional engineer (with marque knowledge) to inspect the vehicle.

Postscript: If the paperwork is not 100% correct, or you are suspicious about the car or the seller, or you just feel "uncomfortable", then walk away......

STEP 4: BUYING A CAR

The Next Step: Assuming all is to your satisfaction, then you are ready to make the seller an offer. Once a price is agreed, you could secure the car by offering a *small* deposit prior to finalising the financial and insurance aspects of the purchase. Refuse to leave a *big* deposit, as you might not see the seller (or the car) again. Remember to obtain a receipt for your deposit. Note that by verbally agreeing to buy a car you have made a "contract" with the seller. Ask the seller how they will accept payment – by cash, cheque or bank draft (but see below).

Negotiating & Paying: Both private sellers and car dealers usually start with an asking price which is higher than they expect to get. In advertisements, the letters "ono" after a price mean "or nearest offer", while "ovno" means "or very nearest offer" indicating the seller is not prepared to drop the price by very much.

Use the faults found when checking the car as a lever to legitimately reduce the price (in proportion to the likely repair costs).

As with any business deal where a price is negotiable, if you look too keen this will weaken your bargaining position. It is better if you look fairly uncommitted.

Method of Payment: It is not ideal to pay cash unless the sum is very small, as there is no official record of the transaction. A (very) small deposit might be paid in cash, if you are prepared to lose it if the seller disappears. It is probably better to pay by an accountable means such as card, cheque or bank draft. Always get a receipt.

Insurance: Next contact your insurers (you should already have an insurance quotation on the type of car you are buying) and ask them to make out an insurance "cover-note" for you. They will probably need to know the car's registration number, engine capacity (in cc), year of manufacture, current value, any significant modifications and very importantly, the precise time and date from which the insurance cover is to be effective. They will also ask you to complete a car insurance proposal form. Remember to get an "agreed value" on your car with your insurers.

Collecting The Car: If your new car is not drivable, consider how you are going to collect it. There are specialist car transport companies who can move it for you. If you decide to do it yourself with a hired or borrowed trailer, do remember to use proper tie-downs.

Left: **A Lenham Sprite/Midget Conversion** strapped down on a trailer, awaiting delivery to its lucky owner.

Before you roar off with your new classic sports car, make sure you have been given:

1. **Receipt:** A signed and dated receipt showing: (a) the amount paid; (b) your name; (c) the seller's name and address; (d) the car's type and registration number. It may also help if the seller states on the receipt that the car is not subject to a finance agreement and that they are the legal owner of the car and entitled to sell it.

2. **Vehicle Registration Certificate:** You need the "New Keeper" part of the Form V5C. Read the instructions on the Certificate to ensure you take the correct part and you have done everything you (and the seller) must do.

3. **Tax Disc:** The current windscreen tax disc.

4. **MoT Test Certificates:** The current and past ones.

5. **Service Records:** Take any supporting invoices and receipts the seller has (for your reference and ultimately to show to a potential buyer when you come to sell the car yourself).

6. **Heritage Certificate** (if available).

7. **Restoration Log:** If there is a restoration logbook, ideally with photos, get that too. It is really part of the vehicle's paperwork and should stay with the vehicle.

8. **Removables:** Check the radio, mats, tools, spare wheel, owner's manual etc are still in the vehicle, do not just assume they are there.

9. **Keys:** Make sure you have all sets of keys, including wheel locks, security devices etc (as appropriate).

STEP 5: THE FINALE....

When buying from a private seller, once the purchase is concluded and paid for, you might try asking the seller a question such as, "Is there anything I need to look at fairly soon?" (or some such query). The answer may be illuminating. It will not alter the sale but will let you know what your first bill is likely to be!

If you have purchased a car privately and you later discover it is not "as described" in the advert, then contact Trading Standards for advice.

If you have bought the car from a dealer and later have a complaint, initially take the matter up with the firm's manager. If that proves unsatisfactory, then contact your local authority's Trading Standards Department or the appropriate motor trade organisation (if the dealer is a member).

If you have not already done so, you should consider joining one (or more) of the relevant car owners' clubs.

10 CLASSIC CAR BUYING TIPS

1. Use the collective expertise of the car clubs.
2. Leave your cash at home when you start your search.
3. Assume "bargains" don't exist.
4. Realise owners often over-estimate their car's value.
5. Forget to check any part and it will turn out faulty.
6. Don't make excuses for any faults you find.
7. Buy the best example you can afford.
8. Don't buy a car if the paperwork is...fawlty.
9. Buying a "pup" is always easy.
10. Selling a "pup" later is not so easy.

Each model in the following pages starts with a data box that gives a summary of key information about that model. Please read the notes below which explain the information given in the data boxes, and its limitations.

Dates: The first year given is usually when a car is launched (often at some major car show), even if production proper does not commence until some time later (if there is a significant delay this will be mentioned in the text). The last year quoted is when production ceased, though quite often cars will be registered or sold at a later date, sometimes much later. Confusion can occur when the "official" end of production occurs late in one year even though some cars are finished off at the very start of the new year, as different sources quote either one or the other year as marking the end of production.

Generally we have not used "model years" which usually refer to the year after the unveiling of a new model, eg a "1970 model" car would probably have been first shown to the public in late 1969.

Number Built: For many models, there is a surprising amount of disagreement as to how many cars were built, despite some sources quoting precise figures. The discrepancy can be enormous in some cases. Further confusion occurs as some sources include prototypes and pre-production cars while others exclude them.

Researching the numbers built can be difficult as many records have been lost due to company closures or factory fires. It seems too that some manufacturers were not conscientious record keepers, and with others there are inexplicable gaps in chassis number sequences. We also know today that some manufacturers understated their sales while others hugely exaggerated them.

Production numbers therefore need to be treated with some caution. Unless there is almost unanimous agreement as to a precise figure, we usually quote an approximate number, with a circa symbol "c." and sometimes add a "?" to indicate greater uncertainty.

Body/Chassis: In the data boxes we have used the general expression "open sports" to describe an open top sports car that usually has a soft-top roof that can be lowered or removed altogether.

Some cars of this era had small bench seats in the rear for "occasional use" and were sometimes classed as 2+2 seaters, but these rear seats were usually very cramped, with little legroom or headroom. Owners are advised to contact their insurers before considering using them as seats.

Engine (Power): In the past, manufacturers often made optimistic claims for the power output of their engines, but most articles and books (including this book) quote the manufacturer's figures as there is usually no other data available. Further confusion can arise as figures sometimes vary (slightly) from one sales brochure to another for what appears to be the same model.

Note that a descending pair of figures (eg 285-270bhp) means that later engines were rated at the lower power output. This is usually due to emission controls.

Layout: This describes the location of the engine, which wheels were driven and what types of gearbox were used.

Performance: The top speed and acceleration figures in this book are those that a typical car in good condition might achieve. Automatic transmission versions will tend to be more sluggish as will cars exported to the US with emission control equipment. Over-reading speedometers, following winds or slight downhill stretches of road can often convince drivers that their cars are capable of greater performance than quoted.

We also know today that some, or maybe many, of the cars supplied to reputable magazines for road tests, were in fact specially tuned (in secret) by the manufacturers. The published performance figures were therefore often better than an owner could ever achieve.

Price Today: The driving factors behind the value of any classic car are its *desirability*, *condition*, *authenticity*, *originality* and *rarity*. Due to the last factor, where known, we have given some indication of the approximate number of surviving cars. Cars with a *racing history* will usually carry a premium. Prices fluctuate according to market trends and often soften towards winter.

In general, it is perhaps fair to say that owners of classic cars sometimes overvalue their vehicles. This is natural and could be for several reasons – they may have personally spent a great deal of money restoring their car (and are now trying to recover this investment), their enthusiasm for the marque may again inflate their perceived values and finally they may have seen cars like theirs advertised at high prices (but this does not reveal what the cars finally sold for).

If you ask the car owners' clubs as to likely values they quite often quote a figure higher than the published guides. This might be simply because they tend to own and see better than average cars so what is "normal" to them are cars in a good to very good condition.

Note that values for insurance purposes may be higher than the likely retail price.

To compile our price bands, we looked at auction prices and published price guides, but the most important factor was information given to us by clubs and owners.

We have used **£** symbols to give an indication of the likely purchase price for a road-legal car from a private seller. Each **£** symbol has two values (as shown in the table):

To the left are values for cars in reasonable condition with a current MoT certificate. The cars are usable, but have some visible cosmetic blemishes and will require some mechanical work. If already restored, the work was done many years ago and hence new work is required.

To the right of the **£** symbols, the values are for cars in very good condition with a current MoT certificate and they will also look good (but will not be in a "show" or "concours" condition). There will also be no obvious mechanical work required. If restored, the work would have been done recently and there would be a restoration log available.

Car in reasonable condition Some cosmetic blemishes Old restoration/Unrestored **Private Sale**		Car in very good condition Looks good (not concours) Recent restoration **Private Sale**
Up to about £1-3,000	**£**	Up to about £3-5,000
Up to about £5-7,000	**££**	Up to about £7-10,000
Up to about £9-13,000	**£££**	Up to about £13-19,000
Up to about £14-20,000	**££££**	Up to about £20-29,000
Up to about £20-25,000	**£££££**	Up to about £30-40,000
Over about £20-25,000	**HiValue**	Over about £30-40,000

Other Notes:

1. **Values in this book are only an approximate guide.**
2. "Immaculate", "excellent", "show" or "concours" cars can cost considerably more.
3. A plus symbol suffix, eg **££+**, indicates the top value is probably more than a straight **££**.
4. Two price bands together, eg **££/£££**, indicates the value is in the middle, between the two. It does not mean the value range is from the bottom of **££** to the top of **£££**.
5. Cars in the **HiValue** category require specialist valuation and extra care when purchasing.
6. Note there is always the odd car that is sold outside the "normal" price bands.
7. "Contact Club" is where pricing is difficult, as may be the case where the cars are rare and few change hands.
8. Prices are never static! Contact the clubs for the latest information and subtleties that no price guide can reflect.

The classic car magazines all publish useful general price guides, but do remember that these are merely "guides" and prices are not set in stone. This is particularly true for rarer cars, examples of which do not come up for sale often, making them difficult to value. It is easier to value mass-produced models such as MGs and Triumphs which are traded in greater numbers.

In the main text for each entry, we include information on model changes and specific checks. Please read the notes below which explain the information given:

Model Changes: Even with the mass-produced sports cars there were many minor changes, which can bedevil restorers who find that replacement parts do not fit. We have highlighted only the main model changes. Although these are often quoted in official literature as happening at a specific date or precise chassis number, the actual model changeover process can be more blurred, with the last cars of the previous model incorporating aspects of the newer model and the newer model incorporating older aspects. This often occurs as the old components have run out before the official model changeover or conversely the manufacturers are simply using up old parts. The situation is further complicated by owners retrofitting parts intended for later models. In practice this means that when you are checking a specific car which, for instance, might be classed as a "Mark II", you might find it incorporates some "Mark III" features.

Specific Checks: In the text we have tried to include additional checks which are specific to each model. These highlight some of the known weaknesses (but may not be exhaustive) and should be read in conjunction with the general 100-point Vehicle Checklist later in this book. Note that some car owners' clubs produce a buyer's guide which can provide useful additional information.

Photo Captions: We have tried to ensure the descriptions given in the photo captions are correct, but usually we have had to rely on information given to us by the owner, the photographer, or as indicated by the car's badges. Therefore a photo caption may, inadvertently, not accurately describe the car illustrated.

Abbreviations	
bhp	brake horse power
c.	circa (ie approximate)
cc	cylinder capacity (in cubic centimetres)
cyl	cylinder
DHC	Drop Head Coupé
dohc	double overhead camshafts
DVLA	Driver and Vehicle Licensing Agency (UK)
FHC	Fixed Head Coupé
ft	foot
FWD	Front Wheel Drive
GRP	Glassfibre Reinforced Plastic
IFS	Independent Front Suspension
in	inch (cu in = cubic inch)
IRS	Independent Rear Suspension
K	thousand (eg £3K is £3,000)
kg	kilogram
L	Litre
lb	pound weight
LHD	Left Hand Drive (ie steering wheel on left)
MoT	"Ministry of Transport" Test Certificate (UK)
mph	miles per hour
NK	Not Known (ie no reliable data known)
ohc	overhead camshaft
ohv	overhead valves (ie pushrod actuated valves)
RHD	Right Hand Drive (ie steering wheel on right)
RWD	Rear Wheel Drive
sec	seconds
sohc	single overhead camshaft
V6/V8	6 or 8 cylinders arranged in a V-formation
VAT	Value Added Tax (UK)
VIN	Vehicle Identification Number

Dates: Ace: 1953-63   Aceca: 1954-63

Numbers Built: Ace: c.723   Aceca: c.330

Body/Chassis: Aluminium body over steel tubing on steel chassis, 2-seater open sports (Aceca: rear-hatch FHC).

Engines: AC 1991cc, 6-cyl in-line, ohc, 85-105bhp; Bristol 1971cc, 6-cyl in-line, ohv, mostly 120-125bhp; Ford 2553cc, 6-cyl in-line, ohv, (bhp – See text).

Layout: Front engine, rear wheel drive, 4-speed manual gearbox (with optional overdrive).

Performance: Dependent on engine fitted – See text.

Prices Today: HiValue.

Above & Below: **The pre-Ace 2.6 cars have a distinctive top lip. This example is one of the last Ace Bristols.**

The Ace was first shown as a prototype at the 1953 London Motor Show. Its all-independently sprung chassis (almost unique in British production cars at the time) was based on John Tojeiro's sports racer and the attractive styling was inspired by a Ferrari *barchetta*. Coupled to AC's own 2-litre engine and a Moss gearbox, the attractive and competent Ace was a success.

The chassis had two main tubular longitudinal members (3-inch diameter) cross-braced in the middle. Small section round and square tubes were welded to the chassis producing a framework which supported the aluminium body panels. The front and rear suspension had transverse upper leaf springs with lower wishbones. The light AC engine, designed in 1919 by John Weller (co-founder of AC), had a single overhead camshaft, five main bearings and an alloy block with cast iron head. With this engine, the Ace could do about 105mph and reach 60mph in 11-12 seconds.

From 1956 a Bristol engine (with Bristol gearbox) was offered and cars so fitted were known as Ace Bristols. The Bristol engine was silky smooth and was happiest above 3,000rpm. Ken Rudd (of Ruddspeed) is usually credited with having encouraged AC to offer the Bristol engine as an alternative. Some 463 Aces had Bristol engines and typically they could top 115mph and reach 60mph in under 9 seconds. Front disc brakes and overdrive became optional extras.

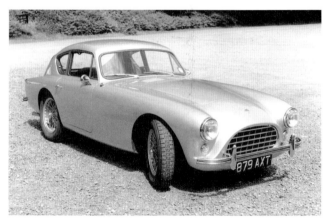

Above & Below: **The nice lines of the Aceca are evident in these photos.**

From 1961, again at Ken Rudd's initiative, the Ford Zephyr 2.6-litre engine was used and these cars are often known as the Ace 2.6 and have "Ruddspeed" on their rocker covers. Although heavier, the Ford engine could be easily tuned, with performance to match, and was also cheaper to maintain. The weight of the Ford engine necessitated an extra leaf in the front transverse spring and heavy duty dampers. The Ford engine was also lower and this permitted a lower nose profile and smaller grille (later to be adopted by the Cobra). Another bonus was that the engine was much cheaper allowing a lower price for the Ford-engined cars. Though only 38 Ace 2.6 cars were made, most survive today. Their performance was very much related to the level of tuning as five stages were offered, up to a claimed 170bhp.

Early cars had Alfin drum brakes, but with increasing performance, front disc brakes were introduced, initially as an option then later as standard.

Among its racing successes, a suitably modified Ace Bristol was a class winner in the 1959 Le Mans.

A year after the launch of the Ace, AC unveiled the good looking Aceca which was a fastback coupé with a rear-hatch (still quite a novelty at the time). Mechanically the car was based on the Ace, using the same engine and gearbox, and with a similar chassis, except the two 3-inch main chassis tubes were increased in wall thickness from 14swg to 12swg. There was also an extra chassis brace and a non-resonant GRP bulkhead that included the facia and footwells. The rear-hatch used an ash frame with a Perspex rear window. To insulate the occupants from noise the differential used Metalastik bushes.

With the extra bodywork the Aceca weighed about 155lb (70kg) more than the Ace and this reduced its performance slightly. With AC's 90bhp engine it could do over 100mph and reach 60mph in about 13 seconds. Some 151 Acecas had the AC engine, while a further 171 had the much more powerful Bristol unit and this enabled the car to exceed 115mph and reach 60mph in around 10 seconds. A further 8 cars had the Ford Zephyr 2.6-litre engine fitted.

Specific Checks: First, check the paperwork then contact the AC Owners' Club for further information. For corrosion, check in particular the outriggers and sill tubes. The AC engines can suffer galvanic corrosion of their alloy blocks. For information on the Bristol engines, refer to the entry for the Bristol 2-litre cars. Tuned Ford engines have a tendency to blow cylinder head gaskets, especially if the optional alloy head was fitted.

Prices Today: The Ace Bristol and Ace 2.6 cars are the most valuable of the Ace/Aceca group while AC-engined Aces are valued less. The Acecas are valued less than the Aces.

Below: **The AC Acecas had curved windscreens and wire wheels were a standard fitment. All Acecas had the distinctive top lip.**

Left: **The AC Greyhound had an auxiliary driving light located on each side of the grille.**

Right: **Below the wraparound rear Perspex window was the boot. It had a fold-down lid that allowed more luggage to be carried when it was open.**

Dates: 1959-63	**Number Built:** 84
Body/Chassis: Alloy body on steel chassis, 4-seater FHC.	
Engines: Mostly Bristol 1971/2216cc, 6-cyl in-line, ohv, 105-128bhp.	
Layout: Front engine, RWD, 4-speed manual (optional overdrive).	
Performance: c.110mph, 0-60 in c.11-12sec.	**Price Today:** £££+

The Greyhound was AC's answer to those potential owners who wanted an AC with more seats. Launched at the 1959 London Motor Show, the car used a new chassis with box section longerons instead of the Aceca's tubes (for increased rigidity). It was also longer (the wheelbase was now 8ft 4in) and the engine was moved forward to create space for a rear seat. However, the main innovation was the all-independent suspension which was coil spring with wishbones and telescopic dampers.

The Greyhound also had rack and pinion steering, front disc brakes, rear Alfin drum brakes, a split hydraulic circuit (but no servo) and wire wheels were standard.

AC used a variety of materials in the construction of these cars including some timber formers and GRP for a number of internal body parts such as the bulkhead, transmission tunnel, wheelarches and rear seat pan.

The Greyhound was built at the same time as the Ace and Aceca and most Greyhounds had Bristol engines (many were the more powerful Bristol D2 engines, producing 125-128bhp). Bristol's own gearbox was also used. Only a handful of cars had the AC 1991cc engine. Today, a dozen or so cars have non-standard engines.

Specific Checks: First, check the paperwork then contact the AC Owners' Club for advice. Inspect the chassis particularly around the suspension mounts, jacking points and outriggers. Look also for corrosion at the foot of the A-post where it meets the sills (check by opening each door and waggling it slightly). Check also for sagging suspension springs. Rear end "clunks" can come from the drive train, rear hub splines or differential mounts.

Prices Today: The Club estimates that over 70 cars still survive. The Greyhound is one of the more affordable AC sports cars today and the Club is well organised for sourcing and manufacturing spares for the car.

Dates: Since 1962 (See text).   **Number Built:** See text.

Body/Chassis: Aluminium body over steel tubing on steel chassis, 2-seater open sports. (CRS: Carbon Fibre body).

Engines: Ford 260cu in (4.2-litre), V8, ohv, 220bhp (estimated);
Ford 289cu in (4.7-litre), V8, ohv, 271+bhp;
Ford 427cu in (7-litre), V8, ohv, 400+bhp;
Ford 302cu in (5-litre), V8, ohv, 320+bhp.

Layout: Front engine, rear wheel drive, 4-speed manual gearbox (MkIV: 5-speed) or 3-speed automatic (rare).

Performance: See text.

Prices Today: HiValue.

Above: **An AC Cobra 289 (from 1964).**

The Cobra is one of the world's great sports cars. The car was born out of an idea by the American, Carroll Shelby, who was a former national sports car driving champion and co-winner of the 1959 Le Mans (in an Aston Martin). Shelby took a modified Ace chassis into which he installed Ford's new 260 cubic inch (4.2-litre) V8, which used the latest thin-wall casting techniques to give a relatively light engine. The result was a car with electrifying performance. Shelby arranged for AC to build complete cars (minus the engine and transmission) and ship them to his workshops in California where the Ford engines and transmissions were fitted and the cars sold. Initially the Cobra was for export to Shelby only, but home market sales commenced in 1964.

Externally the only bodywork changes to the Ace were swaged lips around the wheelarches to permit the use of larger section tyres and the petrol filler was repositioned to the centre (as the petrol tank had been relocated directly above the rear axle). From mid-1963 side vents were added and the wheelarches were widened. Beneath the skin the Ace chassis had been considerably strengthened with an extra crossmember and additional fillets. Disc brakes were fitted on all wheels.

The first 75 cars had the 260 cubic inch V8 engine but thereafter a larger 289 engine was used. After a further 51 cars, the steering was changed to rack and pinion (from the worm and sector steering inherited from the Ace but not ideal for the Cobra). The 4-speed manual gearbox was made by Borg Warner for Ford. A total of 517 of the leaf spring Cobra 289s were supplied to Shelby, plus a further 62 cars were sold by AC themselves.

A Cobra was the first British car home in the 1963 Le Mans and the following year Cobras won the GT class.

In the search for even more performance, in 1965 Shelby launched a new model, the 427 Cobra, with Ford's big block 427 cubic inch (7-litre) engine. The other major change with this model was its new chassis, which was made far more rigid by using 4-inch diameter tubes. The new coil spring suspension was developed with the assistance of Ford's Competitions Department in Detroit, and it made a significant improvement to the car. The Cobra 427 was easily recognisable with its flared wheelarches to cover 7.5x15 inch cast alloy wheels (previous cars used wire wheels). Also the grille aperture was more elliptical in shape to increase the airflow through the radiator.

In total, 315 of these coil spring cars were supplied to Shelby. Some had the cheaper 428 (345+bhp) engine fitted, but few of that engine type remain as most have been retrofitted with the better 427 engine.

In 1966, Shelby ended production due to various factors, including increasingly stringent American safety legislation, and he sold the name "Cobra" to Ford. Meanwhile, back in England, AC continued to make the coil spring chassis car, now called simply the AC 289 Sports (as they were not permitted to use the Cobra name). 27 of these desirable cars, with the small block 289 engine and wire wheels, were made 1966-69.

In 1982, the AC (Autokraft) MkIV appeared, an updated version of the coil spring Cobra, but with a 302 cubic inch (5-litre) Ford V8 engine. The car now had a 5-speed gearbox with servo-assisted ventilated front disc brakes. Some 400 cars were made including a number of "Lightweights".

Below: **The Cobra's distinctive rear bumper on a 1965 leaf spring car.**

Although outside the period covered by this book, there followed the Superblower (supercharged) car from 1997 and the CRS (with its carbon fibre body) from 2000.

In terms of performance, all Cobras are blisteringly fast cars, but exact figures will depend on the state of engine tuning, gear ratios and the wheels/tyres fitted. A leaf spring 289 with c.270bhp tested by *Motor* in 1963 reached 135mph and sprinted to 60mph in 5.2 seconds. The later 427 was, not surprisingly, even quicker.

Specific Checks: First, check the paperwork then contact the AC Owners' Club for further information. Note there are fakes purporting to be real Cobras (in addition to the replicas and tens of thousands of look-alike kit cars), so it is particularly important to know exactly what you are looking at. In all cases, checking an example really needs the services of a qualified Cobra expert.

The aluminium bodies can suffer from dents, cracking and corrosion. Check also the chassis for rust and road accident or race damage. Lack of frequent greasing and maintenance can give suspension problems which are expensive to rectify. The 427's rear suspension, in particular, requires a specialist to set up.

The reliability of stock Ford V8 engines is legendary but advanced tuning can have an adverse effect on longevity, and a full rebuild is expensive. A clue to condition is the oil pressure when the engine is fully warmed up (refer to handbook). Also, check the gearbox carefully as it can lose its synchromesh and maybe even jump out of gear.

Prices Today: First, you are unlikely to find a "basket case" car requiring restoration as that will have been done already. Prices for early Cobras are six figures (Sterling). The most affordable are the MkIV cars which can cost significantly less. Valuation of any Cobra requires expert advice.

Top Two Photos: **Official Ford Motor Co. photos of a 427 Cobra.**
3rd From Top: **The AC Cobra MkIV (a 1991 example).**
Lower Right: **The AC Cobra MkIV CRS (Carbon Road Series).**
Below: **A 1965 leaf spring car, seen in the late 1970s.**

Left: **The handsome AC 428 by Frua.**

Right: **The AC 428 was also made in convertible form.**

Left: **The very modern and stylish lines of the AC 3000ME.**

Right: **The raised part of the engine cover is to clear the large air filter.**

Dates: 1965-73	**Number Built:** 81
Body/Chassis: Steel body on steel chassis, 2-seater FHC or DHC.	
Engine: Ford 428cu in (7-litre), V8, ohv, 345bhp (gross).	
Layout: Front engine, RWD, 3-speed auto (some 4-speed manual).	
Performance: c.140mph, 0-60 in c.6sec.	**Price Today:** HiValue.

Dates: 1973-85	**Number Built:** c.107
Body/Chassis: GRP body on steel chassis, 2-seater FHC.	
Engine: Ford 2994cc, V6, ohv, 138bhp.	
Layout: Mid engine, RWD, 5-speed manual.	
Performance: c.120mph, 0-60 in c.9sec.	**Price Today:** ££+

In 1965, AC sent a coil spring Cobra chassis to Frua in Italy for them to produce the bodywork for a new GT car. The result was a stunningly good-looking design based on a lengthened chassis. The AC 428 was first shown in convertible form at the 1965 London Motor Show and a fastback coupé version soon followed. The initial engine was the Cobra's Ford 427 but production cars had the 428 unit as used in the US Ford Galaxie.

The car had a rudimentary rear "seat" but is effectively a 2-seater. Wire wheels with disc brakes all round (with twin servos) were standard, but the steering was not power assisted.

To build the AC 428, bare chassis (derived from the normal AC twin longitudinal tube design) were shipped to Frua in Italy who would fit the steel body and return the car to AC's factory for finishing, including installing the engine and transmission (usually Ford's own auto box). Early cars had the dash trimmed in leather to match the seats, while later cars had black vinyl and smaller dials with rocker rather than toggle switches.

The potential cost of meeting the impending UK Type Approval regulations, coupled with the 1973 Oil Crisis, resulted in only 81 cars being made of which 51 were fastback coupés and 30 were convertibles.

Specific Checks: First, check the paperwork then contact the AC Owners' Club for further information. Unlike other AC cars of the period, the bodies were made of steel and can rust badly. The cast iron Ford engine is solid and reliable but can run hot and any pressure failure in the coolant system will lead to overheating. With low ground clearance (about 4 inches under the exhaust) check for a damaged underside due to grounding.

Prices Today: The Club estimates that over 60 cars survive. A handful of chassis have been converted to Cobra replicas.

The 3000ME was based on a prototype designed by Peter Bohanna and Robin Stables. This was first exhibited in 1972 as the Diablo with an Austin Maxi engine and gearbox. The design was acquired by AC Cars and given the Ford "Essex" V6 engine and a custom made 5-speed gearbox, chain driven from the engine. Other custom parts included brake/suspension items.

Under its new AC parentage, it appeared at the 1973 London Motor Show as the 3000ME (the name reflected the car's 3-litre Mid Engine). Then followed six long years of development and modifications to meet the ever more stringent UK Type Approval regulations. The car finally entered production in 1979 but after 77 cars were made (plus prototypes) the parent company sold the project in 1984 to a new company, AC Scotland, who made a further 30 cars before ceasing to trade. These Scottish-built cars can usually be distinguished by body-coloured grille, air intakes and bumpers. One prototype was fitted with an Alfa V6 engine.

The chassis consisted of a central steel tub with front and rear tubular subframes bolted to the tub. A small number of cars have had rustproof steel replacement tubs, but this is expensive. The Ford V6 engine was mounted transversely amidships and a small number were turbocharged but this caused overheating and some have had their turbos removed.

The AC 3000ME had a high specification, including sunroof, Sundym tinted glass, electric windows, Wolfrace wheels and disc brakes all round.

Specific Checks: First, check the paperwork then contact the AC Owners' Club for further information. Inspect for rust in the centre tub and chassis crossmembers and check the gearbox carefully as repairs can be expensive.

Prices Today: About 100 cars have survived. The AC 3000ME is possibly undervalued.

Dates: 1946-59 (See text).   **Numbers Built:** See text.

Body/Chassis: Alloy/steel body, ash framed on steel chassis, 2-seater open sports (plus 4-seaters and saloons).

Engines: Mostly Ford 3622cc, V8, side-valve, 85-90bhp; plus Mercury 3917/4375cc, V8, side-valve, 95-100bhp; (J2, J2X, J2R & Palm Beach – See text).

Layout: Front engine, rear wheel drive, 3-speed manual gearbox.

Performance: See text.   **Prices Today:** Contact Club.

Above & Below: **The Allard J1 with its distinctive "waterfall" grille.**

Above & Below: **The K1, with a larger "waterfall" grille than the J1.**

Sydney Allard built a dozen Allard Specials prior to WW2 and in 1946 three production models were announced: the 2-seater Sports (K type - 270 cars produced), 4-seater Tourer (L type - 191 produced) and 4-seater Coupé (M type - 525 produced). These models were followed by the 2-door, 4-seater Saloon (P type - 559 produced) and the J series competition cars (J1, J2, and J2X types - 185 cars produced).

Allards used mainly Ford components along with the venerable UK Ford side-valve V8 engine and the smaller Ford 1508cc 4-cylinder and 2262cc 6-cylinder engines. Other V8s were also used in exported cars.

Prior to the tubular chassis, Allards were all built on the same ladder-frame type configuration, generally having 100in wheelbases for the J series, 106in for the K type and 112in for the L, M and P types. The tubular chassis Palm Beach Mk1, Mk2 and JR had 96in wheelbases and the P2 types had a 112in wheelbase. With the exception of the Palm Beach Mk2, all Allards used a split axle front suspension along with a de Dion type rear axle on J2, J2X, JR and GT coupés.

A tubular chassis was used on the later P2 types: Monte Carlo Saloon (11 cars produced), Safari Estate car (10 produced), K3 Tourer (62 produced), the JR series competition cars (7 produced) and 81 Palm Beach Mk1 and Mk2 cars (including two GT coupés).

With a striking, purposeful appearance and a rocket-like performance, the early cars initially sold well. This was helped by a considerable number of racing successes often led by Sydney Allard himself. In 1949 he was the British Hill Climb Champion and in 1950 his team, with a J2, were placed 3rd in the Le Mans 24-hour race. His greatest racing achievement was winning the 1952 Monte Carlo Rally – the only person ever to win the rally driving his own make of car, a P1 saloon.

Allard car production started to decline in the early 1950s and only a small number of cars were made in the final years, with production finally ending in 1959. A total of 1,901 Allards had been made.

J1/K1: With a large V8 engine, rapid acceleration, racing heritage and readily identifiable "waterfall" grille, these cars were a great success. 151 K1 cars were made 1946-48 together with a further 12 J1 competition cars. This latter model usually had the larger Mercury 3.9-litre engine. Typical performance for the K1 was just under 90mph top speed with an 0-60mph time of 13-14 seconds, while a J1 could reach 60mph in under 13 seconds (depending on tuning, rear axle ratio and tyre size).   Continued....

J2/J2X: Following the success of the J1 came the J2 with even larger V8 engines. UK customers usually had the Mercury engine bored out to 4.4-litres (120bhp) or 140bhp with the Ardun overhead valve cylinder head conversion. Cars exported to the US were usually sold without an engine and customers fitted either the Mercury V8, 5.4-litre Cadillac V8 (160bhp) or Chrysler V8 (172bhp).

With a J2, *Motor* magazine achieved a top speed over 110mph and 0-60mph in 7.4 seconds, incredibly fast for 1951. The cars had coil springs up front (rather than leaf spring) and a de Dion setup at the rear. The J2X featured the new X-type chassis with the engine set forward 7 inches to improve the weight distribution and increase leg room. The bodies of the J2 and the J2X were similar but the J2X was 6 inches longer to accommodate the forward facing radius rods. For racing, twelve J2X cars had fully enveloping front bodywork. Some tuned J2X cars could achieve speeds approaching 150mph and reach 60mph in around 5-6 seconds. 90 J2 cars were made 1949-51 and a further 83 J2X cars were made 1951-52. A Cadillac powered J2 driven by Godfrey Imhof won the 1952 RAC Rally. The very rare J2R had a very different, modern-looking body. It was a sports-racer, usually with a tuned 5.4-litre Cadillac V8 (7 cars made 1953-55).

K2: With its opening boot, the K2 was a more civilised version of the K1. For the UK market the car had Ford V8 or Mercury engines. Cars exported to the US (as usual, without engines) had Cadillac or Chrysler units fitted once they arrived. Between 1950 and 1952, 119 of the K2 cars were made. (The K3 cars, with their unique 3-across bench seating, were mostly exported to the US and Mexico in 1953-54 and featured modern bodywork like the early Palm Beach but used V8 engines. 62 were made).

Palm Beach: With Allards being increasingly exported, this model was aimed squarely at North America. The car had a tubular chassis, being a lighter and smaller version of the P2/K3 frame. It had hydraulic drum brakes and split axles on the Mk1 and MacPherson type front suspension on the Mk2. The Mk1 Palm Beach 21C (8 built) had a Ford Consul 4-cyl 1.5-litre 47bhp engine while the Mk1 Palm Beach 21Z (65 built) had a Ford Zephyr 6-cyl 2.2-litre 68bhp engine. The aluminium bodywork was completely different to the earlier roadsters but the Ford 3-speed gearbox was retained. The Palm Beach Mk2 (1956-59) had a restyled and attractive body but only 8 cars were made, including 5 with Jaguar engines and two GT coupés with fixed-head bodies. With the Jaguar XK engine, a Mk2 could do 120mph.

Specific Checks: Watch out for replica J2 and J2X cars which are created from P, L and M types. Check the chassis plate model prefix and contact the Allard Owners' Club.

Mechanically, weak points include the 3-speed Ford gearbox and excessive wear on the front suspension and steering joints due to a lack of maintenance.

Prices Today: Allards are difficult to price, but most models are probably in the **££££** range except for the J2, J2X and J2R which are in the "HiValue" category.

Above & Below: **The Allard J2, the car in the lower photo has a non-standard roll-over safety bar.**

Above: **The Allard K2.** Below: **The Allard Palm Beach Mk1.**

Dates: 1948-67 (See text).   **Numbers Built:** See text.

Body/Chassis: Steel body with alloy roof, doors, bonnet and boot, ash framed on steel chassis, 2-seater roadster or 4-seater sports saloon or drophead coupé.

Engines: TB14: 1892cc, 4-cyl in-line, ohv, 68bhp; Others: 2993cc, 6-cyl in-line, ohv, 93-150bhp.

Layout: Front engine, rear wheel drive, 4-speed (5-speed TE/TF21) manual gearbox (some overdrive; auto option from TD21).

Performance: See text.   **Prices:** Saloons: £££   DHC: ££££

Above: **Unlike the production Alvis TB14 above, the show car had its headlamps hidden behind the grille.**

Below: **This TA21 was Graber's first Alvis-based saloon and was the actual 1953 Geneva Show car.**

Above: **The TB21 used essentially the same body as the TB14 but with a different grille.**

Below: **The enduring, elegant lines of a Graber built TC108/G. The UK-built cars were subtly different.**

After WW2, Alvis launched the TA14, a 1.9-litre car of essentially prewar design, available as a saloon or a drophead. In 1948 came the TB14 sports version and in 1950 they launched the first of their 3-litre cars. This used an all-new 6-cylinder engine designed mainly by Chris Kingham and it had a new ladder-frame chassis with coil spring IFS and leaf springs at the rear. The 3-litre engine and chassis was steadily modified until the last Alvis car was made in 1967 (and the engine power output was progressively increased).

With virtually all Alvis cars, Alvis only made the engines and chassis which were then despatched to selected coachbuilders to have their bodies added.

These 3-litre cars are large, luxurious sports tourers, weighing 1½ tons empty and measuring 15ft 9in long, except for the TB21 which is both shorter and lighter.

During the 1960s, car making was very much a minor part of Alvis production, the bulk being military vehicles (such as the Saladin, Saracen and Stalwart). Car production ended in 1967 after the company merged with Rover, but military vehicle production continued.

TB14: The TB14 was launched in 1948 but it took until 1950 before cars reached customers. It had the same chassis as the TA14 but with twin carburettors the TB14 could reach about 85mph. The brakes were mechanical. 100 cars were built before the new 3-litre chassis was introduced and the model was replaced by the TB21.

TA21 (Graber): The huge majority of the over 2,000 TA21 and subsequent TC21 & TC21/100 cars that were made were Mulliners saloons or Tickford dropheads. But from 1951 the Swiss coachbuilding firm of Hermann Graber took 9 of these early 3-litre chassis to create the first of the Graber-bodied Alvis cars that would have an important bearing on the remaining years of Alvis car production. Of these early Grabers, 8 were convertibles.

TB21: Mating a modified body from a TB14 roadster to a TA21's chassis created the TB21 roadster. As the car had only two seats it gave it a long sleek look. With 93bhp and a changed rear axle ratio, 95mph could be attained. Only 31 cars were built 1950-54.

TC21/100: The TC21/100 is covered on page 166.

TC108/G: When Alvis faced a major problem with supplies of bodies drying up from their two main coachbuilders, Mulliners and Tickford, they turned to Graber who built two prototypes for Alvis. These handsome, elegant cars with their timeless lines defined the Alvis "look" until the end. Production TC108/G cars were also made by Willowbrook in England but the whole process took much longer than anticipated so only 14 cars were built 1955-58 (while Graber made a further 24). A wraparound rear screen identifies the Willowbrook-built cars.

TD21: The TD21 was launched at the London Motor Show in 1958, the bodies being mainly built by Park Ward (though Graber continued to fit his own bodies, often subtly different). The TD21 had a modified Graber-designed body which provided more headroom in the back and improved the rear visibility. Another change was that the gearbox was no longer by Alvis, but sourced from Austin (with optional overdrive) and an automatic gearbox was available. After the first 25 cars, an improved cylinder head was used which increased the power output to 115bhp. Later cars also had front disc brakes for the first time. There were two main series of cars, the Series I from 1958-62 (784 cars) and the Series II from 1962-63 (289 cars). The latter can be identified by their spotlamps which are fitted concentrically into circular air intakes. The Series II cars also had disc brakes on all wheels, alloy rather than ash door frames, a revised A-post and eventually a 5-speed ZF gearbox. The TD21 could do about 105mph and reach 60mph in under 15 seconds.

TE21/TF21: These cars are easily identifiable, with their double headlamps arranged vertically. The two models look identical though the TE21's instruments were central on the dash, whereas the TF21's instruments were in front of the driver. Power output was now up to 130bhp on the TE21 and 150bhp (with triple SU carbs) on the TF21. 352 TE21 cars were built 1963-66 and 106 TF21 cars were built 1966-1967. Graber's last one was made in 1968.

Specific Checks: Contact the Alvis Owner Club as most cars are known to them and when going to check a car, take a qualified Alvis expert with you.

The box section chassis can rust. Check also the body panels which are expensive to replace. If there are bubbles in the paintwork at the rear of the front wings (near the doors) this is a bad sign as it may indicate corrosion of the complex bulkhead section below. On pre-TD21 Series II cars, open the doors wide and check the front and rear door jambs which are ash and can rot.

Engines are long-lived but can overheat and rebuilds are expensive.

Refurbishing those wonderful interiors is expensive, especially the drophead roofs.

Note that a good-looking car, even with a valid MoT, may still require £10K-£30K spent on it, but at least there is good spares availability.

Prices Today: Dropheads are much more valuable than saloons. Graber cars command a premium as only 129 were ever made, so for their values, and that of the TC108/G, contact the Alvis Owner Club for advice.

Above: **Another Graber interpretation.**

Below: **TD21 Series I. The bungs on bumpers conceal jacking points.**

Above: **TD21 Series II. Gorgeous drophead convertible by Park Ward.**

Below: **The fastest of the 3-litre Alvis cars, the TF21, was capable of 120mph and 0-60mph in under 12 seconds.**

Dates: 1950-53	**Number Built:** c.407

Body/Chassis: Aluminium body on tubular steel chassis, 2-seater sports saloon or drophead coupé.

Engine: 2580cc, 6-cyl in-line, dohc, 105+bhp (See text).

Layout: Front engine, rear wheel drive, 4-speed manual gearbox.

Performance: Top speed c.110mph, 0-60mph in c.12sec; Vantage: c.120mph, 0-60mph in 10-11sec.

Prices Today: Saloon: £££££ Drophead: HiValue.

Above: **Frank Feeley, who was responsible for designing the bodywork, is shown seated in this early Aston Martin DB2 which was David Brown's personal car. The identity of the person standing beside the car is unknown. The miniature "DB2" is a child's pedal car (lucky kid!).**

Though prototype cars were raced during 1949, the production version was not launched until 1950 (in New York). The DB2 was Aston Martin's first postwar large-scale production car, following their earlier Two Litre Sports (sometimes retrospectively referred to as the DB1, with 15 cars built 1948-50). The "DB" prefix was the initials of David Brown, owner of Aston Martin. The DB2 used the 2.6-litre Lagonda engine, which is often referred to as the "Bentley engine" because W.O. Bentley was the Chief Engineer at the time, though the main designer was William Watson.

The car's chassis was derived from Claude Hill's chassis design for the DB1 but had a 9-inch shorter wheelbase. The chassis was highly triangulated and constructed of rectangular section steel tubing. Coil spring suspension was used all round, with hydraulic drum brakes. The handsome bodywork, by Frank Feeley, featured a large one-piece opening front, forward-hinged for good access to the engine. This was an innovative feature on a road-going car of that era.

The early cars had large hot air extractor grilles on each front wing and the radiator grille had vertical slats and was flanked by two smaller grilles. By 1951, the wing grilles had disappeared and the radiator grille (now with horizontal slats) became one-piece, incorporating the small flanking grilles. Some cars, mainly the early ones, had a distinctive rubbing strip along the sills (just visible in the top photo) which was another innovative feature. The saloon's rear window was quite small and some owners have increased its size. The rear boot lid was only to provide access to the spare wheel, luggage having to be passed behind the seats.

The engine was available with different compression ratios, partly to suit local petrol grades. The powerful "Vantage" version had an 8.16:1 ratio and larger SU carbs to produce 125bhp (or more with further tuning). The DB2 used a David Brown 4-speed manual gearbox with either floor or steering column gear change, but some of the latter have been converted to floor changes.

DB2 cars were raced successfully at Le Mans (and elsewhere), a high point being their 1st, 2nd and 3rd placings in the 3-litre class at the 1951 Le Mans.

Specific Checks: Start with the paperwork, then to verify the car's authenticity and learn about its background, contact the Aston Martin Heritage Trust. Checking a DB2 really needs the services of a qualified Aston Martin expert. Note that many of these cars have been raced or rallied. Check the chassis for corrosion and accident damage, also the bodywork which is susceptible to small dents. Test the engine carefully as a rebuild is expensive and the block can crack horizontally, which is bad news. Note the gearbox works best when fully warmed up. Any imprecise steering, wandering or unusual suspension sounds point to wear in that department.

Prices Today: The drophead is valued at about one and a half times that of the saloon.

Above: **The styling was advanced for 1950. Wire wheels were standard.**
Below: **Approximately 102 dropheads were made.**

Dates: 1953-59 (See text).

Numbers Built: DB2/4: c.565   MkII: c.199   DB MkIII: c.551

Body/Chassis: Aluminium body on tubular steel chassis, 2+2 seater sports saloon, drophead coupé or coupé.

Engines: 2580cc, 6-cyl in-line, dohc, 125bhp; 2922cc, 6-cyl in-line, dohc, 140+bhp (See text).

Layout: Front engine, rear wheel drive, 4-speed manual gearbox (DB MkIII: optional overdrive or 3-speed automatic).

Performance: 2.6L: Top speed c.110mph, 0-60mph in c.12sec; MkII: Top speed c.120mph, 0-60mph in c.10sec; DB MkIII: Top speed c.120mph, 0-60mph in c.8-9sec.

Prices Today: Saloons: £££££   Dropheads: HiValue.

Above: **From the front, the one-piece windscreen and bumper overriders help to distinguish the Aston Martin DB2/4 from the earlier DB2.**

To increase the market for the DB2, in 1953 Aston Martin launched the DB2/4 which, as its name suggests, was a four seater (in fact, it was really a 2+2). To achieve the extra seating, the roofline was raised at the rear, the cross-bracing above the rear axle was removed, the fuel tank was set lower (and reduced by 2 gallons to 17) and the spare wheel was placed below the fuel tank rather than above it. Access to the luggage area in the DB2 was not good so the DB2/4 introduced a rear-hatch.

Other improvements included a one-piece windscreen, and bumpers with overriders.

The DB2 2.6-litre engine in Vantage form was fitted as standard until 1954 when a larger 3-litre engine (VB6J) was used. About 565 cars were made, of which over 102 were dropheads. Three Works cars were entered for the 1955 Monte Carlo Rally and won the team prize.

In 1955 the car was revised and exhibited at the London Motor Show as the DB2/4 Mark II. Although the chassis and mechanical specification was unchanged, including the 140bhp VB6J engine (optional 165bhp), the bodies were now made by Tickford rather than Mulliners and there were many subtle changes. These included the roof being raised by 0.75in for more headroom (with a chrome strip above the windscreen), revised rear lights, indicators rather than trafficators and the lower wings behind the front wheels became part of the fixed bodywork rather than being part of the opening bonnet. This change was to eliminate bonnet shake by making the bonnet smaller, lighter and more rigid. Inside the car the improvements included better seats and a fly-off handbrake. About 199 Mark II cars were made, of which about 16 were drophead coupés and about 34 were fixed-head coupés (also known as "hardtops" though the roof was not removable), the remainder being what Aston Martin called "saloons".

In 1957 came the final version, the DB Mark III, which was immediately identifiable by its elegant, flowing grille. In addition, the chrome strip above the windscreen disappeared, the tail lights were revised again and the rear three-quarter windows were openable. Inside the car, the facia was changed completely, with the new shape resembling the front grille.

For the first time, front disc brakes were now available, initially as an option, then as standard (known

Below: **The DB2/4 featured a beautifully sculptured rear end which incorporated an innovative hatch. This particular car was one of the winning team of three Astons in the 1955 Monte Carlo Rally.**

Below: **This is from a series of publicity photos showing the new DB2/4 arriving at Lympne aerodrome (in Kent). Interestingly, the photos all emphasise the car's luggage capacity (note the cases visible in the rear), rather than its new 2+2 capability.**

as the IIIB specification). For the DB Mark III, Tadek Marek effectively redesigned the 3-litre engine, which was now designated DBA and had a stiffer crankcase and a new cylinder block, crankshaft and manifolds. Power output was now 162bhp (178bhp with optional twin exhausts). Ten cars had the optional DBB engine with 195bhp and 47 cars had the DBD 180bhp engine. These last cars could do over 120mph and accelerate to 60mph in about 8 seconds. The clutch was now hydraulically actuated. For 1959 an optional automatic gearbox was available for the first time.

The Mark III was nearly 9in longer and weighed c.350lb (160kg) more than a DB2. About 551 Mark III cars were made, of which approximately 84 were dropheads and five were fixed-head coupés. Nearly two thirds of the Mark III cars were exported to the US.

Specific Checks: Start with the paperwork, then to verify the car's authenticity and learn about its background, contact the Aston Martin Heritage Trust. Checking one of these cars really needs a qualified Aston Martin expert. Check the chassis for corrosion, especially the cruciform diagonals near the door rears. Mark I cars have alloy sills, whereas the later cars have steel (the inner sills are structural). Check the bonnet and hinges carefully, and the front suspension turrets for corrosion or cracks. Inspect the bodywork as it is susceptible to small dents.

Test the engine thoroughly as a rebuild is expensive and the block can crack horizontally, which is bad news. The bearing clearances in the all-alloy 2.9-litre engine are particularly fine and this can lead to overheating or low oil pressure when hot. These engines can also blow their cylinder head gaskets. Note the David Brown gearbox works best when fully warmed up. Any imprecise steering, wandering or unusual suspension sounds point to wear in that department.

Prices Today: The dropheads are valued at about one and a half times that of the saloons.

Photo Top Right: **The DB2/4 drophead.**
2nd From Top: **The DB2/4 Mark II coupé (also called "hardtop").**
3rd From Top: **The DB2/4 Mark II drophead with Windsor Castle behind. This well-known publicity shot is interesting because the car was in fact a Mark I with the photo retouched to make it appear like a Mark II.**
Lower Right: **The DB Mark III saloon. This car is one of the last made.**
Below: **The DB Mark III drophead.**

Dates: 1958-63 (Zagato: 1961-2000)

Numbers Built: DB4: c.1,110   DB4GT: 75   Zagato: 25

Body/Chassis: Aluminium body over steel tubing on steel platform chassis, 4-seater sports saloon or convertible; DB4GT & Zagato: 2-seater sports saloon.

Engine: 3670cc, 6-cyl in-line, dohc, 240bhp (net) (See text).

Layout: Front engine, rear wheel drive, 4-speed manual gearbox with optional overdrive or 3-speed automatic (very rare).

Performance: DB4: Top speed over 140mph, 0-60mph in c.8sec; DB4GT & Zagato: Over 150mph, 0-60mph in c.6sec.

Prices Today: HiValue (See text).

Above: **The handsome Aston Martin DB4. There were five Series; the car shown above is a Series 2. Wire wheels were standard, though chrome plating of the wheels was usually an extra cost.**

The DB4, launched in 1958, represented an entirely new car for Aston Martin rather than simply a development of their earlier models. Styled by Touring of Milan, it used the "Superleggera" (ie super-light) principle where slender steel tubes formed the shape of the roof and rear sections, and were welded to the chassis then covered with light aluminium bodywork.

The new chassis, designed by Harold Beach, was a complex and substantial steel platform construction. The independent front suspension was by coil springs with co-axial telescopic dampers and transverse wishbones. The live rear axle had coil springs with lever type dampers, parallel trailing links and transverse Watts linkage. Steering was by rack and pinion and there were servo-assisted disc brakes all round.

Below: **With the DB4, Aston Martin returned to a conventional rear boot rather than a rear-hatch as used on the earlier DB2/4.**

The engine was also new. Designed by Tadek Marek, this superb 3.7-litre six-cylinder all-alloy double overhead camshaft engine had been race developed. After early overheating/low oil pressure problems had been overcome, it was ultimately to power many Aston models. The standard gearbox for the DB4 was a 4-speed David Brown manual unit.

There were just over 1,100 DB4 cars made in five Series. The first 50 cars had frameless door windows but this was not satisfactory at high speed so chrome frames were introduced. A total of 150 Series 1 cars were made before the Series 2 arrived in 1960. These had bonnets hinged at the front (for safety reasons), better front disc calipers, a bigger oil sump with optional oil cooler and opening rear quarter lights. 350 Series 2 cars were made.

The following year came the Series 3, with three separate circular rear lights and other minor improvements. 165 were made before the Series 4 cars arrived later that same year (1961). Most of these cars had the DB4GT front styling with headlight fairings. There was also a new design of grille with 7 vertical bars (see right) and the bonnet air scoop was reduced in height. The oil cooler was now standard. In total, 230 Series 4 cars were made, plus a further 30 pretty convertibles. The DB4 Vantage was also launched in 1961. It had a 266bhp "Special Series" engine with a tuned head and triple SU carburettors. 136 DB4s were fitted with this engine plus 32 Series 4 and 5 convertibles.

Below: **Only 70 of these attractive and desirable DB4 convertibles were made. They were based on the Series 4 then Series 5 cars. Note the quarter light door windows which were not on the saloon version, also the new grille design which appeared on the Series 4 and 5 cars. The convertible was not called a "Volante" at this stage.**

In 1962 came the final version of the DB4, the Series 5. This had its body lengthened by about 3.5 inches to give more space and it had 15-inch (rather than 16-inch) wheels. Most were to Vantage specification. 145 Series 5 saloons were made, plus a further 40 convertibles.

In the meantime, in 1959, an exciting derivative of the DB4, the 2-seater DB4GT, had been launched. It was about 5 inches shorter in both wheelbase and length than the saloon, had headlight fairings and was lighter than a comparable DB4 by c.180lb (80kg). The highly tuned engine had twin spark plugs per cylinder, triple Weber carbs and gave over 300bhp (net), so the car was suitably quick. The prototype, driven by Stirling Moss, won its first race and set a new lap record at Silverstone. In total, 75 DB4GT cars were made. The GT engine was also used in about 14 DB4 Vantage GT cars.

At the London Motor Show in 1960 there appeared the fabulous DB4GT Zagato. Based on the GT chassis, it was even lighter, having a thin gauge aluminium body, perspex side windows and lighter trim. Styled by Ercole Spada, the Zagato was intended to compete with Ferrari. With highly tuned engines these Zagatos were very fast cars. Initially 19 of these road/race cars were made (plus one Bertone-bodied coupé) then in 1991 a further four "Sanction 2" Zagatos were completed. These were followed by two more cars in 2000, often referred to as "Sanction 3" cars. Note that over the years a number of DB4 cars have had Zagato type bodies fitted.

Specific Checks: Start with the paperwork, then to verify the car's authenticity and learn about its background, contact the Aston Martin Heritage Trust. Checking one of these cars really needs the services of a qualified Aston Martin expert. With the DB4 range, the main worries are chassis and engine condition and note that generally parts can be very expensive.

The important sills are mostly hidden by the bodywork, so to assess them look underneath, into the wheelarches, examine the sill paintwork for oxidisation due to underlying rust, and you might request the owner to jack up the car (to test the car's structural integrity). Check also the chassis in the scuttle and footwell area and where the rear suspension arms are mounted. The door bottoms and hinges are also prone to corrosion. The light alloy bodywork can dent and may suffer from electrolytic corrosion wherever it meets steel.

Test the engine carefully as a rebuild is hugely expensive. The alloy block can crack, which is bad news, and the cylinder liners can corrode with their O-ring failure leading to oil and water mixing (also bad news). Weeping from six tiny indicator holes on the block side might indicate O-ring failure. Note the gearbox works best when fully warmed up and may baulk when worn. Note too that many of these cars, particularly the GTs and Zagatos, have been raced or rallied.

Prices Today: Vantage versions carry a small premium. The drophead is valued about one and a half times that of the saloon, while the DB4GT is valued at considerably more and the Zagato is higher still. Competition history can add substantially to the value of a car.

Above: **The DB4GT was a 2-seater and was shorter than the saloon. Note that many of the DB4 Vantage cars also had the faired headlights.**

Below: **The fabulous DB4GT Zagato. Only 25 were made, in 3 batches, between 1961 and 2000. Initially difficult to sell, today they are highly sought after and hugely expensive to buy.**

Below: **The DB4GT Zagatos were all very individual cars with minor differences between them. To save weight, no bumpers was normal.**

| Dates: | 1963-65 | Number Built: | c.1,034 |

Body/Chassis: Aluminium body over steel tubing on steel platform chassis, 4-seater sports saloon, convertible or estate.

Engine: 3995cc, 6-cyl in-line, dohc, 282bhp (See text).

Layout: Front engine, rear wheel drive, 4-speed manual with overdrive (later 5-speed) or 3-speed automatic gearbox.

Performance: Top speed over 140mph, 0-60mph in c.8sec; (Vantage slightly faster).

Price Today: HiValue (See text).

Above: **The Aston Martin DB5 looks similar to the Series 5 DB4 Vantage (with faired headlights), though the DB5 has two petrol fillers (but confusingly, so do some late DB4 cars).**
Below: **123 of these pretty DB5 drophead convertibles were made.**

The DB5, launched in 1963, was a natural development of the DB4 Series 5, with a larger engine and, after the first 40 cars, a 5-speed ZF gearbox rather than the David Brown 4-speed unit with overdrive. The engine had triple SU carburettors as standard and the increase in power helped to compensate for the greater weight of the DB5. The added c.250lb (113kg) was due to more standard equipment such as electric windows, Sundym tinted glass, an alternator, four silencers (rather than two), Girling tandem brake master cylinders and twin vacuum brake servos with disc brakes on all wheels. Included in the options list was air-conditioning (fitted to most cars exported to the US), Selectaride adjustable rear dampers and 3-speed Borg-Warner automatic transmission. As usual, wire wheels (15-inch) were standard.

A Vantage engine with triple Weber carburettors was again offered as an option (from autumn 1964), this time producing 314bhp (later an optimistic 325bhp was quoted). There were 65 Vantage cars made.

The DB5 is inextricably linked in the popular consciousness with the fictional hero, James Bond (007), who drove a much modified DB5 in many of his films.

Another interesting variant came about because David Brown wanted an estate version for himself and had the factory convert a DB5 for his personal use. Then customers saw his car and wanted similar conversions so the coachbuilding firm of Radfords was contracted to do these Shooting Brake conversions and a total of 12 more were made (plus seven DB6 based cars).

Specific Checks: Start with the paperwork, then to verify the car's authenticity and learn about its background, contact the Aston Martin Heritage Trust. Checking one of these cars really needs the services of a qualified Aston Martin expert. With the DB5 the main worries are chassis and engine condition and note that generally parts can be very expensive.

The important sills are mostly hidden by bodywork, so look underneath, into the wheelarches and examine the sill paintwork for oxidisation due to underlying corrosion. You might request the owner to jack up the car to test the car's structural integrity. Check also the chassis in the scuttle and footwell area and where the rear suspension arms are mounted. The door bottoms and hinges are also prone to corrosion. The alloy bodywork can dent and may suffer from electrolytic corrosion wherever it meets steel.

Test the engine thoroughly as a rebuild is hugely expensive. The alloy block can crack, which is bad news, and the cylinder liners can corrode with their O-ring failure leading to oil and water mixing (also bad news). Weeping from six tiny indicator holes on the block side might indicate O-ring failure. Note that some of the saloons have been raced or rallied.

Prices Today: Vantage versions carry a small premium. The drophead is valued significantly more than the saloon. A car with automatic transmission is worth slightly less than a car with a manual gearbox. Note that competition history can add substantial value.

Below: **Later DB5 cars had "DB5" badges by the rear number plate.**

Dates:	1965-70
Numbers Built:	DB6: c.1,573 Volante: c.215
Body/Chassis:	Aluminium body over steel tubing on steel platform chassis, 4-seater sports saloon, convertible or estate.
Engine:	3995cc, 6-cyl in-line, dohc, 282bhp (See text).
Layout:	Front engine, rear wheel drive, 5-speed manual or 3-speed automatic gearbox.
Performance:	Vantage: Top speed c.145mph, 0-60mph in c.6sec.
Prices Today:	HiValue (See text).

Above & Below: **The DB6 looks similar to the DB5 but has split bumpers, a Kamm tail, rear spoiler and "DB6" tail badge. Also, the DB6 saloon has quarter lights, whereas the DB5 saloon does not. This is a Mk1 car.**

The DB6, launched in 1965, was the third and last of the Italianate Astons and the most numerous. The DB6 had a slightly higher roof, longer wheelbase (by 3.75in), a more steeply raked windscreen (by 4 degrees) and opening quarter lights. The leather trim on the Mk1 cars had large, distinctive "V" seams. Power steering, air-conditioning and automatic transmission were options.

The same engines were used as for the DB5, though the Vantage engine was progressively modified through three stages, coded A to C, but the same 325bhp was quoted. Vantage engines were fitted to many cars.

In 1969 came the Mk2, identified by its flared wheelarches to accommodate wider tyres. All these later cars had power steering, Selectaride rear dampers and 46 also had fuel injection. 248 Mk2 saloons were made.

The convertible version of the DB6 was given its own inspired name, the "Volante". The first 37 cars were built on the DB5 chassis and are called, not surprisingly, the "Short Chassis Volantes". They have features of both the DB5 and DB6, but no Kamm tail. The full DB6 version was launched at the London Motor Show in 1966. 178 Mk1 and Mk2 Volantes were made, 38 with Vantage engines and half with automatic transmission.

Radfords converted another seven to Shooting Brake estates while another coachbuilder, FLM Panelcraft, created a few more.

Specific Checks: Start with the paperwork, then to verify the car's authenticity and learn about its background, contact the Aston Martin Heritage Trust. Checking one of these cars really needs the services of a qualified Aston Martin expert. With the DB6 and Volante the main worries are chassis and engine condition and note that generally parts can be very expensive.

The important sills are mostly hidden by bodywork, so look underneath, into the wheelarches and examine the sill paintwork for oxidisation due to underlying corrosion. You might request the owner to jack up the car to test the car's structural integrity. Check also the chassis in the scuttle and footwell area and where the rear suspension arms are mounted. The door bottoms and hinges are also prone to corrosion. The alloy bodywork can dent and may suffer from electrolytic corrosion wherever it meets steel.

Test the engine thoroughly as a rebuild is hugely expensive. The alloy block can crack, which is bad news,

and the cylinder liners can corrode with their O-ring failure leading to oil and water mixing (also bad news). Weeping from six tiny indicator holes on the block side might indicate O-ring failure.

Prices Today: Vantage versions carry a small premium. The Volante is valued at one and a half to two times that of the saloon. A car with automatic transmission is worth slightly less than a car with a manual gearbox. Note that competition history can add substantial value.

Below: **215 of these pretty Volantes were made in total, including the first 37 Short Chassis cars with their non-Kamm tails. The soft-top roof was powered. The car below is a Mk1 Volante.**

Dates: DBS: 1967-72   Vantage: 1972-73

Numbers Built: DBS: c.786   Vantage: 70

Body/Chassis: Aluminium panels on steel superstructure mounted on steel platform chassis, 4-seater sports saloon.

Engine: 3995cc, 6-cyl in-line, dohc, 282bhp (See text).

Layout: Front engine, rear wheel drive, 3-speed automatic or 5-speed manual gearbox.

Performance: Top speed c.140mph, 0-60mph in c.7-8sec.

Price Today: £££/££££

Above: **The attractive lines of the Aston Martin DBS were styled by William Towns. This is a Series 2 car.**

The DBS continued the Aston Martin DB series of cars and was built alongside the earlier DB6, until the latter was phased out in late 1970. The DBS was based on a modified DB6 chassis which had been lengthened by one inch and widened by 4.5in, though the overall car was 1.5in shorter and 6in wider. The DBS also used the same 6-cylinder engine as the DB6, though the new car had in fact been designed for a V8 unit, the production of which was running behind schedule due to technical problems. A major change from the DB6 was the de Dion rear end which replaced the DB6's live axle arrangement. The front suspension of the DB6 was retained, which comprised double unequal wishbones, coil springs with co-axial shock absorbers and anti-roll bar.

The 6-cylinder engine still produced a quoted 282bhp with SU carbs. In Vantage form, with triple Webers, it was optimistically quoted as 325bhp. Fuel injection was an option. The clutch was quite heavy to use so most buyers opted for the excellent Borg-Warner 3-speed automatic gearbox. All cars had limited slip differentials as standard and as with all Astons up to that time, the DBS had wire wheels. Also standard were Sundym tinted glass and electric windows, while power steering and air-conditioning were optional extras.

At 6ft wide, half-an-inch over 15ft long, weighing almost two tons laden, and capable of exceeding 140mph, the DBS was a seriously large and fast machine.

The initial DBS Series 1 cars (approximately 550 made) are identified by the ventilation extractor slots in the C-post behind the rear three-quarter windows. The Series 2 cars (from early 1970), had their extractor slots under the rear window, plus deeper panels under the nose, sills and rear. The Series 2 cars also had a revised gear console and facia, and power steering became standard.

In 1972, after David Brown's departure, the company dropped the "DB" prefix (reintroduced in the 1990s) and the car became known simply as the Aston Martin Vantage. It was produced for just over a year. The Vantage can be identified by its new front which had two 7in headlights rather than the DBS's four 5.5in headlights. This was the same as the Aston Martin V8 launched at the same time, but unlike the V8, the 6-cylinder Vantage still had wire wheels. There was still a market for this

Below: **The 6-cylinder DBS can be readily distinguished from the similar DBS V8 by the wire wheels which were used only on the DBS.**

Below: **A pre-production car. The ventilation extractor slots in the C-post are clearly visible. These were a Series 1 feature.**

smaller engined car (due to the V8 model costing nearly one third more), but it was to be Aston Martin's last 6-cylinder car.

Specific Checks: Start with the paperwork, then to verify the car's authenticity and learn about its background, contact the Aston Martin Heritage Trust. Checking a DBS or Vantage really needs the services of a qualified Aston Martin expert. With these cars the main worries are chassis and engine condition and note that generally parts can be very expensive.

Due to the cost, many of these cars have had poor body repairs or have not been serviced properly (ideally every 2,500 miles) so a full recent service history is essential and if not available, one must assume the worst.

When checking the bodywork, note that aluminium can crack with age and stress, so look especially around the windscreen pillars' bases and the boot lid area. Generally, where the aluminium panels meet the steel inner structure or chassis, corrosion can occur despite Aston Martin taking care to prevent this.

To check the important sill area, you might ask the seller if you can remove the chrome cover plates. Beware of cars that have had a new sill outer panel simply welded over rusty inner ones. Also check the jacking points and inner wings for other indications of corrosion. The rear end is also prone to rust and if it affects the suspension mountings the repair can be very expensive.

As it wears, the automatic gearbox begins to drip oil – check the ground where the car is usually parked.

Prices Today: Along with the DBS V8 and the V8, these are the (relatively) affordable Astons at today's prices, but maintenance bills will reflect their hand built supercar status. Manual gearbox cars are worth more than automatics, while Vantage versions are at a slight premium.

Photo Top Right: **An Aston Martin DBS with Vantage engine.**
2nd From Top: **The racing driver, Innes Ireland, in an early DBS.**
3rd From Top: **An Aston Martin Vantage with its revised front including single headlight units.**
Lower Right: **The luxury interior with automatic transmission.**
Below: **Ouch! This crash test at MIRA in September 1968 involved driving the DBS into a 200 ton concrete block at 30mph. It passed.**

Dates: 1969-90

Numbers Built: DBS V8: c.400   V8: c.1,607   Vantage: c.369
Volante: c.663 (plus c.187 Vantage).

Body/Chassis: Aluminium panels on steel superstructure on steel
chassis, 4-seater sports saloon or convertible.

Engine: 5340cc, V8, dohc/bank, (fuel injection & bhp -See text).

Layout: Front engine, rear wheel drive, 3-speed automatic or
5-speed manual gearbox.

Performance: V8: Top speed c.160mph, 0-60mph in c.6sec;
Vantage: Top speed c.170mph, 0-60mph under 6sec;
Volante: Top speed c.150mph, 0-60mph in c.8sec.

Prices Today: DBS V8 & V8: ££££   Vantage & Volante: HiValue.

Above: **An Aston Martin DBS V8.**

It had always been intended to power the DBS with a new V8 engine, which was initially designed by Tadek Marek. The engine required significant development by others before it was ready for production. Once fully sorted, the V8 was a technical triumph with its four overhead camshafts and all-alloy construction. Initially the engine was fuel injected. Although at that time Aston Martin did not quote the power output of their engines, it seems that the new V8 produced around 300-320bhp.

Power steering was standard on the car. Due to concerns about the wire wheels' ability to cope with all the torque, these cars had special GKN alloy wheels instead of wire wheels. The disc brakes were now ventilated. Although the manual ZF gearbox was a good one, the clutch was heavy and many buyers opted for the excellent Chrysler 3-speed automatic gearbox. Air-conditioning was standard from late 1971.

In 1972, after David Brown's departure, the company dropped the "DB" prefix and launched a much modified car known simply as the Aston Martin V8. It had only two 7in headlights and the same frontal design as the 6-cylinder Aston Martin Vantage. Other improvements included more boot space (created by stowing the spare wheel flat), better sound insulation and electronic ignition. After about 288 of these cars had been made, there came a new model in 1973, its main change being the adoption of Weber carbs rather than fuel injection. This required a larger bonnet bulge air intake and the bulge itself was extended to the back of the bonnet. These cars had many other detail improvements such as better engine cooling and revised interiors. With increasing emission controls, power output fell, but with some mild tuning in 1977, it was restored to 304-305bhp. Approx. 969 of these Weber cars were made to 1978.

In October 1978 came the "Oscar India" cars, using the phonetic alphabet for OI, which stood for "October Introduction". There were minor changes: the bonnet bulge front was blanked off, a small rear spoiler was added and the interior was updated to include a burr walnut facia. The heating and ventilation system was revised (again), with better air-conditioning. 1980 saw the V580 engine introduced, giving improved fuel consumption. In the next few years, the car's specification continued to be enhanced, eg central locking, electric door mirrors and a lock-up facility on the auto gearbox.

About 291 Oscar India cars were made before the last series of the standard V8 cars appeared in 1986. These reverted to fuel injection (305bhp being quoted) and were easily identifiable with their cross-spoke BBS alloy wheels and lack of any bonnet bulge. Only 59 cars were made before production ended in 1989.

From 1977 buyers could specify the Vantage version. These had an uprated engine with revised valves, camshafts, manifolds, carburettors etc and generated some 375-380bhp, and were initially available only with a manual gearbox. This was the fastest production car in the UK at the time. The Vantage was recognisable by its blanked-off front grille, deep glassfibre front air dam and rear spoiler. The air intake on the bonnet was closed. A new version arrived in October 1978, sharing many features of the standard Oscar India cars. From 1983, BBS wheels were fitted. The final version appeared in 1986. These last cars had 16-inch wheels of various makes and some cars were automatics. The V580X engine was considerably tuned to raise its power output to a claimed 400+bhp. In total, c.369 of these Vantage cars were made.

In 1978 the delectable Volante convertible became available. This had a powered and lined soft-top, leather upholstery, burr walnut veneer, air-conditioning, etc. In 1986 came a new version with fuel injection and no bonnet bulge. Later in the same year appeared the Vantage Volante – the most desirable of the range. About half of these cars had automatic gearboxes. The Vantage Volante had a bodykit, but HRH Prince Charles, a long time Aston owner, ordered one without the bodykit. Another two dozen buyers followed suit, so these cars are often known as the "POW" (Prince of Wales) version.

Below: **An early Aston Martin V8. Note the different front to the DBS V8.**

During the 1980s, due to emission controls, the Federal specification cars were slower than the performance figures quoted in the data box.

The company, after changing hands several times, was eventually taken over by Ford in 1987. In 1990 the Aston Martin V8 range was replaced by the new Virage.

Specific Checks: Start with the paperwork, then to verify the car's authenticity and learn about its background, contact the Aston Martin Heritage Trust. Checking a V8 car really needs the services of a qualified Aston Martin expert. Remember that generally parts can be very expensive. Due to cost, many of these cars have had poor body repairs or not been serviced properly (ideally every 2,500 miles) so a full recent service history is essential and if not available, one must assume the worst.

When checking the bodywork, note that aluminium can crack with age and stress, so look especially around the windscreen pillars' bases and boot lid area. Where the aluminium meets the steel inner structure or chassis, corrosion can occur despite Aston Martin taking care to prevent this.

To check the important sill area, you might ask the seller if you can remove the chrome cover plates. Beware of cars that have had a new sill outer panel simply welded over rusty inner ones. Also check the jacking points and inner wings for other indications of corrosion. The rear end is also prone to rust and if it affects the suspension mountings the repair could be very expensive.

The V8 engines can suffer from blown head gaskets. To check for this, pre-warm the engine then run it up to over 4,000rpm while on your test drive. Although a blown head gasket can manifest itself in a number of ways, the most common one with this V8 is to raise the header tank coolant level or even blow out the coolant. A compression test on each cylinder is advisable. Check also the idle and running oil pressures are as per the car's manual, and listen to check that the engine is not "rumbling".

As it wears, the automatic gearbox begins to drip oil – check the ground where the car is usually parked.

Prices: Today, along with their 6-cylinder sister, the DBS, the DBS V8 and V8 saloon (non-Vantage) cars are the (relatively) affordable Aston Martins, but maintenance bills will reflect their hand built supercar status. The V8 engine cars are slightly more expensive to buy than the 6-cylinder ones. Manual gearbox cars are worth more than automatics, the Vantages are worth around double the standard cars and the Volantes are higher still.

Above: **The purposeful rear of William Towns' V8 design.**
Below: **The Volante had a fully lined, powered, soft-top roof.**

Above: **The Vantage Volante had a controversial bodykit.**
Below: **The "POW" Volante was so-called because the Prince of Wales preferred his Volante without the bodykit (shown above).**

Left: **An Aston Martin V8 Zagato (1986-88). 89 built (including 37 Volantes). 5.3L 432bhp engine. 186mph and 0-60 in under 5 seconds. HiValue.**

AUSTIN-HEALEY 100 & 100-Six

Dates: 1952-59

Numbers Built: 100: c.14,630   100-Six: c.15,440

Body/Chassis: Steel and aluminium body with steel chassis, 2-seater (100-Six: 2 or 2+2 seater) open sports.

Engines: 100: Austin 2660cc, 4-cyl in-line, ohv, 90bhp; 100-Six: Austin 2639cc, 6-cyl in-line, ohv, 102-117bhp.

Layout: Front engine, rear wheel drive, 3-speed (later 4-speed) manual gearbox (some with overdrive).

Performance: 100: Top speed c.105mph, 0-60mph in c.11sec.

Prices Today: £££+   100M, 100S: Contact Club.

AUSTIN-HEALEY 3000

Dates: 1959-67

Numbers Built: MkI: c.13,650   MkII: c.5,450   MkIIa: c.6,110
MkIII: c.17,700

Body/Chassis: Steel and aluminium body with steel chassis, 2 or 2+2 seater open sports.

Engine: Austin 2912cc, 6-cyl in-line, ohv, 124bhp; MkII: 132bhp; MkIII: 148bhp.

Layout: Front engine, rear wheel drive, 4-speed manual gearbox (some with overdrive).

Performance: Top speed c.115mph, 0-60mph in c.11sec; MkIII: Over 120mph, 0-60mph in under 10sec.

Prices Today: MkI, MkII: £££/££££   MkIII: ££££+

Above: **A charming period photograph of an Austin-Healey 100. Note the characteristic sweep of the door lines.**

A feature of the 100 was that its windscreen could be raked backwards for racing. There was a full race version, the 100S, built in 1955, but only 55 were made so it is extremely rare and very valuable today. Its considerably different specification included alloy external body panels, special oval grille, disc brakes on all wheels, uprated suspension, large fuel tank and a tuned 132bhp engine.

There was also the more numerous 100M "Le Mans" version. This had a tuned engine producing 100-110bhp, and usually a louvred bonnet with leather bonnet strap. About three-quarters of the cars had two-tone paintwork. Probably around 640 cars were factory-built in 1955-56 and are known as 100M cars, while a further 500 or so "Le Mans" conversion kits were sold to dealers or owners (or fitted by the Donald Healey Motor Company at Warwick). Only the factory-built 100M cars have chassis numbers that identify them. As the 100M is desirable, it requires care when purchasing one today as there are cars advertised as one of the original 640 100M cars when they are not.

In 1956 came the first of the 6-cylinder cars, the 100-Six, designated the BN4. It was a 2+2 seater and could be readily distinguished from the earlier 100 by its oval grille, bonnet air scoop and external door handles. The

The 1952 London Motor Show was the venue for Donald Healey to show his handsome new Healey 100 prototype. The "100" designation reflected his intention that it should be a true 100mph sports car. The car was a sensation and Leonard Lord, then head of Austin, made a deal with Healey that Austin would manufacture and market the car. Hence the famous Austin-Healey marque was born.

The car had been sketched by Donald Healey with final styling by Gerry Coker. Donald, his son Geoffrey, and Barry Bilbie had produced the chassis design. A number of pre-production cars were made in late 1952 and production proper commenced the following year. Jensen Motors were contracted to make the body/chassis units which were then transported, fully painted, to the main Austin assembly plant at Longbridge.

The first Austin-Healey 100 cars had 3-speed manual gearboxes (with overdrive) and are known as Series BN1 cars. Interestingly, this gearbox was in fact a 4-speed Austin unit with the lowest gear blanked off as it was deemed unnecessary. The later BN2 series cars (c.4,600 made) had stronger 4-speed gearboxes (again with overdrive) and better brakes (but still drum brakes on all wheels).

Below: **This car is a BN1 converted to 100M "Le Mans" specification. Note the intriguing side flash which is the wrong way round.**

cars were longer (2 inches in the wheelbase), the windscreen was now fixed and overdrive was optional. In 1957 the engine power output was increased by a quoted 15bhp by fitting a new cylinder head and six-port inlet manifold, also larger carburettors. Some owners upgraded their older cars. From late 1957, assembly of the cars was moved to the MG Plant at Abingdon in Oxfordshire and in 1958 a 2-seater, the BN6, was launched and about 4,100 were made.

In 1959 came the Austin-Healey 3000. Developed from the earlier, visually almost identical, Austin-Healey 100-Six, the 3000 had a larger engine and better brakes (discs on the front for the first time). The car came in two forms – the 2-seater BN7 (c. 2,800 made) and the 2+2 seater BT7 (c.10,800 made). Like its predecessor, the new 3000 was also assembled at the MG Plant.

In 1961 the MkII models, still designated BN7 (c.350 made) and BT7 (c.5,100 made), came out with triple SU carburettors and high-lift camshaft producing 132bhp. The front grilles on these cars now had vertical bars rather than horizontal bars. The carbs were difficult to keep in tune, so in 1962 Austin-Healey reverted to twin carburettors with a new model, the MkII Convertible, designated BJ7 (and unofficially sometimes known as a MkIIa). It was a 2+2 seater convertible with a new curved windscreen, quarter lights and wind-up windows for the first time. A 2-seater version was never reintroduced.

The BJ7 was replaced by the more powerful MkIII (BJ8) the following year. This new model was made in larger numbers than all the previous models. It had new carburettors and revised camshaft to give a further increase in power, a revised interior with a new wood veneer dashboard and centre console. It also had a quieter exhaust and servo-assisted brakes. The first 1,390 examples are referred to these days as "Phase I" cars because in the Spring of 1964 a revised version was introduced without any fanfare or publicity. These later Healeys (now referred to as "Phase II" cars) were much improved. They had revised rear suspension to increase ground clearance by about 1.5in and the rear springs were softer too. The front disc brakes were uprated, hubs strengthened and door handles changed to push-button. In 1965 came the final change which was to provide separate indicators front and rear. These cars are sometimes referred to as "Phase III".

Suitably modified 3000s were rallied successfully by Pat Moss, the Morley brothers, Timo Makinen, Paddy Hopkirk and Rauno Aaltonen, amongst others.

Most "Big Healey" production went to North America, though quite a number have returned to the UK and been converted to right-hand drive. Original left-hand drive cars can be identified by an "L" on their chassis/car number (some later MkIII cars have a "U" in the chassis/car number designating a North American specification).

In 1967 production ceased because the company said the car could not comply with the new US safety and emission regulations and partly because the car's design was beginning to be outdated by the competition.

Continued....

Above: **An Austin-Healey 100 with non-standard "Le Mans" headlights.**
Below: **An Austin-Healey 100-Six. Note the different grille.**

Above: **A 100-Six with after-fit rear indicators (the middle lights).**
Below: **A 3000 MkII 2+2 with non-standard Le Mans type headlamps.**

Specific Checks: When inspecting an Austin-Healey 100, 100-Six or 3000, first check the paperwork, ensuring the numbers match those on the vehicle, then later verify the car's authenticity by contacting the Heritage Motor Centre Archives, Gaydon (unless the car already has a Heritage Certificate).

When examining the car itself, start with the chassis. This consists of two main longitudinal rails with cross-members and outriggers. In an accident the rails get kinked. Hence check these are straight (and not rusted). The outriggers are particularly prone to corrosion. The chassis is welded to the floor and bulkheads which makes repairs more difficult.

The front and rear shrouds (ie the bodywork between the bonnet and front wings and the bodywork between the rear boot lid and rear wings) are aluminium and are prone to dents and electrolytic corrosion where they meet the steel wings. As with most open cars, the door fit is a good guide to the condition of the bodywork and chassis – the gap between the door and body should be the same from top to bottom. If the gap at the top is less than at the bottom, it may indicate that the whole car is sagging, which is not a good sign. Look also at the swage line that runs along the side of the car – this will also reveal any misalignment of the doors.

The Austin engines are fairly reliable but consume oil and are leaky. The gearboxes are also reliable (the BN1 unit perhaps less so) and so are the rear axles. Ground clearance was never great and reduces with age which increases the likelihood of damage to the underside and loss of exhausts.

Options included a hardtop, heater, overdrive (where it was not standard) and wire wheels. A brake servo was optional from late 1961 (standard on MkIII).

Note: The term "100-4" is an unofficial name sometimes used for the original "100" model to distinguish it from the later 6-cylinder 100-Six.

Prices Today: In terms of value, the 2-seaters generally cost more than the 2+2 seaters, while the late MkIII cars are the most valuable as they are the most popular. However, there is relatively little difference in value over the whole range (excluding the 100M and rare 100S). The condition of a car is the most important factor.

Below: **A late Austin-Healey MkIII.**

Above & Below: **The 3000 MkII 2+2 was the last model with sidescreens.**

Above & Below: **An early MkIII, with standard steel disc wheels (rare).**

Dates: 1958-71   **Number Built:** c.129,500

Body/Chassis: Steel unitary, 2-seater open sports.

Engines:
  1958-66: 948cc then 1098cc, 4-cyl in-line, ohv, 43-59bhp (net);
  1966-71: 1275cc, 4-cyl in-line, ohv, 65bhp (net), (US: 65-55bhp).

Layout: Front engine, rear wheel drive, 4-speed manual gearbox.

Performance:
  MkI: Top speed just over 80mph, 0-60mph in c.20sec;
  MkIV: Top speed over 95mph, 0-60mph in c.13sec.

Prices Today: Frogeye: ££   Others: £+

Above: **An Austin-Healey Sprite MkI (Frogeye). To keep the price down, even the front bumper was an extra.**

Designed by the Healey team with Barry Bilbie, Gerry Coker and later, Les Ireland, and with final input by MG, the Sprite was intended to be low cost. To achieve this it used many components (modified as required) from the Austin A35 saloon, such as the A-series engine, gearbox, rear axle and front suspension. The rear suspension, however, was different to the A35, using quarter elliptic springs and trailing arms. Twin SU carburettors helped to boost the modest engine power. It was Britain's first mass-produced open sports car that was of unitary construction and it was assembled at the MG Plant at Abingdon. With its headlights sprouting from the bonnet, this much-loved car soon became known affectionately as the "Frogeye" (or the "Bugeye" in North America).

The car abounded with little quirks, such as the lack of external door handles, the lack of an opening rear boot lid (to put luggage in the rear you had to get it past the seats) and the huge one-piece rear-hinged bonnet that opened like a clam shell. Although the performance is modest by modern standards, it was adequate for its era and the car had the added benefits of good handling and a quick gear-change, which helped the sporty feeling. All this added up to just the sort of car that gets a cult following!

During the MkI's short production life there were very few changes, but sliding side screens became standard in 1960. Nearly 49,000 of these MkI (AN5) "Frogeyes" were made. Note the AN5 annotation is the vehicle number prefix.

In May 1961 the Sprite MkII (H-AN6) was announced to replace the MkI. The main difference between the MkI and MkII was that the one-piece front of the car now became more conventional with fixed wings and an opening bonnet. Also the rear was restyled with a boot incorporating an external, lockable, lid. The rear wheel-arches were squared off too. Mechanically, the 948cc engine was uprated to produce 46.5bhp and the gearbox was fitted with a close ratio gear set. At the same time, it was decided to resurrect MG's famous "Midget" name so an almost identical car to the Sprite was launched as the MG Midget. Both the Sprite and Midget were built at Abingdon and since both cars were identical except for the grille and trim, it gave rise to the collective expression "Spridget".

In October 1962, the H-AN7 version was introduced with a 1098cc A-series engine of 55bhp, improved rib cased gearbox and front disc brakes for the first time. The interior trim was also improved. Wire wheels became an option during the production run of this version.

In March 1964 came the Sprite MkIII (H-AN8) with wind-up windows, openable quarter lights, more curved windscreen, external door handles and semi-elliptical rear springs (replacing the quarter elliptics). The interior was updated with a black crinkle finish facia. The A-series engine was uprated to 59bhp with an improved cylinder head and exhaust system. The crankshaft now had larger diameter main bearings to make the running smoother and improve longevity.   Continued....

Below: **Good engine access on the MkI "Frogeye". This show car has the optional front bumper, heater and windscreen washers fitted.**

Between 1959 and 1966, about 4,000 cars were exported as CKD (Completely Knocked Down) kits, mainly to Australia. These cars were then assembled using some locally sourced items, eg tyres, trim and various electrical parts.

The definitive MkIV (H-AN9) appeared in 1966. It had the bigger 1275cc engine of 65bhp and a soft-top roof that was permanently fixed to the rear bodywork (and was therefore much easier to put up and down). In early 1967 a small number of MkIV cars (659 according to MG Factory records) were also built at Cowley.

In 1969 the H-AN10 version of the car appeared. It was attractively restyled with a matt black grille, black sills (with the word SPRITE prominent), Rostyle steel wheels and slimmer bumpers. Today these cars are sometimes unofficially known as MkV Sprites.

In 1971, due to the end of the agreement between Austin and Healey, the car was re-badged simply as an Austin Sprite (AAN-10). 1,022 examples were made and they were only sold on the home market.

In good condition, the Sprite is very reliable when serviced properly, the front suspension requiring regular greasing to avoid an expensive overhaul.

Optional extras on Sprites included a hardtop, radio, heater and wire wheels.

Specific Checks: First check the paperwork, ensuring the numbers match those on the vehicle, then later verify the car's authenticity by contacting the Heritage Motor Centre Archives, Gaydon (unless the car already has a Heritage Certificate).

Next check the car itself. The most important item is body corrosion and in particular rusting of the sills, which are structurally critical and often expensive to rectify. Take out the rubber bungs in the sills to look behind them for rust or dirt. Watch out for new oversills hiding rusty inners behind them. The early design of unitary construction is complex and though it creates a very stiff structure, it makes repair more difficult due to "hidden" sections. If rust is visible, assume there is much more which you cannot see. For instance, if the outer wheelarch is rusted, the inner will probably be rusty too. In the Sprite, structural areas that are often affected by rust include the complex sill sections, "chassis" rails, outriggers, rear spring attachments, the floor and the door pillars. Open the doors and inspect the bottom of the A-posts (a particular rust trap which is usually worse than what can be seen).

If the car looks a bit down at the rear, the rear spring mounting has probably rusted badly and/or the springs have sagged. Look also for broken leaves. Check for rusty floor pans (under the carpeting) just behind the seats as this is where the leaf spring front mountings are located. While in this area, check also for corrosion of the cross-members just in front of the seats. The leaf spring rear mounting area can be inspected inside the boot.

Check the gap at the front and rear edges of the doors. The gap should be even, but if narrower at the top it may indicate a sagging bodyshell, which is a bad sign!

Above: **A new MkI at Abingdon, ready for despatch. The small rear bumpers were standard. Note the normal fitment of fabric side screens. Sliding perspex panes in an aluminium frame were fitted when a hardtop was ordered, or as an option. These were later fitted as standard.**

Below: **A delightful period photo of a MkII Sprite. Note the sill section is the same as the MkI with that distinctive upturn behind the front wheel. The MkII's wings were fixed, though the opening line of the MkI's bonnet is retained as a seam line.**

Below: **A MkIII Sprite's features included wind-up windows, quarter lights, more curved windscreen and exterior door handles. Underneath, the quarter elliptic rear springs were replaced with semi-elliptics.**

Check too for rust by the bonnet hinges, battery tray and around the brake and clutch master cylinders. Note that new Heritage bodyshells are available for some versions of the Sprite.

On the MkI (Frogeye), check also for corrosion of the large one-piece front, as a replacement steel unit is expensive. And remember to take a torch to look into the rear boot area behind the seats.

The Sprite's engine is the trusty A-series, which is relatively easy and cheap to work on, but leaks oil and the tappets can be noisy, as can a worn timing chain. The 948cc engines can run very hot, the 1275cc versions less so. An oil cooler can assist matters. Gearboxes tend to whine, especially in 1st gear, and the gear levers make a sizzling noise but this is usually not serious.

The rack and pinion steering should be light and precise. If not, it probably means things are worn or seized. A common occurrence is king-pins becoming worn and seized due to lack of regular greasing and this often necessitates the replacement of the complete suspension unit. Note that springs may creak in hot dry weather. Handbrakes are sometimes ineffective due to worn clevis pins on the linkage and seized reaction arms in the brake drums.

If a MkI (Frogeye) is fitted with wire wheels, check it is the rare Healey conversion. There was no factory wire wheel option and other conversions may not be safe.

There were a number of adaptations or specials based on the Spridget, such as the Arkley and Lenham. In Italy, Innocenti produced an attractive spider and coupé using Sprite running gear but with their own body. (For more information, refer to the Other Models section from page 156).

From the late 1980s, the Frogeye Car Company on the Isle of Wight produced the Frogeye replica, which was approved by Geoffrey Healey. Though it looked like a Sprite MkI, it had a GRP body on a galvanised box-section tubular steel chassis with 1275cc A-series, later 1.4-litre K-series engines. Production ended in the late 1990s, with c.130? made.

Prices Today: The most valuable Sprite is the MkI (Frogeye) which can be 50-100% more than a later Sprite in the same condition. MkI cars sometimes have GRP fronts fitted, but this modification reduces the car's value. Other modifications, such as larger A-series engines fitted to earlier cars, should not affect value other than with show cars where originality is important. The actual condition of a car is the key factor in valuation, though colour can also affect the price.

Photo Top Right: **A 1967 MkIV Sprite with hardtop fitted. This is an early example prior to reversing lights being introduced.**
2nd From Top: **A 1967 MkIV (H-AN9) car, with optional wire wheels.**
3rd From Top: **A 1970 studio photo of a H-AN10 car. The car has early pattern Rostyle steel wheels and optional anti-roll bar. The black windscreen frame was only on the first 21 cars.**
Lower Right: **A 1971 H-AN10, with optional wire wheels.**

41

Dates: 1963-70

Numbers Built: GT: 451   GT4S: 2,505

Body/Chassis: GRP body on steel chassis, 2+2 seater fixed-head coupé (GT4S: 4-seater).

Engine: Triumph Spitfire 1147cc, 4-cyl in-line, ohv, 63-67bhp; From 1967: 1296cc, 4-cyl in-line, ohv, 75bhp.

Layout: Front engine, rear wheel drive, 4-speed manual gearbox (with optional overdrive on the 1300GT).

Performance: Top speed c.85-90mph, 0-60mph in c.10sec; 1300GT: slightly faster.

Price Today: £ (See text).

Above: **The Bond Equipe GT had nice proportions.**
Below: **The small tail fins identify this car as a GT.**

The Bond Equipe was launched at the 1963 London Motor Show at Earls Court. Before the Equipe, the company was better known for its small 3-wheelers. The new car was a clever blend of Lawrie Bond's handsome design of glassfibre body mated to a Triumph Herald chassis with a Triumph Spitfire engine and gearbox. The Spitfire sports car had only been launched the previous year. The Equipe also used the Spitfire's front disc brakes, together with the Herald's doors, scuttle structure (bulkhead) and windscreen. In common with many Triumph models of the time, the Equipe had a large one-piece forward-hinged bonnet which gave good access to the engine. This was in contrast to the poor access to the rear boot space as there was no boot lid. The car, however, was well equipped for the time with a wood-rimmed steering wheel, rev counter, carpets and heater. The Equipes were sold through Triumph dealers who also serviced the cars.

A year later (in 1964), Bond launched the new GT4S which addressed a number of criticisms of the original car, such as the limited rear headroom and poor access to the rear boot space. The original car (now known, retrospectively, as the Bond Equipe GT 2+2) ceased production in October 1964. The new version had a revised bodyshell and its title, GT4S, emphasised the car's 4-seater capability having extra headroom in the rear (the roofline was raised by 2 inches). It now had a rear boot lid, and a "Kamm" tail (this is where the back is "chopped" to reduce its aerodynamic drag, the idea having come from Wunibald Kamm).

The car was readily identifiable with its twin headlights and revised grille. A GT4S was in fact the first car to drive on Britain's first section of motorway, the M6 Preston bypass.

In 1965 the car's engine (in common with the Spitfire Mk2) had its power boosted slightly to 67bhp due to a different camshaft and exhaust manifold, and now its top speed was closer to 90mph.

There continued to be minor improvements – the seats were made slightly flatter, and a heated rear window and a Webasto sunroof were added as options. In 1967 the engine size was increased, again in line with that of the Spitfire Mk3, to 1296cc. A total of 571 of these Bond Equipe 1300GT cars were produced.

Above: **The Equipe GT's fastback roofline limited the rear headroom.**
Below: **The one-piece opening front was very "Triumph". Note the rear three-quarter windows can hinge open.**

Road tests of the period praised the bucket seats and build quality of the car, but criticised the Triumph rear suspension's tendency to jack up on hard cornering. Performance was always slightly less than the equivalent Triumph Spitfire due to the Equipe's greater weight.

Some cars were exported world-wide due to Triumph's extensive dealer network, so cars went to France, Spain, Portugal, Greece, North America, Australia, New Zealand and even the Cook Islands. Production of the Equipes ceased in August 1970, shortly after Reliant took over the Bond company.

Typical options you might find on these cars include wire wheels and, on the 1300cc cars, overdrive.

Specific Checks: When inspecting an Equipe GT or GT4S, first check the paperwork, ensuring the numbers match those on the vehicle.

As the car has a mainly GRP body, it is possible to have a car that looks fine but in fact has a highly corroded chassis. Hence start with checking the car's underside fully. The outriggers and rails rust quite readily and in all likelihood the chassis will have been replaced or repaired by now, which usually requires the body to come off. Footwells and floors can also rust, as can the Herald's scuttle, doors and the windscreen frame. Visually check the gap between each door's rear edge and the bodywork. It should be the same from top to bottom. If not, it could mean the whole structure is seriously rusted, has residual accident damage or the body has been poorly refitted.

If the bonnet to door gap is good, this may be one sign of a competent restoration.

The GRP body may have crazing or star cracks which are quite difficult to repair properly (requiring grinding out and re-glassing) before repainting. When the bodies were originally made, steel items were laminated into the bodywork in key locations – they rust and expand and require removal and replacement (ideally with stainless steel items).

Mechanically the cars are pure Triumph while trim parts are a mixture of Triumph and Bond.

Typical modifications include having an alternator and electric fan fitted, both worthwhile. Early cars may also have later Spitfire engines fitted or even be upgraded to a Triumph Vitesse 2-litre specification.

Prices Today: The Bond Owners' Club estimates there are probably far less than 10% of the cars still left today. There is not much difference in price between the GT and GT4S, the main criterion being the car's condition, assuming the paperwork is in order.

Photo Top Right: **This Equipe GT4S has been slightly lowered.**
2nd From Top: **The higher rear roofline of the Equipe GT4S permitted four people to travel more comfortably.**
3rd From Top: **The nice lines of the Equipe GT4S are evident.**
Lower Right: **The Equipe GT4S is readily distinguishable from the earlier Equipe GT by the twin headlights and different grille.**

Dates: 1967-70

Numbers Built: Mk1: 591   MkII: 841

Body/Chassis: GRP body on steel chassis, 4-seater fixed-head coupé or convertible.

Engine: Triumph Vitesse 1998cc, 6-cyl in-line, ohv, 95bhp (105bhp from 1968).

Layout: Front engine, rear wheel drive, 4-speed manual gearbox (with optional overdrive).

Performance: Top speed c.100mph, 0-60mph in c.11-12sec.

Price Today: £ (See text).

Above: **The Bond Equipe 2-Litre was not intended to replace the earlier GT4S but to be an addition to the range, with its larger 6-cylinder engine.** Below: **Early design sketches were by Trevor Fiore, who went on to design the similar looking Trident Clipper.**

In 1967, Bond launched a new model, the Equipe 2-Litre, to be made in parallel with the Equipe GT4S. They both used a Bond glassfibre body mated to a Triumph chassis with Triumph mechanical parts. Whereas the original GT models used the Triumph Herald/Spitfire as their basis, the 2-Litre used the Triumph Vitesse, and this time the car had its own windscreen and steel door skins.

For the new car, initial sketches were submitted by Trevor Fiore (and later this emerged as the TVR/Trident Clipper). But in the case of the Bond Equipe 2-Litre, apparently the final design was created in-house by Alan Pounder, who was Bond's Chief Engineer, with the assistance of Specialised Mouldings Ltd, who made the pre-production bodies. The new body had sharper lines than the earlier GTs and was most attractive.

In late 1968 the MkII was launched with a slightly more powerful engine, but perhaps more importantly the rear suspension was at last modified to reduce the tendency to jack up if lifting off the throttle on hard cornering. The MkII cars also had revised interior trim with black leatherette replacing the polished wooden dashboard. A practical feature of the MkII cars was that they had roof gutters which reduced leaks and resultant floorpan corrosion.

Above: **Similarities to the Trident Clipper are also evident in this view.** Below: **The 2-Litre had sharper lines than the GT/GT4S and a new fastback design.**

An exciting development with the 2-Litre was the launch of a stylish convertible version, and this eventually accounted for approximately half the production of the MkII. But the Bond Equipe 2-Litre cost a third more than a Triumph Vitesse, which therefore restricted its sales. Together with the GT4S, production ceased in August 1970, shortly after the company's takeover by Reliant. A MkIII prototype was made by Reliant but with access to the Triumph dealer network denied, the project went no further.

Optional extras you may find on Bond Equipe 2-Litre cars include wire wheels, overdrive and fabric sunroof (on the fixed-head version).

Specific Checks: When inspecting an Equipe 2-Litre, first check the paperwork, ensuring the numbers match those on the vehicle.

As the car has a mainly GRP body, it is possible to have a car that looks fine but in fact has a highly corroded chassis. Hence start with checking the car's underside

fully. The outriggers and rails rust quite readily and in all likelihood the chassis will have been replaced or repaired by now, which usually requires the body to come off. Footwells and floors can also rust, as can the Vitesse's scuttle, the doors and the windscreen frame. Check the gap between each door's rear edge and the bodywork. It should be the same from top to bottom. If not, it could mean the whole structure is seriously rusted, has residual accident damage or the body has been poorly refitted.

If the bonnet to door gap is good, this may be one sign of a competent restoration.

The GRP body may have crazing or star cracks which are quite difficult to repair properly (requiring grinding out and re-glassing) before repainting. When the bodies were originally made, steel items were laminated into the bodywork in key locations – they rust and expand and require removal and replacement (ideally with stainless steel items). In the 2-Litre, there is also a piece of wood laminated into the bodywork just above the boot opening.

Mechanically the cars are pure Triumph while trim parts are a mixture of Triumph and Bond.

With the convertibles, and with the owner's help, put the soft-top roof fully up and then down, and inspect the interior for water ingress (eg soggy carpets) and for water damage to seats and trim.

Typical modifications include having an alternator and electric fan fitted. Unlike other Equipes which had telescopic dampers, MkII cars had lever arm dampers and these can be converted to telescopics at the rear to improve the handling. Fitting a brake servo is also a popular modification.

Prices Today: The Bond Owners' Club estimates there are probably far less than 10% of the Equipe 2-Litre cars still left today. In terms of prices, the 2-Litre fixed-head cars cost slightly more than the GT or GT4S, while the convertibles cost considerably more than the fixed-head versions.

Above: **The Equipe convertible was a natural option as the underlying Triumph chassis also appeared in a convertible version.**
Below: **An Equipe convertible with its soft-top roof up.**

Above: **The front wing side grille is non-standard on this convertible.**
Below: **Bond's Chief Engineer, Alan Pounder, at the wheel of this convertible.**

Below: **This restored car is owned by Jazz legend Dame Cleo Laine.**

Dates: 1946-61 (See text). **Numbers Built:** See text.

Body/Chassis: See text.

Engines: Types 400-405: 1971cc, 6-cyl in-line, ohv, 75-125bhp.
Type 406: 2216cc, 6-cyl in-line, ohv, 105bhp.

Layout: Front engine, rear wheel drive, 4-speed manual gearbox (overdrive on some cars).

Performance: See text. **Prices Today:** Contact Club.

Above: **The Bristol Type 400. Note the distinctly BMW-style grille.**
Below: **The Type 400 had front opening (rear-hinged) doors.**

At the end of WW2, the Bristol Aeroplane Company had to diversify as the requirement for military aircraft had dropped dramatically with the onset of peace. One of their solutions was to manufacture luxury cars. A key feature of all the early Bristol cars (Types 400-406) was the BMW-derived 6-cylinder 2-litre engine with advanced design of cylinder head and unusual layout of pushrods (18 in total, including six that crossed the cylinder head).

The cars themselves were all cleverly designed, well built and embodied many interesting features. The manufacturer's aviation background is often evident and it is perhaps not surprising that these were expensive cars. Today, Bristols are very much prized as drivers' cars and are typically owned long-term.

Type 400: The first model, the Type 400, was based closely on prewar BMW models (as reflected in the BMW-style grille) and was launched in 1946 with deliveries starting the following year. It was a 4-seater with two doors (rear-hinged) and sliding door windows. It had a substantial chassis with a steel body on an ash frame (but the door skins, bonnet and boot lid were aluminium as were the spare wheel cover and bumper aprons on later cars). It had either the rare Bristol 85 engine with one Solex carb that produced 75bhp or more usually the 85A engine that had triple SU carbs and produced 80bhp. A rare optional 85B engine produced 90bhp. Performance with the 80bhp engine was a maximum speed over 90mph and an 0-60mph time of about 20 seconds. Approximately 470 cars were made from 1946-51.

Above: **A feature of the Type 400 was its opening rear window.**
Below: **The Type 401.**

Type 401: Although the 401 was mechanically almost the same as the 400, it had a distinctive "Aerodyne" body designed by Touring of Milan for a prewar Alfa and modified by Bristol's Dudley Hobbs. It had been wind-tunnel tested and featured wind-cheating aspects such as recessed push button door releases and faired-in bumpers. Furthermore, it used the "Superleggera" method of body construction, which consisted of aluminium panels over a light tubular steel framework. Two other interesting features of this car were, first, both bumpers could slide up to 1.5 inches on impact and, second, to gain access to the engine, the bonnet could swing open from either side of the car as the hinges doubled as catches. The car used the Bristol 85C engine that produced 85bhp and it would get to 60mph in about 15 seconds and could just reach 100mph. During the 401's production life it evolved and there were many

improvements to the engine, silencer, suspension, dashboard, upholstery etc. About 600 cars were made from 1948-53.

Type 402: This was a rare convertible version of the 401 with approximately 20 examples built. It was introduced in 1948 and discontinued in 1950.

Type 403: This was essentially an upgraded version of the 401. The only external differences were a chromed radiator grille and "403" badges on the bonnet and rear. The main mechanical changes on the 403 were: the 100A (100bhp) engine, a front anti-roll bar, "Alfin" drum brakes and improved heating and ventilation. The performance was now a top speed that exceeded 100mph and an 0-60mph time of about 13 seconds. Later 403s had the 100B and finally 100B2 (105bhp) engines. The latter was combined with a remote short shift gearbox with overdrive on top gear. About 280 cars were made from 1953-55.

Type 404: Designed by Dudley Hobbs, this car had a completely new and modern body with two small tail fins and a grille apparently inspired by a Bristol aero engine intake. The 404 was a 2-seater with a shortened wheelbase (8ft rather than the 9ft 6in common to all other 2-litre Bristols). The body construction was now aluminium on an ash frame. The 404 was the first Bristol to house the spare wheel in a compartment behind a front wheel, with a similar compartment on the other side housing the battery and other bits (a nice design feature, and used also on subsequent models). There was no rear boot lid so access to the rear luggage compartment was from inside the car.

The 404 had the 105bhp Bristol 100B engine which was identical to the 100A except that the compression ratio was raised from 7.5:1 to 8.5:1. An optional (rare) 125bhp 100C engine was also available. The same gearbox as the 403 was used, but it was fitted with a neat remote-control selector and a short gear lever. This gear lever somehow seemed to further improve an already excellent gearchange, and so they have sometimes been retrofitted to older cars. Overall the Type 404 was lighter than the 403 and it could do about 110mph. Only 52 cars were made from 1953-56.

Type 405: This was Bristol's only four-door car. Unlike the 404, it had a rear boot lid. The engine was the 100B or 100B2 (105bhp) unit and overdrive was fitted as standard to the car. Front disc brakes were an option. The 405 was a popular design with just over 300 made from 1954-58. This included about 40 (or perhaps fewer) attractive 2-door drophead coupés, the coachwork being made by Abbotts of Farnham.

Continued....

Photo Top Right: **The rare Type 402 Drophead.**
Middle Photos Right: **The Type 401 and Type 403 look identical except for the chromed grille and badges on the 403. These photos are both Type 403 cars.**
Lower Right: **The Type 404.**

Type 406: The 406 was a larger car than its predecessors, and more of a luxury car than a sports saloon. Mechanical changes relative to the 405 were: the Bristol 110 engine was enlarged to 2.2 litres by extending both the bore and the stroke. Power output was still 105bhp, but produced at 4,700rpm instead of 5,000rpm and with better torque characteristics. There were various other detail refinements, for example this is the only Bristol engine with a timing chain tensioner. The car had servo-assisted disc brakes all round and the rear axle was located by a Watt linkage, rather than the A-frame which had been used since the 400. The 406 was to be the last 6-cylinder Bristol and about 180 were made between 1958 and 1961 in addition to 7 beautiful (and very expensive) Zagato Type 406 variants.

Engines & Gearboxes: There were three main series of Bristol engine, with a number of variations existing within each series: The original Type 85 engine was essentially a modified prewar BMW 328 unit, built with Whitworth rather than metric threads. The 85 series engines were fitted as standard to the Bristol 400, 401 and 402 models. The 100 series engine (fitted to the Bristol 403, 404 and 405) had larger valves, greater valve overlap, larger main bearings and a revised oil pump. Valve gear was lightened to improve refinement at high rpm and they normally produced 100-105bhp, though higher power versions were available. The 110 series engine was introduced for the Bristol 406. An increase in both bore and stroke brought the capacity up to 2,216cc.

The gearboxes were also Bristol built and had synchromesh on the upper three gears but 1st gear had a "free-wheel" which enabled its selection at any road speed. The gearboxes are durable and well-engineered, and with a light, slick change that adds greatly to the pleasure of driving the cars. The free-wheel can fail under harsh acceleration leading to gear fracture, thus some have been replaced with a fixed 1st (non-synchromesh) gear. The clutch is the same as that used in the MGA.

General: Since the Type 400-406 cars are all based on essentially the same chassis, the component inter-changeability is close to 100%. It is therefore not unusual to find early cars with later engines, disc brakes, and overdrive (most worthwhile and fitted as standard to the 405 and 406).

With the electrical system, many owners fit flashing indicators (semaphores were standard on Types 400-404) and higher-intensity tail and brake lights. Alternators are often fitted in place of original dynamos. It should be noted that there are only two fuses on the entire car, and that many circuits have no fuse at all.

With some makes of car, originality carries a high price premium, but this seems less relevant to Bristol values, provided the changes enhance the car's usability and have been done competently.

Specific Checks: When going to check any 2-litre Bristol, take a qualified expert with you (first contact the Bristol Owners' Club for advice).

After checking the paperwork, examine the car's body. The 400 has a mainly steel body on an ash frame.

Above & Below: **The rare Type 405 Drophead.**

Above: **The Type 405 was Bristol's only 4-door car.**
Below: **The Type 406 had a larger 2.2-litre engine.**

The 401, 402, 403 and 406 have aluminium bodies built up on a framework of steel tubes – the Touring "Super-leggera" method of body construction. The 404 and 405 have their aluminium bodies on an ash upper frame. This combination of steel chassis, aluminium body and timber frame on the 404 and 405 is particularly vulnerable to deterioration and care should be taken to ensure that the structure (including wooden items) is sound. On the "Superleggera" body cars, corrosion will appear where steel meets aluminium, particularly where insulation between the two metals breaks down. On the 401-403, this tends to be on the sills and immediately above the front bumper. Although seldom terminal, this can be unsightly and is expensive to repair. All body panels for these cars have to be made from scratch.

Next turn to the chassis – this is 6.5 inches deep and is an almost indestructible box-section frame. It is unlikely that you will find serious corrosion in the main chassis, but it is possible that you will find fairly extensive corrosion in the extension legs behind the rear wheels. This is time-consuming and expensive to fix, and is an MoT failure point.

The engines were well made and should be very durable if used sympathetically and serviced regularly. However, it could cost up to £10,000-£12,000 to rebuild a worn out engine, so it pays to make sure you get a good one. It is also worth checking to see that the starting handle is present (on the 400 it is located in the boot, while on other models it is clipped to the right hand side of the engine bay). The starting handle is useful for setting valve clearances and for fitting fan belts (as well as starting the engine if the battery is flat).

The 401, 402 and 403 cars have aluminium fuel tanks held in place by steel straps. If moisture has been allowed to penetrate between the tank and the straps, corrosion will follow. Removing and repairing the tank is a time-consuming process. On all models (except the 400 which has no fuel reserve), the fuel feed unit consists of two copper pipes of different lengths (for main and reserve feed) descending into the tank from above. Occasionally these pipes crack, resulting in a car which seems to run out of fuel even though the tank is still half full.

On the front suspension, the exposed ends of the leaf spring should be covered with leather gaiters, intended to keep grit and dirt away from the leaves. The gaiters deteriorate with age and it is not unusual to find that they have been removed. New gaiters are available. Early cars have Bristol's own lever arm shock absorbers, later examples (from chassis 1006) have telescopic dampers. As with the rear suspension, modern dampers can be made to fit.

There is a one-shot lubrication system which supplies oil to the king-pins and steering rack. This is a reliable system, but it does appreciate being used regularly. It often gets disconnected and replaced with grease nipples, necessitating a lot of work to put the one-shot system back into operation. If the one-shot system is working properly, it is usual to see oil dripping down the insides of the front tyres when the car is parked. If you see a stream of oil on one side but not the other, it is possible that the system might be blocked on that

Above: **The Type 406 was the last model of the Bristol 2-litre cars.**

side. It is also possible for the non-return valve to stick open, so that oil seeps out regardless of whether the pedal is pressed or not.

The rubber-insulated wiring is highly likely to have deteriorated considerably after fifty years. Rewiring is a substantial but worthwhile project.

The interior was trimmed in high-quality leather. A car today should ideally have an attractively patinated original interior or had a high-quality retrim. A vinyl or cloth interior, or an original leather one that is tatty to the point of falling apart, would typically cost over £6,000 to replace.

Prices Today: In value terms, the 402, 404 and 405 Drophead are the "premium" models that command the highest prices and the Bristol Owners' Club believes that perhaps two thirds of those have survived, while about a third of the other models have survived too. It is hard to be precise with values as relatively few change hands and many of those are between Club members. Contact the Bristol Owners' Club for further guidance.

Below: **A very rare, and handsome, Type 406 Zagato.**

Dates:	Since 1973	**Number Built:** Still in production.

Body/Chassis: S3: GRP and aluminium body (S4: mainly GRP) with steel spaceframe chassis, 2-seater open sports.

Engines: Ford 1297cc, 4-cyl in-line, ohv, 72bhp;
Ford Cortina GT 1599cc, 4-cyl in-line, ohv, 84+bhp;
Lotus 1558cc (later: 1598cc), 4-cyl in-line, Twin Cam, 126bhp.

Layout: Front engine, rear wheel drive, 4-speed manual gearbox (5-speed from 1986).

Performance: Ford 1600: Top speed 100+mph, 0-60mph under 8sec;
Lotus: Top speed 110+mph, 0-60mph under 7sec.

Price Today: ££ (Early Models).

Above: **The original Caterham Super 7, with sidescreens in place.**

In 1973, Caterham Cars, who were the exclusive distributors of the Lotus 7, also took over the manufacture of the car, which henceforth was known as the Caterham 7 and did not carry Lotus badges. Initially Caterham made what was then the current model, the glassfibre bodied S4. After about 40 had been made, in 1974 they decided to revert to the S3 and this formed the basis for their subsequent cars. The new Caterham version of the S3 was improved and had a strengthened chassis (with extra triangulation) and the early cars used the Lotus Twin Cam engine (in "Big Valve" form), or the Ford crossflow engine.

From 1977, the Caterham 7 was fitted with the Vegantune-made Lotus Twin Cam engine and by 1978 the engine had become the "tall block" 1598cc version. Eventually supplies of the Twin Cam engine began to dry up and Caterham used the Ford 1600 GT "Kent" engine in various states of tune, including one with a special twin cam Vegantune head called the VTA, but it is quite rare today. The last Lotus-engined car was made in 1981.

The cars continued to be developed and new engines were introduced (including the Sprint and Cosworth in the mid-1980s). From 1985 a de Dion rear suspension was available and a 5-speed box from 1986.

Before 1984, due to Type Approval regulations, all Caterhams were sold in component form with new parts. After 1984, there were also part-complete kits, allowing buyers to add their own (usually second-hand) parts; in the UK these cars attract Q-plate registrations.

Options included full-weather protection, heater, alloy wheels and roll-over bar. From 1981 there was the long cockpit chassis, which later became standard.

Specific Checks: There are fake Caterham Sevens, so before purchase, note the chassis number and the frame maker's number (which will be different). Then check the car's identity with the Lotus Seven Club.

The body/chassis unit is the most important aspect to check as the steel tubing can rust and can suffer from poorly repaired accident damage. Remove the bonnet and nose cone to facilitate your inspection. The S4's design, with its enveloping GRP body, makes chassis inspection and repair more difficult, though new GRP panels can be made to order.

If the car's handling is not perfect it may be due to wear in the suspension, which is relatively cheap to rectify, but it may also be due to chassis distortion or damage, which could be expensive. With luck, it might just be because the tyre pressures are incorrect.

On early cars, check the rear axle has had the Caterham modification of a welded-on strengthening plate (otherwise the loads from the rear suspension can cause cracks in the axle, leading to oil loss). In addition, look out for engine overheating due to inadequate cooling and check that the riveted gearbox crossmember is not working loose from the transmission tunnel.

S3 car spares are usually available but some S4 parts (eg windscreen support brackets, top half of doors and hood supports) are difficult to find.

Prices Today: Many of these cars were exported or have since been taken abroad. As with the Lotus 7, demand for cars in good condition often outstrips supply, therefore values remain high. The S4 cars have values lower than other early Caterhams, for cars in a similar condition.

Left & Below: **A 1982 car with some modifications to meet local (New Zealand) regulations. It also has changes to accommodate a supercharger to the 1600 x-flow engine.**

Dates: Crusader: 1971-74   Clan & Clover: 1982-87

Numbers Built: Crusader: c.350   Clan: c.130   Clover: c.27

Body/Chassis: GRP monocoque, 2-seater fixed-head coupé.

Engines: Crusader: Imp Sport 875cc, 4-cyl in-line, sohc, 51bhp;
Clan: Imp Sport 998cc, 4-cyl in-line, sohc, 65 or 78bhp;
Clover: Alfa Romeo 1490cc, flat-four, ohc, 105bhp.

Layout: Rear engine, rear wheel drive, 4-speed manual gearbox;
Clover: Mid-engine, rear wheel drive, 5-speed gearbox.

Performance: Crusader: Top speed c.100mph, 0-60mph under 13sec;
Clover: Top speed c.115mph, 0-60mph in c.8sec.

Prices Today: £ (See text).

Above & Below: **The Clan Crusader was well designed and built.**

This attractive car was conceived by a group of Lotus engineers (who were known as the "clan") under Paul Haussauer, together with John Frayling who did the clean-cut styling and Brian Luff who helped with the car's development. The cars were made in a new, purpose-built, factory in Washington, County Durham. The Clan's glassfibre monocoque structure had marine plywood stiffening and was very strong. An example was crash tested successfully (the author saw the crashed car later). The rear engine cover was unusual, being made of slatted black ABS plastic and it opened sideways.

The Clan Crusader used virtually standard Imp Sport front and rear sub-assemblies, comprising the complete engine and transaxle (with rear mounted radiator), suspension (but with custom coil springs), drum brakes all round and Imp steering.

From his 1978 notes, the author records that with his own Clan Crusader, "The overall finish and trim are to a high standard. It's very easy to drive around town and the servo-assisted brakes are very powerful, but the car can be twitchy at high speed when there is a cross wind."

The Clan Motor Co. Ltd ceased trading in late 1973, but several part-finished cars were completed and sold in 1974. Of approximately 350 cars made, there were 15 LHD cars exported to Holland and 19 competition cars.

Over the years Clans have been successful on the track. On its very first outing in 1972, a Clan Crusader came 2nd overall in the Manx International Rally.

When the company closed, bodyshells and other Clan parts became available from Brian Luff Ltd. Then in 1982, a new business, Clan Cars Ltd in Northern Ireland, purchased Brian Luff's moulds and started to market a revamped car, now called simply the "Clan". It was good-looking with retractable headlamps, moulded-in bumpers, glass sunroof and a 998cc engine. The cars are generally referred to as the "Irish Clans" and were available as kits or completed cars. The company produced approximately 120 road cars, plus 10 for competition work. About this time, a rival business, Clan Marketing, also sold about a dozen cars or bodyshells.

In 1985, Clan Cars Ltd launched a new version called the Clan Clover. It had a restyled body with an Alfa Romeo 1.5-litre engine mounted amidships, but the company ceased trading in 1987 after completing only six kits and 20 fully built cars (plus one part-finished car). The

McCoy was a mid-1980s front-engined Mini-powered kit car derived from the Clan, but with fixed Mini headlamps and all the GRP panels were different.

Specific Checks: Engine cooling is marginal even with a standard 875cc engine, so the cooling system must be in tiptop condition. Some cars have fitted electric fans and front radiators (refer also to the Ginetta G15 entry for other Imp engine checks). The body should last a long time, but check the glassfibre carefully where the suspension is mounted as it may need reinforcing, also inspect the marine plywood.

Prices Today: All three models have similar prices with condition being the critical factor. They are probably undervalued, especially the original Crusader.

Left: **An "Irish Clan". It had a neat flat GRP rear engine cover with spoiler.**

Right: **A Clan Clover. Its front was similar to the "Irish Clan", but the rear was quite different.**

Dates: 1959-64	**Number Built:** 2,648

Body/Chassis: GRP body on steel chassis, 2-seater open sports.

Engine: 2548cc, V8, ohv, 140bhp.

Layout: Front engine, rear wheel drive, 4-speed manual gearbox (with optional 3-speed automatic gearbox).

Performance: Top speed over 120mph, 0-60mph in under 9sec.

Price Today: £££/££££

Above: **A recent photo with a Daimler SP250 (Dart) in a period setting. Note the removable hardtop on this car.**

Originally called the "Dart" by Daimler, the name had to be dropped as Dodge had already registered this name, but to many it is still the "Dart". It followed the unsuccessful Daimler Conquest roadster (119 made), using a brand-new V8 engine designed by Edward Turner, who was also responsible for the all-conquering Triumph Twin racing motorcycle engines of the 1950s.

The Dart's new V8 proved to be a good-looking design providing power with smoothness, flexibility (155lbft of torque) and economy – and it produced a glorious sound. The grille design with its large "V" reflected this new V8 engine.

Since the tooling to make steel bodies would have been very expensive and take longer to produce, Daimler opted instead to use glassfibre. The car had disc brakes on all wheels, which was an advanced feature. However the development time allowed to produce the car was too short and this showed up in various shortcomings that had to be quickly sorted out after the car's launch.

Jaguar took over Daimler in 1960 and they increased the chassis/body rigidity as part of the "B" specification cars launched the following year. Later "C" specification cars had better trim, including a heater as standard.

Several cars were seriously raced in the 1960s and 1970s and a few still participate in racing in the US. In the UK, the value of the cars tends to preclude this today but they still take part in classic rallies and other less risky forms of motorsport. The race-bred engine is notably high revving and can produce astonishing power outputs when tuned.

Optional extras included a radio, 3-speed automatic gearbox, wire wheels and removable hardtop.

Below: **Edward Turner's impressive V8 engine.**

Specific Checks: Start with the paperwork, then later contact the Jaguar Daimler Heritage Trust Archives to verify the car's authenticity (unless the car already has a Heritage Certificate).

With the car itself, start by looking for corrosion of the chassis steelwork, particularly at the front cross-tube, in and under the front suspension towers, the rear springs' forward mountings and the main rails under the rear axle. If looking at a "B" or "C" specification car, check for corrosion of the A-posts in front of the doors and the additional side-rails below the doors.

Next look for signs of damage to the GRP bodywork, indicated by stress-cracking and starring. This requires a specialist to repair properly.

Below: **The "V" motif on the grille signifies the V8 engine.**

With the engine warmed up, take a note of the engine oil pressure when idling and when driving. Later you can discuss this information with the owners' club. The "A" specification engines tend to have slightly lower oil pressures than the later "B" and "C" specification engines. Check too for oil leaks from the front and rear of the engine and listen for rumbling sounds. With the transmission, check for noise and backlash in the gearbox and rear axle. Listen for a "clack-clack-clack" noise in 1st gear that might indicate a broken gear tooth.

Finally, check operation of door locks and window winders, the fit of the doors and look for worn hinges.

Today, all servicing items are available and virtually all the mechanical components can be rebuilt or reconditioned. Most replacement GRP panels are available and the chassis is straightforward to repair, even with the bodywork in place.

It is relatively easy to upgrade these cars. For relaxed motorway cruising the original 4-speed manual gearbox can be retrofitted with overdrive or it can be replaced by a Toyota 5-speed unit. The heavy and imprecise original steering system can be replaced by a lighter and more agile rack and pinion system, and the handling can now be greatly improved by fitting telescopic dampers to the live rear axle. Oil filter replacement used to be a difficult job but now a modern spin-on canister can be fitted. Note that many Darts are used regularly and have accumulated high mileages.

Prices Today: It is thought that about half of the original number of cars produced still survive with about 300 in the UK, 350 in New Zealand, 100 in Australia and 500 in the US (in fact, 1,200 of the cars made were LHD). There do not appear to be any significant variations in value between the different "A" to "C" specification cars, the condition of a car being the main factor.

Photo Top Right: **The Dart's soft-top roof folds down neatly.**
2nd From Top: **Soft-top roof up and the optional wire wheels fitted.**
3rd From Top: **Note the standard steel wheels on this Dart have the optional full wheel covers instead of nave plates.**
Lower Photos: **The period tail fins are very evident in these photos.**

Dates:	1975-83 (See text).
Number Built:	c.8,583 (See text).
Body/Chassis:	GRP body with stainless steel panels on epoxy coated steel chassis, 2-seater fixed-head coupé.
Engine:	PRV 2849cc, V6, ohc, fuel injection, US: 130bhp (UK:160bhp).
Layout:	Rear engine, rear wheel drive, 5-speed manual or 3-speed automatic gearbox.
Performance:	Top speed c.120mph, 0-60mph in 9-10sec.
Prices Today:	LHD: £££ RHD: ££££

Above: **The DeLorean's sharp styling by Giugiaro (who also penned the first Lotus Esprit) still looks modern and dramatic today.**

The man behind this stunning car was John Z. DeLorean, a former vice-president of General Motors. He had a vision for a car that would be exciting, safe and would outlast most of its rivals. He called in Giugiaro (of Ital Design) to do the styling and Lotus to develop the chassis and prepare the car for production.

Originally the car was to be made of a revolutionary new material called ERM (Elastic Reservoir Moulding – a compressed sandwich of glassfibre mat around resin-impregnated urethane foam) with subframes front and rear attached to the ERM body. However, it was decided that the technology was not yet fully proven so a conventional steel chassis with glassfibre skeletal body was chosen for the production version. What was not conventional, in fact unique, was the use of unstressed brushed stainless steel cladding panels, bolted to the glassfibre below. The finish was highly distinctive.

The large, and heavy (c.90lb, 40kg) gull-wing doors, were another exciting feature of the car, and are easy to use as they are counterbalanced, rising on cryogenically preset torsion bars, with gas struts.

Although the car was first shown in prototype form in 1975, production did not commence until early 1981. The cars were assembled at a new state-of-the-art factory (complete with its own test circuit), which had been built in record time on a 72-acre site in Northern Ireland, with financial backing from the British government.

The rear-mounted engine for the new car was a PRV (Peugeot-Renault-Volvo) all-aluminium unit that was already proven and could meet US emission regulations – for though the car was built in Northern Ireland, it was aimed principally at the US market. In normal PRV installations the engine is front-mounted but by turning over the crown wheel in the transmission it could be rear-mounted in the DeLorean. Although the engine overhung the rear axle line, any potential handling problems were solved by using larger (and wider) 15-inch cast alloy wheels at the rear and 14-inch wheels at the front, together with a correctly set up suspension. A planned twin turbo engine did not make it further than two prototypes, but today there are a number of tuning options for those wishing more power.

The Lotus input is evident from the distinctive backbone chassis, which will be familiar to Lotus car owners. In the case of the DeLorean, the fuel tank is cleverly wedged between the Y-forks at the front. This comfortable car had a comprehensive specification with leather seats and air-conditioning, as well as power assisted disc brakes on all wheels. US cars have an 85mph speedometer, as required by the then US regulations, but this can be readily converted to a 140mph unit as on the "Euro-spec" cars.

Being relatively light at the front meant the steering did not require power assistance. The cars were all built as LHD though a few were converted to "Euro-spec" LHD and RHD to act as demonstrators for the planned later entry into the British and continental markets. These very rare UK RHD cars have a number of minor differences to the US models.

During its short production life there were a number of subtle changes made to the car which the *cognoscenti* can spot, and these changes can help an expert to establish the likely production date of any car being inspected. One readily noticeable change was the evolution of the bonnet. The very early examples included a separate small "Gas Flap" and two pressed grooves, but soon the flap was discontinued and later the grooves too, ending with simply a plain bonnet.

Below: **The rear slats and segmented tail lights are identifying features of the DeLorean when seen from the rear.**

There was also the introduction of grey as an alternative to the uniform black interiors of the early cars.

Sadly, the DeLorean was launched at a time of high inflation in Britain, plus a poor dollar-to-pound exchange rate which greatly increased the car's selling price in the US. Furthermore, the US market was suffering from a recession, the worst winter on record in 1981 and to cap it all there were early quality control issues resulting from the inexperienced workforce. The company went into receivership and production of the car ended in December 1982, though a few more were assembled off-line in the US during 1983. Although the official production figure is quoted as 8,583, there is speculation that the actual figure could be about 9,000 cars.

Specific Checks: Today the cars have met and surpassed their design objective of being long-lasting, for perhaps as many as 6,000 of them are still around. They have also proven to be relatively reliable cars. When checking a DeLorean, ideally take along someone who knows the cars. If the car is a re-imported DeLorean, ensure it is properly road-legal in the UK, that all import taxes have been paid and the paperwork is correct. Then moving on to the car itself, examine the epoxy coating on the steel chassis as that is the one major structural component that can corrode. Next look for accident damage (especially on cars which have been painted), and scan the panel shut lines, as repairs to the stainless steel panels can be expensive. Also check the operation of the doors and, in particular, the central locking.

The engines seem to be almost indestructible and the stainless steel exhausts are long-lived. Early alternators, early fuel pumps and horns have been known to fail. Many early 80Amp alternators have been uprated. There have been a number of safety recall modifications and it is important to check these have been done – contact the Club for more information.

Examine the interior trim which can be badly affected by sun damage, especially cars from sunny parts of the US. Replacement trim parts are available. Fully check all electrical systems, especially if additional kit has been added, and look for bodged wiring. Make certain the air-conditioning works properly. Other than that, these are usually reliable cars, provided they are regularly serviced and cared for.

Prices Today: The DeLorean Owners' Club estimates there are about 300 cars in the UK of which half are in private collections and museums and the rest are used fairly regularly. As the cars are relatively new and were built to last there are few "restoration" cases and most cars should be in fair or better condition. Although all cars were completed with the unpainted brushed stainless steel panels, a few cars have since been painted and this devalues them significantly. RHD cars are the most valuable.

John DeLorean died in 2005, aged 80.

Above: **Door windows were fixed but had a small, inset, electrically openable section, which can be seen in the photos above and below.**

Below: **The rear location of the engine is not obvious, but the different sized wheels (15-inch rear, 14-inch front) can be seen clearly.**

Below: **Gull-wing doors opened in front of Crathes Castle in Scotland.**

Left: **An Elva Courier MkII.**

Right: **The wheels and roll-over bar are non-standard.**

Left: **The style of the one-piece forward-hinged bonnet changed several times during the car's production life.**

Right: **The car did not have bumpers. This is a Mk1, which was the best seller and the most common survivor today.**

Dates: 1958-65   **Number Built:** c.600?

Body/Chassis: GRP body on steel chassis, 2-seater open & FHC.

Engines: Mostly MG 1489-1798cc, 4-cyl, ohv, 72-95bhp.

Layout: Front engine, RWD, 4-speed manual (overdrive rare).

Performance: c.100mph, 0-60 in 11-13sec.   **Price Today:** ££/£££

Dates: 1957-73   **Number Built:** c.400? (See text).

Body/Chassis: GRP body on steel chassis, 2-seater open sports.

Engines: Standard-Triumph 948-1296cc, 4-cyl, ohv. (Optional Ford).

Layout: Front engine, RWD, 4-speed manual (overdrive very rare).

Performance: Mk1: c.75mph, 0-60 in c.18sec.   **Price Today:** £

Frank Nichols made the first Elva sports car in 1955. The name was from the French "Elle va" ("She goes"). Elva made almost 1,000 cars, mainly for racing, and most were exported to the US. The good looking Courier was their road-going sports car, designed by Nichols and Peter Nott, and launched in 1958. Its GRP body was bonded to a tubular ladder-frame chassis. Initially the car used the MGA 1489cc engine and gearbox, with a Riley rear axle. The engine was set well back giving a nearly 50:50 weight distribution and neutral handling. Many Couriers were raced (and the Courier Spyder was a dedicated lightweight racer).

The MkII (late 1959) had a single, curved, windscreen (rather than split screen) and revised facia. The engine was now the larger MGA 1588cc unit. In 1960 came a hardtop coupé with a reverse rake rear window. After Elva had built a total of some 400 cars, they ran into financial difficulties, and production was taken over by Trojan. The Trojan-built version, the MkIII, had the MGA 1622cc engine, and apart from the first 25 cars, a new box-section chassis. The MkIV roadster (from late 1963) had smoother lines, larger cockpit, wind-up windows, improved chassis and optional "T-type" all-independent suspension.

Trojan built 210 Couriers (175 roadsters, 35 fastback coupés) and 152 were LHD. Engines were as follows: MGA (in 104 cars), MGB (94), Ford 1500GT (8), Lotus Twin Cam (4, including 2 lightweight "Sebring" racers). The last 38 cars (built by Ken Sheppard) are considered the best.

Specific Checks: Check for chassis corrosion. Early tubular frames can bend near the engine mounts. Most spare parts are available and moulds exist in the UK and US for pre-Trojan cars and for sections of the MkIV. Most Couriers will have been raced or driven hard.

Prices Today: The Elva Owners' Club estimates that c.60 Elvas survive in the UK, but most are abroad.

In 1952, former Air Vice-Marshal "Pathfinder" Bennett started Fairthorpe Ltd, named after Bennett's home in Toowoomba, Australia. After making a few Atom and Atomata light saloons, in 1956 came the Electron sports with a Climax FWA 1098cc engine (under 20 cars made).

In 1957 Fairthorpe launched the Electron Minor, designed by John Green and powered by a Standard 10's 948cc, 38bhp unit. By mid-1958 the nose shape had been improved with the earlier protruding headlights and triangular-shaped grille being dropped. An Electron nose was an option. The car was now available in kit form to avoid Purchase Tax and this brought the price down by over 40% and sales rose. Electron Minors were relatively cheap, light, with good performance and handling, so that many of them were raced. The Mk1 finished production in 1960 with perhaps over 300 made and some exported (no production records survive for the Electron Minors, so these numbers are club estimates).

The Mk2 (1960-63) had many changes, the front from the Fairthorpe Zeta (a Ford 2.5L sports car – 5 made). A wider chassis permitted a range of engines including Ford, though the Herald unit was standard. The Mk3 (from 1963) had the Spitfire 1147cc engine and could do 95mph, while the Mk4 had a new chassis and the Spitfire 1296cc engine, but only c.10 were made. The Mk5 (from 1970) had a revised chassis and longer tail section – c.5 cars made and the final Mk6 used a Triumph GT6 chassis, but only 2 were made.

Specific Checks: Check for chassis corrosion, especially the rear outriggers and on early cars around the front suspension. The Fairthorpe Sports Car Club own the body moulds so these parts can be made to order. Parts for Standard 10-based front suspension are becoming scarce.

Prices Today: The club estimates that c.100 cars survive. Prices depend on originality and condition.

Dates: 1960-66	**Number Built:** c.202

Body/Chassis: GRP body on steel chassis, 2+2 seater sports saloon.

Engine: 1800GT: MGB 1798cc, 4-cyl in-line, ohv, 95bhp (See text).

Layout: Front engine, rear wheel drive, 4-speed manual gearbox (with optional overdrive).

Performance: See text.

Price Today: Contact Club.

Above: **The grille on this Gilbern GT is non-standard; the normal grille had horizontal slats.**

Gilbern owes its name to its two founders – GILes Smith and BERNard Friese. They formed the company in 1959 and the following year production commenced on the GT. The car had an unstressed glassfibre body riveted and bonded to a semi-spaceframe chassis, made of mainly square steel tubing. The Gilbern GT's first public show was at the 1961 Racing Car Show in London and it was well received due to its detailed design, good proportions and well-finished construction.

A handful of early cars were based mainly on Austin mechanical parts and were powered by the 948cc Austin-Healey Sprite A-series engine in various states of tune (including supercharged). At least one car was fitted with a 1.1-litre Coventry Climax FWA engine. In 1962, Gilbern adopted the 1622cc MGA engine and made other improvements. Probably only a dozen of those cars were made. By 1963 the 1798cc MGB engine became standard and the car was then known as the 1800GT. The car also used the MGB's gearbox, rear axle and front suspension, complete with disc brakes and wire wheels. The earlier car had used worm and peg steering but this changed with the 1800GT to rack and pinion. An important improvement with the 1800GT was its chassis, which was stiffened by additional triangulation. About 175 Gilbern 1800GT cars were made.

The performance depends very much on the engine fitted. In 1961, *Autocar* magazine tested a supercharged 948cc GT and achieved 96mph and an 0-60mph time of 17.5 seconds while in 1964, *Motor* magazine timed a tuned 1800GT at over 110mph with the 0-60mph dash being made in 12 seconds.

Various extras were available such as Borani wire wheels, long-range fuel tanks, various engine tuning parts, ZF-gearbox and limited-slip differential. By 1964, overdrive was available and this increased the top speed.

Most of the cars made were the 1800GT version and the main market was the UK, though four LHD cars were exported to the US and two RHD cars went to Australia. Total production numbers of the GT/1800GT used to be quoted at between 400 and 600 but today the Gilbern Owners' Club thinks the actual number to be about 202.

Specific Checks: When considering buying one of these sturdy and well built cars, the main area of deterioration is the 16 gauge 1.25-inch square steel tube chassis, which rusts and can crack. The vulnerable hollow sills can be checked by first removing the rear wheels and then shining a torch into the sills. Look also for stress cracks around the engine mountings. The glassfibre body is bonded and riveted to the chassis which can make

removal time-consuming but is not particularly difficult. For strength, the doors, bonnet and boot hinges are all bolted through the glassfibre to the steel spaceframe chassis structure below. The Gilbern Owners' Club has the glassfibre moulds so body panels can be purchased and the square tube chassis can be repaired in sections or a new one purchased complete. Some trim parts are difficult to source. The large rear window, if perspex, can become crazed and less transparent with age, but later ones were glass. The 1800GT versions, being MGB based, benefit today as their spares are readily available.

Prices Today: The Club estimates that possibly as many as 100 cars survive today. Valuation is difficult as so few cars come onto the market.

Above: **A side view of the good-looking Gilbern GT.**
Below: **The car had a well-equipped interior.**

Dates:	1966-76 (See text).	**Number Built:** c.800

Body/Chassis: GRP body on tubular steel chassis, 2+2 seater sports saloon or estate.

Engine: Ford 2994cc, V6, ohv, 141bhp (MkIII: 157bhp).

Layout: Front engine, rear wheel drive, 4-speed manual gearbox (some with overdrive) or 3-speed automatic (rare).

Performance: Top speed over 115mph, 0-60mph in c.9sec.

Price Today: £/££

Above: **The Gilbern Genie, Invader MkI and MkII all looked very similar. The side styling was apparently inspired by the Alfa Romeo Giulia coupés. The car illustrated is a Genie.**

The Gilbern Genie was launched at the 1966 London Motor Show. This luxurious and sturdy car had an unstressed glassfibre body riveted and bonded to a semi-spaceframe square tube steel chassis (mainly 16 gauge). It used the new Ford 3-litre "Essex" V6 (in fact, Ford had offered Gilbern an early example to try out prior to the official launch of the engine). The engines required minor modifications to fit, and the better exhaust manifolds used by Gilbern gave some extra power.

The suspension was an amalgam of MG and Gilbern parts with coil springs, and a live rear axle. Early wire-wheeled Genies (the first 41 cars) had primarily MGB-based suspension and Austin-Healey rear axles, while later cars (from Spring 1968 and up to the Invader MkII) had MGC-based suspension and rear axles. About 9 Genies were fitted with fuel injection but were later converted to carburettors.

Extras on the Genie included overdrive, electric windows, fabric sunroof, wire wheels (standard on the very first cars) and Gilbern alloy wheels were fitted to the last 150 Genies. Nearly 200 Genies were made including two convertibles and one estate. Only three cars were exported.

By early 1969 the original founders (Smith and Friese) had sold out and left the company.

In mid-1969 the car was renamed the Invader and it appeared with a redesigned chassis and a more luxurious interior, which included a walnut facia and electric windows (with fixed quarter lights). Other changes included smaller rear lights and recessed door handles. An optional automatic gearbox was also available, though they are quite rare. About 80 Invader MkI cars were made.

The Invader MkII (launched in late 1970) looked similar except that the bonnet had a discrete bulge rather than a recessed air intake. More importantly it had an improved front chassis. About 210 MkII cars were made, plus a further 100 or so Estate versions (a higher number than is sometimes quoted). Production of the MkI/MkII included one convertible and 4 cars were officially exported. Gilbern alloy wheels were fitted on the earlier cars and overdrive was a fairly common extra.

Note that the model changeovers were not clear cut and there is a considerable crossover of parts from Genie to MkI and MkII.

Below: **The last 150 Genies were all fitted with Gilbern's own alloy wheels, as were the Invader MkI, MkII and Estate. This car has the optional fabric sunroof.**

Below: **The Estate version of the Invader was launched in 1971 and was popular, with just over 100 made.**

In September 1972 came the MkIII with a restyled body. Its handsome and timeless lines look as good today as they did back then. It was easily distinguishable from the earlier Invaders by its full-width grille, flared wheel arches and high-back front seats. For ease of production, the MkIII used mainly Ford components throughout (ie engine, gearbox, suspension and rear axle). It also had the improved Series 2 Ford V6 engines and other modifications such as a revised chassis, complete with a Ford subframe at front. Of the MkIII production of about 210 cars, 11 cars were exported and there was one convertible. One prototype MkIV was also part built – it was a stretched MkIII with more legroom and boot space.

Unfortunately, in mid-1973 Gilbern went into receivership as it had accumulated debts over a number of years. Although the company ceased trading in 1974, there followed many attempts to revive the business, during which time a few more cars were assembled in ones and twos at the factory, until 1976. After that date a few more cars were completed by enthusiasts and some even remain today as unbuilt cars.

Specific Checks: When checking one of these cars, the main area of deterioration is the 16 gauge 1.25-inch square tube steel semi-spaceframe chassis, which rusts and can crack. The vulnerable hollow sills can be checked by first removing the rear wheels and then shining a torch into the sills. Look also for stress cracks around the engine mountings. Unless re-routed, the main front to rear brake pipe runs in the offside sill and tends to corrode unseen.

The unstressed glassfibre body is bonded and riveted to the chassis which can make removal time-consuming but is not particularly difficult. For strength, the doors, bonnet and boot hinges are all bolted through the glassfibre to the steel spaceframe structure below. The Gilbern Owners' Club has the glassfibre moulds so body panels can be purchased and the square tube chassis can be repaired in sections or a new one purchased complete. Some minor trim parts are difficult to source. The cars have a tendency to overheat unless the radiator core is clear and the electric fan works.

Prices Today: The Gilbern Owners' Club estimates that possibly as many as half of the Genies and Invaders made survive today. The Genie and early Invaders have the same value but the MkIII cars carry a slight premium.

Photo Top Right: **The MkIII featured a restyled body with flared wheelarches and full-width grille.**
2nd From Top: **A MkIII with Wolfrace wheels.**
3rd From Top: **The MkIII interior was luxurious.**
Lower Right: **A MkIII in an impressive setting.**

Dates: Since 1961 (See text).   **Number Built:** Over 500 to date.

Body/Chassis: GRP body on tubular steel chassis, 2-seater open sports or coupé.

Engines: Ford or Lotus (See text).

Layout: Front engine, rear wheel drive with normally a 4-speed manual gearbox.

Performance: Dependent on engine, but usually fast or very fast!

Prices Today: Series I-III: £££+   Series IV: ££ (See text).

Above: **An early Series II Ginetta G4.**

Ginetta was founded in 1958 by the four Walklett brothers – Bob, Douglas, Ivor and Trevers (also known as "Trevor"). Most of their cars were for racing and the G4 was no exception, except its design was dual purpose: a weekday road car and a weekend racer. It appeared at the Racing Car Show in London in 1961 and used a spaceframe chassis made of 1-inch, 18 gauge round steel tubing with an attractive glassfibre open top body which had distinctive tail fins and rear wheelarches that partly covered the wheels. The one-piece, forward-hinged bonnet was easily removable and was held closed by two very visible spring clips. The cars were supplied complete, including soft-top, but in component form for user assembly to avoid UK Purchase Tax.

Between 1961 and 1969, there were three Series of the G4 plus the G4R race version. The Series II cars (from 1963) had revised bodywork including the removal of the tail fins, a flat tail panel and the wheelarches were more rounded. The late Series I and Series II cars also had revised suspension with improved ride and a BMC rear axle replaced the original Ford unit. Front disc brakes were now an optional extra as was a curved hardtop incorporating a raked windscreen. Development continued and in 1966 the interior was completely revised and the round tube chassis was changed over to square tubing. The Series III cars (from 1967) had manual pop-up headlamps to meet new headlamp height regulations, plus a smart chrome front bumper. They looked altogether more sleek, but only 20 were made.

Engines were usually Ford and were originally 1 to 1.5-litre pre-crossflow units in various states of tune. Later cars (from 1963) could be specified with the new Ford Cortina 1500GT unit though some cars had Lotus Twin Cam or similar engines fitted, while late Series III cars were fitted with the Ford 1600 crossflow engine. With the G4's racing design and marque pedigree, it is perhaps not surprising that G4 cars have been very successful on the track with numerous wins around the world. The G4R race version had disc brakes on all wheels and its own design of independent rear suspension. Initial production of the G4 ended in 1969.

In 1981 production restarted as the Series IV, usually referred to as the G4/4. This had a new chassis and was 3 inches longer and 2 inches wider to give more interior space. The chrome front bumper was eliminated and though originally launched with pop-up headlamps like the Series III cars, the headlamps soon became fixed.

The G4/4 could take a Ford 1.3, 1.6 "Kent", or 1.6/2-litre "Pinto" engine. Production of the G4/4 ended in 1984 with around 35 made, but in 1989/90 a further batch of Series II cars (c.30) were made mainly for export.

After the Walkletts sold Ginetta in 1989, Trevers and Ivor, together with Trevers' son, Mark, formed Dare UK Ltd and started to produce a further development of the G4 Series II which remains in production today.

Specific Checks: When checking an early G4, look for corrosion of the chassis, especially underneath the bonding where the body is attached. Also inspect the chassis for damage from racing. Check the car's identity with the Ginetta Owners' Club as there are fakes.

Prices Today: There are about 30 Series I-III cars in the UK plus a further 50 or so Series IV and Dare cars. The rest are mainly in Japan or the US. With relatively few Ginetta G4 cars changing hands, they are difficult to value, but Series I-III cars are probably worth approximately twice that of the Series IV cars.

Above & Below: **Two Dare G4 cars.**

Dates: 1967-74	**Number Built:** c.600

Body/Chassis: GRP body on tubular steel chassis, 2-seater fixed-head coupé.

Engine: Imp Sport 875cc, 4-cyl, sohc, 51bhp (net) or 998cc, 65bhp.

Layout: Rear engine, rear wheel drive, 4-speed manual gearbox.

Performance: 875cc: Top speed over 95mph, 0-60mph under 13sec; 998cc: Top speed over 100mph, 0-60mph under 10sec.

Price Today: ££

Above: **A Ginetta G15 Series I. These early cars are quite rare.**

The attractive G15 was developed from a long line of successful race/sports cars and appeared first at the 1967 London Motor Show. The new car used an Imp Sport engine and 4-speed all-synchromesh gearbox fitted in the rear together with the Imp rear suspension. Unlike the Hillman Imp car, the G15 had twin wishbone front suspension incorporating Triumph disc brakes and usually had a front mounted radiator. The fuel tank, battery and spare wheel were also placed up front and they virtually filled the forward compartment but there was luggage space behind the seats. The large upward-opening rear engine cover gave excellent access to the engine. The car also had 13-inch wheels, rather than the Imp's 12-inch ones, and was noted for its excellent handling. The G15 was raced very successfully.

This smart little car (only 12ft long and 44in high), was produced in five Series with mainly small detail changes to distinguish between them. The facia and seats were revised for the Series II cars. The Series III (from 1971) had a number of improvements, such as larger rear three-quarter windows and an electric radiator fan was now available. The front bumper was given a small moulded section between the two chromed halves (which were VW sourced, the rear bumper being from a Riley Elf). Development continued with the car, for example the petrol tank was changed from glassfibre to steel to meet new safety regulations and the door handles became flush-fitting units from mid-1972.

Some cars were fitted with an optional fabric sunroof or alloy wheels. About 80 cars had the more powerful 998cc engine fitted. Towards the end of the car's production life it was required to be crash tested at MIRA and apparently passed satisfactorily.

The advent of VAT tax, in April 1973, removed the huge tax advantage of people buying a car in component form and assembling it themselves, so the Series IV cars, which were post-April 1973, were therefore factory assembled. To make them more attractive they had many extras fitted as standard, but G15 production ended in 1974. However, in 1978, to meet a specific order from the US, two specially modified cars were built which were fitted with VW engines and had cosmetic changes to the bodywork such as flared wheelarches.

Specific Checks: When checking a G15, first check for chassis corrosion particularly the area around the rear trailing arm mountings and upswept chassis section in front of the rear wheels. In addition, sagging or cracking

of the front spring mounting turrets may occur on early cars. Look out also for rusty fuel tanks.

Check also the engine for difficult starting, excessive smoking or lumpy idling. A high water temperature after a long test drive may indicate a blown head gasket. Also listen for unusual noises from the transaxle/gearbox whilst driving. The sliding perspex side windows can suffer from scratches and the metal frames in which these windows are mounted are prone to rusting.

Prices Today: It is thought there may be approximately 400 or more cars left today. Prices are mainly dependent on a car's condition rather than its Series.

Above: **A Ginetta G15 Series III car with the optional fabric sunroof.**
Below: **Engine access was excellent.**

Right: **The Ginetta G21's boot was a practical feature.**

Left: **Normally the headlamps were behind the grille, but this can blank the radiator, hence some cars (like this one) have the headlamps moved out.**

Dates: 1970-78 (See text).	Number Built: 68

Body/Chassis: GRP body on steel chassis, 2-seater FHC.

Engine: Sunbeam 1725cc, 4-cyl in-line, ohv, 85bhp (G21S: 98bhp).

Layout: Front engine, RWD, 4-speed manual (optional overdrive).

Performance: c.110mph, 0-60 under 10sec.   **Price:** Contact Club.

Dates: 1949-50	Number Built: 105

Body/Chassis: Aluminium panels on steel subframe with separate chassis, 2-seater open sports.

Engine: Riley 2443cc, 4-cyl in-line, ohv, 104bhp.

Layout: Front engine, RWD, 4-speed manual gearbox.

Performance: c.110mph, 0-60 in c.11-12sec.   **Price:** HiValue.

The good looking G21 first appeared at the 1970 London Motor Show but sales did not start until 1973. Unlike previous Ginettas, which had racing aspirations, the G21 was designed solely for road use.

The G21 chassis consisted of substantial 2-inch square steel tubing with a deep backbone made of pressed steel. The glassfibre body was bolted to the chassis and the entire front of the car could be easily removed to gain all-round access to the engine. The car passed the MIRA crash test and all cars were factory built. The G21 was 12 inches longer and 6 inches wider than the G15. While alloy wheels, reclining seats, a collapsible steering column, heated rear window and laminated windscreen were standard, overdrive, headrests and sunroof were optional extras.

Originally the car was offered with either a Ford V6 3-litre engine or the smaller Sunbeam Rapier 1725cc unit. However, only two V6 prototypes were built and all production cars were made with the smaller engine, which reduced the final price by almost a third. A Holbay-engined 98bhp version, the G21S, was also available which included overdrive as standard equipment.

Although the car was officially only available until 1978, one or two further cars were made up to 1981. Unfortunately the G21's debut had coincided with a major economic recession in the UK, and it is a pity that more of these fine cars were not made.

Specific Checks: The chassis can rust – look especially at the tube at the front of the passenger footwell that passes over the exhaust, as this is very rust prone. All chassis and body panels are still available, though the rear bumper is hard to obtain.

Prices Today: The Ginetta Owners' Club estimates there may be 55-60 cars left. With few cars changing hands, it is difficult to value the G21 accurately.

After WW2, Donald Healey set up the Donald Healey Motor Co. in Warwick, to produce his ideal sports car. His first models were the Westland roadster (c.64 made, 1946-50), the fast Elliott sports saloon (c.101 made, 1946-50) and the Sportsmobile (c.23 made, 1948-50).

In 1949, Healey launched the Silverstone, named after the nearby circuit. Based on Healey's "D" type chassis, with a body designed by Len Hodges, the new car was intended to be raced and its price had to be under £1,000 to avoid the crippling double Purchase Tax in the UK.

The engine was located some 8in further aft than earlier models, giving the car better handling. The IFS was by coil spring and trailing arms, while the live rear axle used coil springs too, and the drum brakes were hydraulic. The car had several unusual features: the windscreen could partially retract into the scuttle to minimise wind resistance when racing; second, the spare wheel protruded at the rear, acting as a rear bumper and third, the headlamps were set behind the front grille to minimise the car's frontal area.

After c.51 cars were built, in 1950 came an improved version, using Healey's "E" type chassis, and with a wider body and more legroom. Other improvements included a telescopic steering column, larger windscreen (with perspex wind deflectors), more space behind the seats for luggage and stowage and an improved soft-top. The Silverstone was exhibited in New York and a good proportion of the cars made were exported. However, the high cost of the hand built Silverstones restricted their sales potential, despite racing successes.

Specific Checks: Check the car's authenticity with the owners' clubs, as a number of replicas have been created by re-bodying Healey Saloons.

Prices Today: Proper valuation requires expert advice.

Dates: 1948-61

Numbers Built: XK120: c.12,050   XK140: c.8,940   XK150: c.9,380

Body/Chassis: Steel (and aluminium) body on separate chassis,
XK120: 2-seater roadster, fixed-head or drophead coupé;
XK140/150: 2-seater roadster, (2+2) fixed-head or drophead coupé.

Engines: XK120/140: 3442cc, 6-cyl in-line, dohc, 160-210bhp;
XK150: 3442cc, 6-cyl in-line, dohc, 210-250bhp or
3781cc, 6-cyl in-line, dohc, 220-265bhp.

Layout: Front engine, rear wheel drive, 4-speed manual gearbox
(with optional overdrive or 3-speed automatic gearbox).

Performance: (Standard models) Top speed over 120mph,
0-60mph in c.9sec (tuned versions even quicker).

Prices Today: FHC: ££££/£££££   OTS & DHC: HiValue.

Above: **An official photo of the Jaguar XK120 roadster. The rear spats were standard but had to be removed when wire wheels were used.**

The Jaguar XK120 was launched at the 1948 London Motor Show, and was the star of the show. The car's name reflected its new XK engine and the speed the car could achieve. The design had much input from Jaguar's founder, William Lyons, along with William Heynes (Jaguar's Chief Engineer), Claude Baily and Walter Hassan, with an important contribution from Harry Weslake. The XK120 had the world's first production twin cam engine and the attractive car was capable of racing car performance. The price (£998 plus tax) was extremely good too, so not surprisingly orders flooded in.

The first model was the OTS (Open Two Seater) roadster and the initial 240, or so, cars had aluminium bodies, making these desirable and very expensive today. Thereafter, steel was used, though the bonnet, doors and boot lid remained in aluminium with ash frames for the doors and boot lid (though later non-OTS car doors were steel). In 1951 came a fixed-head coupé with wind-up windows and in 1953 came a drophead. Seats were leather trimmed and the fixed-head and drophead convertible had walnut veneer dashboards, while the roadster had a simpler leather-covered dashboard. The engine was available in different states of tune, the SE (Special Equipment) unit generating 180bhp and this version had wire-wheels too. The Americans referred to the SE model as the XK120M ("M" for "Modified").

In its time the XK120 was the fastest production car in the world and in 1949 one flew through a measured mile of the Jabbeke highway in Belgium at an amazing 132mph. This particular XK120 roadster was reputedly standard except that its soft-top roof was removed, its windscreen was replaced by a small metal wind deflector and there was a detachable undershield fitted.

Famous Hollywood film stars such as Clark Gable and Gary Cooper bought XK120s and there were many speed records and competition wins too, such as the Appleyards' victories in the 1951 and 1953 RAC Rallies.

The XK140 appeared in 1954. It can be identified by its more substantial bumpers and fewer vertical slats in the grille. Otherwise the car looked identical to the XK120, but beneath the skin the engine now produced 190bhp in standard form and was moved forward by 3 inches to improve the front/rear weight distribution.

This had the additional benefit that there was more legroom in the roadster and (with an extended roof line) provided space for two small children's seats in the fixed-head and drophead convertible. The door width on the coupé was increased by 5.5 inches.

The XK140 had rack and pinion steering and telescopic dampers on all wheels. Brakes were still drum on all four wheels and some cars (under 400) had automatic gearboxes. The SE version now gave 210bhp and came with wire wheels.

The XK150 appeared in 1957 with some significant changes – a one piece "wraparound" windscreen, raised waistline and cockpit width increased by over 4 inches. The car was the first mass produced car to have disc brakes on all wheels and these brakes were servo-assisted (drum brakes were apparently still available). The grille was widened too and the walnut veneer dashboard was replaced by a leather-covered version. Again there were different states of tuning available, including the rare S option with triple carbs producing 250bhp.

Due to a major fire at the Jaguar factory, the roadster appeared late. It now had wind-up windows for the first time. In 1959 a 3.8-litre engine became available for all XK150s (the S option with triple carbs produced 265bhp).

Under one in five XKs were RHD and the proportion of roadsters varied with each mark of car. With the XK120, two-thirds were roadsters but this dropped to just a quarter with the XK150. In contrast, the proportion of fixed-heads rose from under a quarter with the XK120 to nearly half of all the XK150 cars. Continued....

Below: **The XK120 fixed-head coupé. All post-1951 XKs, like this one, had cockpit fresh air vents in the front wings.**

Optional extras included an automatic gearbox (on the XK140/150 only, and rare today), overdrive, wire wheels and C-type cylinder head (on the XK140).

Specific Checks: Start with the paperwork, then later contact the Jaguar Daimler Heritage Trust Archives to verify the car's authenticity (unless the car already has a Heritage Certificate).

Restoring an XK can be hugely expensive and bodges are common, so checking an XK really needs the services of a qualified Jaguar expert. The critical items are the body/chassis and a good quick guide to condition is to bend down and scan your eyes along the bottom of the car. The front wing, door and rear wing (before the wheel) should all be in a straight line (see photos on right).

Next, open the doors fully – they should not strike the body. The door hinge boxes can rust badly. The sills are critical and should be checked for corrosion from below. Check also that the main longitudinal chassis rails are straight. Poorly repaired accident damage may reveal itself as rippling in a chassis rail just behind the front shock absorbers, which is a weak point. Check too that the long torsion bars at the front run parallel with the chassis rails. If possible, and with the owner's permission, remove each rear wheel to check the chassis section behind the rear axle, especially the front mounting of the rear springs. Look also for broken leaf springs.

The engine is solid and reliable, but leaks oil and, if worn, can burn oil at a prodigious rate. The timing chains should not rattle. With alloy heads, it is essential that antifreeze (with its corrosion inhibitor) has always been used or there will be overheating problems. Check the exhaust manifold for cracking. The Moss manual gearbox is reliable and should be relatively quiet, though 1st and reverse gears may whine. A faulty gearbox can be costly to repair.

The trim and soft-top roof (where applicable) should be in good condition, as a full re-trim is expensive.

Modifications include electric fans to assist engine cooling, alternators (especially if electric fans are fitted) and 15-inch E-Type wheels (as their tyres are cheaper than those for the standard 16-inch XK wheels).

Prices Today: RHD XK120/140s are relatively rare, as are RHD XK150 roadsters. In the UK, any LHD car will cost slightly less than a RHD equivalent. The XK140 and XK150 fixed-head cars are the most affordable. Valuation of any XK really requires expert advice.

Above & Below: **The XK140 roadster is identifiable by its split windscreen and substantial bumpers.**

Above: **The XK150 roadster had a large rear deck, being only a 2-seater.**
Below: **All XK dropheads, like this XK150, had wind-up windows.**

Below: **The XK150S was capable of over 130mph. The "S" cars all carry a significant premium in their values today.**

Dates: 1961-74

Numbers Built: S1: c.38,400   S2: c.18,800   S3: c.15,300

Body/Chassis: Tubular steel front subframe bolted to steel monocoque, 2-seater open sports or 2-seater (or 2+2) rear-hatch fixed-head coupé.

Engines: 1961-64: 3781cc, 6-cyl in-line, dohc, 265bhp (gross); 1964-71: 4235cc, 6-cyl in-line, dohc, 265bhp (gross); US: 245-246bhp (gross); 1971-74: 5343cc, V12, ohc, 272bhp (net); (US: 241bhp).

Layout: Front engine, rear wheel drive, 4-speed manual gearbox (optional 3-speed automatic gearbox on some models).

Performance: Top speed over 145mph, 0-60mph in 6-7sec; (2+2 and US models all slightly slower).

Prices Today: Roadster: £££££   Coupé: ££££   2+2: £££+

Above: **The Jaguar E-Type Series 1 can be identified by its glass headlight fairings and trim line crossing the air-intake. This is an early publicity photo. The girl seems pleased with the new car.**
Below: **Rear view of a very early Series 1 car.**

Above: **A "flat floor" S1 car (with factory hardtop), seen in 2006.**
Below: **Series 1 coupé 2-seater with rear-hatch and bonnet open.**

The Jaguar E-Type is perhaps one of the best known sports cars in the world. It was a direct descendent of the famous C-Type and D-Type racers. The E-Type was designed by William Heynes with its styling by Malcolm Sayer, a talented aerodynamicist, who paid particular attention to the car's streamlining. The E-Type was launched in 1961 and was an immediate sensation. The car not only looked good, but it also had a phenomenal top speed (150mph was possible) and was relatively cheap – an unbeatable combination. The high level of customer demand caught out Jaguar who had to bring production forward and only a few E-Types were actually delivered to customers in 1961.

The E-Type was of semi-monocoque construction with the front subframe bolted onto the monocoque. It also had independent rear suspension and the car originally used the XK150S 3.8-litre engine with triple carbs and Moss gearbox.

In 1964 the engine size was increased to 4.2-litres (identified with tail badges) and an all-synchromesh Jaguar gearbox was introduced. In 1966 a 2+2 seater fixed-head coupé version was added. This was 9 inches longer (all taken up in the now heavier doors), and it also had a higher roofline (by about 2 inches) with an enlarged windscreen and two wipers (rather than three).

Due to Federal regulations the last cars of the first Series, unofficially called Series 1½ or 1A (the "A" for "American"), had their attractive and aerodynamically efficient headlamp fairings removed. In addition, Stromberg carbs were fitted as part of the car's new emissions controls.

In late 1968 came the Series 2, which had its bumpers raised and the front bumper crossing the grille (it had been only a trim line on the Series 1). The side/indicator lights were much larger and were now located below both bumpers. There were improved brakes (with larger calipers), better engine cooling (with enlarged air intake and two fans) and improved safety with rocker switches and a collapsible steering column.   Continued....

The Series 3, launched in 1971, had Jaguar's new silky smooth V12 engine (314bhp gross, 272bhp net or in the US: 241bhp). The car is easily recognisable by its distinctive grille and flared wheelarches (for its wider wheels and tyres). Brakes were upgraded with ventilated front discs, there was anti-dive front suspension and power-assisted steering was now standard. The larger, heavier, Series 3 cars were all built on the longer 2+2 wheelbase, though the roadster was still just a 2-seater.

Of the total number of E-Types made (c.72,500), over 80% were exported. The car was known in the US initially as the XK-E though later as the E-Type.

Production of the coupé ended in late 1973, the roadster going on until 1974. Almost half of all E-Types made were roadsters. The last 50 E-Types built were all painted black (except for one car), were RHD, and had a plaque signed by Sir William Lyons on their dashboard.

Typical optional extras fitted to E-Types included 3-speed automatic transmission (available only on the longer 2+2 seater Series 1½ and 2 cars and both of the Series 3 models), power steering on the Series 2 cars (standard on the Series 3), detachable hardtop, Webasto fabric sunroof (on the fixed-head cars), wire wheels (standard on early cars), air-conditioning and tinted glass. In recent years, many owners have upgraded aspects of their cars such as the suspension and brakes, and some have fitted 5-speed gearboxes.

Specific Checks: Start with the paperwork, then later contact the Jaguar Daimler Heritage Trust Archives to verify the car's authenticity (unless the car already has a Heritage Certificate).

The E-Type is a sophisticated piece of machinery and checking an example really needs the services of a qualified E-Type expert. Due to the often high costs of doing a proper repair on this car, bodged repairs are common. Fortunately the major mechanical parts – engine, gearbox and rear axle are all robust, but most of these cars were driven hard so will either have had major rebuilds or will now require them.

The V12 is so smooth that any untoward noises can signal bad news. If not changed, the timing chains stretch and rattle. Some oil consumption is not abnormal (on all the engines). The cost of an engine rebuild, especially the V12, can be expensive (c.£3K).

Above: **A Series 1 handsome 2-seater coupé.**
Below: **This is a 4.2-litre 2+2 version.**

Above: **A Series 2 roadster. Note the absence of headlight fairings.**
Below: **A trio of E-Types representing, from left to right: S1(2-seater coupé), S2 (roadster) and S3 (2+2 coupé).**

Below: **The cockpit of a Series 2 roadster.**

The big enemy of this car is rust. In addition to all the usual areas to check, there are particular points to look out for, all of which are expensive to rectify. These include: underside corrosion – check especially under the boot and where the rear suspension is mounted at the rear of the floorpan. Look at the floorpan too, and around the wheelarches. Also inspect the rear bodywork carefully for thinning of the metalwork due to corrosion (and possible use of plastic filler).

Check where the front subframe meets the body. In addition, check the front subframe for rust, accident damage, welding and fatigue cracks.

The bonnet should sit correctly when lowered and not be distorted (due to accident damage or corrosion). A replacement bonnet is expensive (c.£3K plus fitting and paint). Also look for rust around the bonnet hinges.

Overall the panel fit can be a good guide as to the bodywork's condition.

Next check the universal joints on the prop-shaft as they are difficult to replace. Failure of these is usually due to a lack of maintenance. The rear silencers (if mild steel) tend not to last long. Inspect both the rear hubs for wear by rocking the wheels when the car is jacked up. Finally, note that the rear brakes (being inboard) are often neglected and repairs can be quite difficult.

Prices Today: The S1/S2 roadsters used to be valued at considerably more than the 2-seater coupés, but the latter's prices are rising so the gap is now closer, while the 2+2 seaters are worth slightly less. Automatic versions are less desirable than manual gearbox cars. An early "flat floor" car carries a premium.

Finally, be wary of coupés that have been converted to roadsters and watch for cars that have been re-imported and converted to right-hand drive as these are usually worth less than original right-hand drive examples. The body/chassis number should reveal what you are buying. Valuation really requires expert advice.

Above: **The fabulous V12 engine of a Series 3.**
Below: **A Federal-spec Series 3 with side repeaters and large over-riders.**

Above: **All Series 3 coupés were 2+2 seaters.**
Below: **The distinctive grille readily identifies a Series 3 car.**

Below: **Series 3 with early "fishtail" exhaust arrangement and optional wire wheels.**

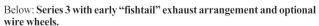

| Dates: | 1975-96 | Number Built: | c.115,300 |

Body/Chassis: Steel unitary, 4-seater fixed-head coupé or
2-seater cabriolet, or 2 or 2+2 seater convertible.

Engines:
1975-93: 5343cc, V12, ohc, fuel injection, 285-300bhp (HE: 285bhp);
1983-91: 3590cc, 6-cyl in-line, dohc, fuel injection, 221-225bhp;
1991-96: 3980cc, 6-cyl in-line, dohc, fuel injection, 223-238bhp;
1993-96: 5994cc, V12, ohc, fuel injection, 308bhp.

Layout: Front engine, rear wheel drive, 3 or 4-speed automatic,
or 4 or 5-speed manual gearbox.

Performance: V12: Top speed over 150mph, 0-60mph in c.6-7sec;
6-cyl: Top speed c.140mph, 0-60mph in c.7sec.

Prices Today: Early Coupé: £   Cabriolet: £+
Late Coupé: ££   Convertible: ££ (Late cars: £££)

Above: **A pre-HE car with its all-black bumpers and Kent alloy wheels.**
Below: **A much later 3.6-litre Jaguar XJ-S.**

Above: **A 3.6-litre model from 1987, with pepperpot alloy wheels.**
Below: **Compare the car above with the post-1991 facelift model below (with its new rear and altered side windows). Lattice alloy wheels fitted.**

Not a successor to the E-Type (and unfairly maligned by the Press when launched), the good-looking XJ-S went from strength to strength, lasting in production for 21 years and enjoying impressive sales. In 1991, the official model designation was changed from XJ-S to XJS.

The car was based on the short wheelbase floorpan of the Jaguar XJ saloon, the -S suffix added for "Sport". It was very well equipped with leather, air-conditioning and alloy wheels as standard. But in 1981 Jaguar had to launch a new model, the HE ("High Efficiency") to address criticism about fuel consumption and build quality. The HE's modified engine with "Fireball" cylinder heads gave better fuel consumption and the car now had traditional Jaguar features such as wood veneer. There were also improvements in build quality. The HE had an "HE" rear badge and "starfish" alloy wheels.

There were two major developments in 1983: first, the introduction of a cabriolet version (the XJ-SC), with a considerably strengthened bodyshell, and second, a smaller 3.6-litre, 6-cylinder engine option. This new engine, the AJ6, was more fuel efficient but only slightly less powerful than the V12. The 3.6-litre car was popular, with just over 10,000 made (pre-1991), including c.1,100 cabriolets. The cabriolet was initially offered with only the smaller engine, but a V12 was also available two years later (c.3,900 cars fitted with the V12).

The 3.6-litre car was available with either 4-speed automatic or 5-speed manual gearbox, the first manual option on the XJ-S since 1978 when a 4-speed unit had been phased out due to lack of demand (only 352 sold).

By 1988 the cabriolets had been replaced by an attractive 2-seater convertible (some cars had already been officially converted from coupés by Hess & Eisenhardt in the US). The year also saw the launch of the Jaguar-Sport XJR-S version to commemorate Jaguar's win at Le Mans earlier that year. The XJR-S had uprated suspension, bigger wheels and styling features such as colour matched bumpers and rear spoiler. The cars were all automatics and ABS was fitted. In 1991 the XJR-S got a 6-litre engine producing 333bhp (US: 318bhp).

1991 saw the first major face-lift and re-engineering of the car, which included a galvanised body with new side windows (no quarter lights), an altered rear and a revised interior. The popular straight-six engine was increased to 4-litres. In 1994 it was replaced by its successor, the new AJ16 engine (238bhp). In 1992 a 2+2 seater convertible was added to the range.

The V12 was raised to 6-litres in 1993 and a 4-speed auto box was now standard in the V12 cars. The bumpers were now larger and body-coloured. Production of the XJS eventually ceased in 1996, the last cars being the "Celebration" models to mark Jaguar's 60th anniversary.

Cars for North America usually had four headlights (these have also been fitted by specialists to some UK cars). The export cars' engines had a lower bhp, eg the 5.3L V12 was rated at 244bhp (HE: 262bhp), the 6.0L V12 was rated at 280bhp and the 4.0L six-cylinder engine was rated at 219bhp. North America also had the "Collection Rouge" and "Classic Collection" special editions.

Specific Checks: To verify the car's authenticity, contact the Jaguar Daimler Heritage Trust Archives (unless there is already a Heritage Certificate).

The XJ-S (XJS) is a sophisticated vehicle that needs regular servicing, so be wary of cars without a full recent service record. Checking a car really needs a qualified Jaguar expert. Fortunately the major parts, ie engine, gearbox and rear axle, are generally robust, but they still all require the usual checks.

Corrosion on early cars can be a major problem and requires knowledge to detect and assess. This can be a safety issue. In particular check the front crossmember, for if badly rusted this can write-off the car. Check also the sills, wheelarches, rear suspension mountings and around the windscreen and A-pillars (this last area can have terminal rust). Even the galvanised cars can rust!

Remember to check that the wheels and tyres are genuine XJ-S items. Pre-1993 cars have inboard rear disc brakes that are difficult to work on and hence often neglected – check the handbrake works. The electrics can give trouble, especially the windows. Check too the air-conditioning. In general, even minor problems can be difficult and/or expensive to rectify. Experts advise against buying the really cheap examples of XJ-S.

Prices Today: Pre-HE cars had quality problems. Post-1991 face-lift cars command the top prices. Cabriolets/convertibles cost 50% or so more than a comparable coupé. The late coupés are possibly undervalued.

Below: **A 2-seater V12 Jaguar XJ-S convertible.**

Above & Below: **The cabriolet (1983-88, c.5,000 made) had a targa roof in front of the centre bar, then either a half hardtop or a folding rear hood (as shown here). Starfish alloy wheels fitted.**

Above: **The convertible had a powered top. This is a 2-seater version.**
Below: **About 31,000 convertibles were made 1988-96. The car shown was the last RHD 6-litre convertible to be made.**

Dates: 1953-63   **Number Built:** 546

Body/Chassis: GRP body (aluminium doors) on steel chassis, 4-seater sports saloon.

Engine: Austin 3993cc, 6-cyl in-line, ohv, (bhp - See text).

Layout: Front engine, rear wheel drive, 4-speed manual (optional overdrive); 541S: 4-speed auto or manual (with overdrive).

Performance: 541: Top speed over 115mph, 0-60mph in c.11sec; 541R: About 125mph; 541S auto: About 110mph.

Price Today: Contact Club.

Above: **The radiator shutter is closed in this photo of a Jensen 541R.**

Launched at the 1953 London Motor Show, this handsome car took its type number from being the first series for 1954 – hence "541", but production proper did not commence until January 1955. Styled by Eric Neale, with technical design by Colin Riekie, it was the first British production car to have a full glassfibre body and it had the distinctive feature of a controllable shutter over its radiator air-intake. It also had noticeable streamlined blisters over its front wheelarches (later versions had them over the rear wheelarches too).

The car used a tuned Austin 4-litre engine with triple SU carburettors mated to an Austin gearbox. Jensen were always shy about quoting the bhp of their engines but it seems likely that the early 541 produced about 117bhp. The car had servo-assisted drum brakes, but with the new *deluxe* version launched in late 1956, Jensen could claim to be the first British company to market a 4-seater production saloon with disc brakes all round. This model also had wire wheels and overdrive. A total of 53 of the *deluxe* version were made, plus 173 standard cars.

The 541R came in 1957, with rack and pinion steering, a Moss gearbox and initially the more powerful, new Austin DS7 engine with twin carbs, producing c.150bhp. It also had the new Austin A90's front crossmember and its complete front suspension. The boot became top-hinged too. At the time, it was one of the world's fastest production cars, and it is visually distinguishable from the earlier 541 by its larger streamlined blisters over both its front and rear wheelarches. There were 193 Jensen 541R cars made, but only 43 with the DS7 engine. The others had the DS5 triple carb engine, which was also fitted to 13 standard 541 cars and 8 *deluxe* ones.

The final version, the 541S, came in 1960. This had a 4-inch wider chassis, a revised bodyshell with more headroom and a wider cabin. It had a more conventional looking grille too. It used the Austin DS5 engine. A manual gearbox version was fitted to 20 cars, but most used the 4-speed GM automatic gearbox, modified by Rolls-Royce. The 541S has the distinction of being the first British production car with front seat belts fitted as standard (though they were only diagonal belts in those days, ie no lap straps), plus a fire extinguisher and first aid kit. There were 127 Jensen 541S cars made.

Specific Checks: When checking one of these Jensens, examine the GRP bodywork for bad repairs, surface crazing and ripples. Although glassfibre is repairable,

this can be quite expensive when done properly. With the chassis, check for corrosion and poorly done accident repairs. In particular, check the 5-inch cylindrical side members – one doubles as a vacuum reservoir for the brake servo. Check also where the front and rear suspension units are mounted. The king-pins and stub axles wear and are difficult to repair or replace.

With the engines, the cylinder heads can crack and replacements are very hard to locate. Note that there are only a few specialist companies that know these cars.

Prices Today: It is thought that perhaps as many as 350 cars still exist. In terms of value, the 541 is difficult to price as relatively few change hands, but manual gearbox cars are more sought after in the UK. Note there were no cars produced in LHD form.

Above: **A Jensen 541R with its top-hinged boot lid.**
Below: **A period photo of the 541S, with its more conventional grille.**

Dates:	1962-66	Number Built:	500

Body/Chassis: GRP body (aluminium doors) on steel chassis, 4-seater sports saloon.

Engines: Chrysler 5916cc (305bhp) or 6276cc (330bhp), V8, ohv.

Layout: Front engine, rear wheel drive, 3-speed auto (or optional 4-speed manual) gearbox.

Performance: Top speed c.130+mph, 0-60mph in c.7sec.

Price Today: Contact Club.

Above: **The Jensen C-V8 is a good-looking machine.**
Below: **The bonnet is released via a small locked panel below the bonnet air intake. Earlier C-V8s had a locking handle instead (see above).**

Above: **The C-V8 with twin silencers from its large Chrysler V8.**
Below: **A MkIII is recognisable as the headlights are of equal size and do not sit in an oval chrome surround (compare this with the cars above).**

The C-V8 was launched at the 1962 London Motor Show, and took its type number from its Chrysler V8 engine. This seriously powerful sporting coupé, noted for its driving experience, was designed by Eric Neale and the Jensen brothers with the very strong chassis design by Kevin Beattie. But the distinctive styling of the four slanted headlights (without their intended perspex fairings) was controversial. The car was lavishly equipped for the time, including diagonal front seat belts (ie no lap straps) fitted as standard. The C-V8 was the first British production car to use an alternator, which was relevant as it had a lot of electrical equipment. The car used the smooth Chrysler TorqueFlite automatic gearbox with a limited slip differential (in fact, only 10 of all C-V8 cars had the optional manual gearbox). Servo-assisted disc brakes on all wheels were necessary to slow down this 1½ ton high-speed projectile.

After only 69 cars had been produced, a Mark II appeared in 1963 with many minor improvements, including rear shock absorbers that could be adjusted by the driver from inside the car. The following year saw the introduction of the even larger 6.3-litre (383 cubic inch) V8 engine. A total of 250 MkII cars were made.

In 1965 came the final, MkIII, version. This had a slightly revised body, dual circuit brakes, a revised facia with walnut veneer (the earlier cars had Formica) and 181 were made.

Only ten C-V8 cars were made in LHD form, as it was not successful in the US market.

There was one convertible made and one car was adapted to fit the revolutionary new four-wheel drive FF system, which was to be such a feature of the model that followed, the Jensen FF.

Specific Checks: First check the GRP bodywork, looking for bad repairs, surface crazing and ripples. Although GRP is repairable, this can be quite expensive when done properly. With the chassis, check for corrosion and poorly done accident repairs. In particular, check the outer box section sill area under the GRP and the bottom of the small compartments just forward of the rear internal wheelarches. Both areas are prone to rusting. Note the front suspension needs greasing every 1,000 miles.

Prices Today: About 200-230 cars still exist in the UK and perhaps 80-90 elsewhere in the world. The C-V8 is difficult to price as relatively few change hands.

Dates: 1966-76 and 1983-90

Numbers Built: Interceptor: c.5,700   FF: 320   SP: 232
Convertible: c.450   Coupé: c.39

Body/Chassis: Steel body/chassis, 4-seater rear-hatch coupé, convertible or fixed-head coupé.

Engines (to 1976): Chrysler 6276cc, V8, ohv, 325-330bhp gross (US MkIII: 220bhp net) or 7212cc, 280bhp net (US: 215bhp net), (SP: 385bhp gross).

Layout: Front engine, rear wheel drive (FF: 4-wheel drive), 3-speed automatic (MkI: optional 4-speed manual gearbox).

Performance: Top speed over 130mph, 0-60mph in under 8sec. (SP: higher top speed).

Prices Today: Interceptor: £££   FF: £££+   Convertible: ££££

Above: **A Jensen Interceptor MkII. Note the Rostyle wheels.**
Below: **An Interceptor MkIII, which is the most numerous version.**

Below: **The enormous glass rear-hatch is a distinctive feature of the Interceptor, FF and SP. Note the vinyl roof covering on this car.**

In 1966 a new Interceptor was launched (Jensen had used the name for an earlier car – see page 167). The new car's striking styling was based on a design by Touring of Milan, and the bodies were built initially by Vignale in Turin with final assembly at the Jensen Motors' factory in West Bromwich, though by 1967 the body production was also transferred to Jensen's. The new Interceptor's chassis was based closely on the C-V8's and it used the same Chrysler 6.3-litre (383 cubic inch) engine and automatic gearbox.

The Interceptor was not only a handsome and powerful car, but also a luxury vehicle with a price tag to match (in 1966 it cost about 1½ times that of a Jaguar E-Type 2+2). The Interceptor's Italianate body was eye-catching, the large glass wraparound rear-hatch was particularly distinctive and the car's performance was electrifying. During its long production life it always had large Chrysler engines (through different Series) matched to smooth TorqueFlite automatic gearboxes, though 24 MkI cars had the optional Chrysler manual gearbox.

Being a hand built car there were many detail changes and trim variations but in 1969, after just over 1,000 cars had been made, came the MkII with a host of improvements. Perhaps the most obvious change was the interior with its completely redesigned dashboard. This had recessed instruments in a vacuum-formed plastic moulding with rocker switches. Under the bonnet the changes included power steering, revised front suspension and Girling brakes (though late MkI cars already had these improvements, and are sometimes known as Mk1.5 cars). Air-conditioning was now available as an option. Just over 1,100 MkII cars were built and the total included over 400 LHD cars, most of which went to North America.

In 1971 came the MkIII, which was to be the most numerous version. The main changes were GKN alloy wheels (which replaced the earlier steel Rostyles), ventilated disc brakes, revised interiors (with leather taking over from vinyl) and there were differences in the US cars due to Federal safety and emission regulations. From late 1971 export cars (and from mid-1972, all production) started to be fitted with the larger 7.2-litre (440 cubic inch) engine and by this time air-conditioning and tinted glass were standard on all cars. A vinyl roof was a commonly requested option and louvred bonnets were available for the 7.2-litre cars.

The 1973 model year J-series cars (with their "J" badges) are sometimes regarded as the best of this generation. In late 1973 came the Series 4 cars ("Series 4" being the Chrysler designation for their engine). The interiors were revised (yet again) and by 1975 the full dashboard was walnut veneer and these were the most luxurious of this luxury car. Over 1,200 Interceptor MkIII Series 4 cars were made but still retained the 'J' badge.

During the Jensen's long production life there were several important Interceptor variants. Perhaps the most important, technically, was the Jensen FF which was launched at the same time as the Interceptor in 1966. This had 4-wheel drive using the Ferguson Formula and Dunlop Maxaret anti-lock brakes which together gave the car astonishing road handling. Jensen had tried these out on a modified C-V8 the previous year (confusingly, they also called that test car a "Jensen FF").

The new FF was easily distinguishable from the Interceptor by its double extractor vents behind the front wheels. The FF was also longer (3 inches overall and 4 inches in the wheelbase) and the engine was mounted slightly further back and moved over to suit the FF transfer box. There were three Marks of FF, which followed the changes to the standard Interceptor model. The FF cars were considerably more expensive than the already pricey Interceptors, so despite tremendous positive publicity, only 320 Jensen FF cars were made before production ended in 1971 (and none were built in LHD form).

To follow the FF, Jensen needed a flagship model and the SP was their answer. Launched in 1971, it had the larger 7.2-litre (440 cubic inch) engine with the "Six-Pack" triple twin-choke carburettor and produced 385bhp. It could be identified by its louvred bonnet and a blue "SP" badge on the grille. The SP could not be marketed in the US as its engine did not meet emission regulations, so most stayed in the UK.

In 1974, the Convertible took over the SP's flagship role. When the Convertible was created, the company was lucky in that the original C-V8 chassis was so rigid that little additional strengthening was necessary. The large soft-top roof was powered and available in many colours. Unfortunately the Convertible was unveiled at a time of conflict in the Middle East, oil shortages in the West and general economic recession, which dampened sales of all luxury cars at the time.

The final variant, the very rare Coupé, appeared in 1975. It utilised the Convertible's body but had a new fixed top designed and installed by Panther Westwinds. A styling feature was a clear panel that extended across the entire width of the roof, but few cars were built (the exact number is unknown).

By the mid-1970s the company was struggling financially and went into receivership with all car

Above: **An Interceptor MkIII.**
Below: An early FF. Detail features are different to the production cars as this one was built by Vignale in Turin. The double extractor vents behind the front wheels identify the car as an FF.

Above: **A production FF with Windsor Castle in the background.**
Below: **An SP, identified by its louvred bonnet and blue grille badge. Non-SP cars with bonnet louvres have a shorter run of louvres.**

production ending in 1976. But this was not quite the end of the story as a further 13 cars were assembled in the 1980s. These had 5.9-litre (360 cubic inch) V8 engines and other minor changes.

Specific Checks: These cars (and especially the FF) are all sophisticated pieces of machinery, and checking an example really needs the services of a qualified Jensen expert. First, contact the Jensen Owners' Club for advice.

Due to cost, many of these cars have had poor body repairs or not been serviced properly (every 4,000 miles) so a full recent service history is essential and if not available, one must assume the worst.

The good news with these cars is the chassis, engine and gearbox are all sturdy items and the trim used was generally of the best materials, but the bad news is that the bodies can rust badly. Panel fit should be good so step back and look along the sides of the car – if panels do not appear to fit perfectly, it is not a good sign.

The sills/side members are complex and hidden behind trim strips but you might ask the seller to jack up the car using the original jack which could reveal a badly corroded sill. The side members can be checked through the drain holes in the outer sills with a probe. This should touch the inner box section and not go in more than 0.5 inch, if it does then the section has rotted away.

The engines do run hot (hence the louvred bonnets on some models) but this is generally only a problem if coolant is expelled, the fuel evaporates or the heat in the engine compartment causes the wiring to become brittle or it creates other problems. Normal modifications to be found with the cooling system include up-rated fans and radiators.

A look under the bonnet may also reveal bodged wiring – a common problem, but a good modification is the proper addition of more relays to reduce loads on the switches including the ignition switch.

With a car weighing nearly two tons (laden) it needs good brakes and good suspension. The front end needs regular maintenance and the rear end tends to sag (you should get two fingers between the rear wheelarches and the tyres).

Spares are easier to find for the MkIII than earlier cars. There are some spares problems with the FF units but these are generally reliable cars.

Prices Today: It is thought that world-wide perhaps as many as half the Interceptors are still in existence plus around three-quarters of the FF cars, two-thirds of the SPs, and most of the Convertibles and Coupés, but there is insufficient data to be precise. In terms of prices, the Convertible is the most sought-after version, with values around twice that of the other (non-FF) cars. The FF is valued around one and a half times that of a standard Interceptor and the Coupé is too rare to value accurately. In every case, the car's condition is the most important factor in a valuation.

Above: **The Jensen Convertible was an attractive variant.**
Below: **The Convertible's large soft-top roof was powered.**

Above & Below: **The Coupé, with its clear roof panel, is rare. The car above has non-standard wire wheels (which were not an option).**

Dates: Healey: 1972-75   GT: 1975-76

Numbers Built: Healey: 10,498   GT: 509

Body/Chassis: Steel unitary. Healey: 2-seater open sports;
GT: 2+2 seater sports estate.

Engine: Lotus 1973cc, 4-cyl in-line, dohc, 140bhp (144bhp from
late 1974; GT: 144bhp).

Layout: Front engine, rear wheel drive, 4-speed manual gearbox
(from late 1974: 5-speed).

Performance: Top speed c.120mph, 0-60mph in c.8sec.

Prices Today: Healey: ££   GT: ££

Above: **An early Jensen-Healey. Note the stainless steel capped bumpers, in contrast with the later rubber bumpers as seen on the next page.**
Below: **The car's styling was mainly by Bill Towns, with input from Donald Healey and Kjell Qvale (who owned Jensen).**

The Jensen-Healey was launched in 1972 as a fast, luxurious and competent convertible sports car aimed principally at the US market. In performance terms it was a worthy successor to the "Big Healeys". It used conventional Vauxhall mechanical parts other than the gearbox (originally a Chrysler unit) and the new 16-valve Lotus 907 engine. This technically advanced, but as yet untried, engine was key to both the car's excellent performance and its early problems. The 907 was canted over at 45 degrees which allowed a low bonnet line, but made access to certain under-bonnet parts difficult. The UK market cars had Dellorto carburettors while those for the US had Strombergs to meet emission controls.

A Vauxhall subframe was used at the front, complete with Vauxhall steering and suitably modified suspension and disc brakes. At the rear, a Vauxhall live axle, modified coil spring suspension and drum brakes were used.

The front and rear wings for this handsome car were all bolted on to facilitate accident repair and the alloy wheels were specially designed for the car.

After its launch, the new Jensen-Healey almost immediately ran into problems due to build quality issues and the poor reliability of the Lotus engine. However, this was soon overcome and a much improved Mk2 version appeared in 1973. The Mk2 also had better soundproofing and a host of other minor improvements to make it altogether a better finished machine. Whereas almost all Mk1 cars had black vinyl trim, the Mk2 cars were offered with either black or tan. From late 1974 the car had a Getrag 5-speed gearbox. In addition, large 5mph rubber bumpers were fitted to meet US regulations. A factory hardtop was also available as an optional extra, but there were no automatics.

Two-thirds of Jensen-Healeys were Mk2 cars and three-quarters of the Jensen-Healeys made were exported as LHD cars. Interestingly, the Jensen-Healey represents over half of all Jensen cars ever made.

In 1975 a "sports estate" GT version was launched with plus 2 (children only) rear seating. By this time the connection with Healey had ended, so it was known simply as the Jensen GT. The new car was virtually identical to the earlier convertible other than its roof and tail section (with its rear-hatch). The interior was different and there were a few minor mechanical changes such as a larger brake servo and a front anti-roll bar. There was also a viscous coupled engine cooling fan to save

Above: **The car had a neat soft-top roof.**
Below: **The low profile of the bonnet was achieved by canting the Lotus engine over at 45 degrees (as can be seen in the photo over the page).**

power (this fan had also been fitted to the last Jensen-Healeys).

The GT's luxury specification included electric windows, tinted glass, walnut facia and US cars had air-conditioning (optional in the UK). The GT had the same trim options as the Jensen-Healey, apart from the seat facings which could be in different colours and fabrics, including leather. Production ceased with the demise of Jensen in 1976. Of the 509 cars made, 291 were LHD cars for export.

Specific Checks: These cars are unfortunately prone to rust (as were most steel cars of this period) so a very careful check is necessary. The main areas to inspect include the sills (which are expensive to replace properly), early bumpers, bonnet front, boot lid lip, edges of front and rear wings, panel seams, floorpan and where the front suspension is mounted. New panels are still available along with other body parts.

Another check is front end alignment and the gaps between the wings, headlight surrounds and bonnet. The build quality in this area was not good during manufacture and can be difficult to correct.

The Lotus engine is expensive to repair and longevity requires not only regular servicing but also the owner must check fluid levels weekly. Failure to do so can be financially painful. The gearboxes tend to be relatively reliable. A modification you might find today is overdrive fitted to some 4-speed gearbox cars. The basic Vauxhall supplied suspension, brakes and steering systems are all reasonably reliable.

Prices Today: It is thought that world-wide perhaps as many as two thousand Jensen-Healeys are still in existence plus around three-quarters of the Jensen GTs made, but there is insufficient data to be precise. Despite the relative rarity of the Jensen GT, its value is broadly similar to the convertible.

Donald Healey, who was Chairman of Jensen when the Jensen-Healey was created, died in 1988, aged 89.

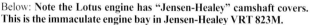
Below: **Note the Lotus engine has "Jensen-Healey" camshaft covers. This is the immaculate engine bay in Jensen-Healey VRT 823M.**

Above: **This later Jensen-Healey Mk2 has the larger bumpers.**
Below: **This is a customised Jensen GT, using non-standard wheels.**

Above: **Note the rear wiper parks off the opening rear-hatch.**
Below: **The Jensen GT had pleasing proportions.**

Dates:	1950-54	Number Built:	c.825 (See text).

Body/Chassis: Alloy panels with steel frame on steel chassis, 2-seater open sports.

Engine: 1486cc, 4-cyl flat-four, ohv, 60-62bhp.

Layout: Front engine, rear wheel drive, 4-speed manual gearbox.

Performance: Top speed c.85-90mph, 0-60mph in c.15-16sec.

Price Today: £££

Above: **A gleaming Jowett Jupiter Mark 1a.**

Although a Jupiter chassis appeared at the 1949 London Motor Show, the car was not properly launched until the following year. The innovative chassis, with its large bore tubes, was designed by the Austrian engineer Robert Eberan von Eberhorst (well-known for his work at Auto Union and Cisitalia). The Jupiter's curvaceous body was styled by Reg Korner.

The front suspension used double wishbones and longitudinal torsion bars while the rear axle was on twin parallel trailing arms with transverse torsion bars. All Jupiters have perforated steel wheels and, apart from the very first cars, hydraulic drum brakes all round.

The car was made to high standards of coach-building, with wind-up windows, a leather upholstered bench seat and a column-mounted gearchange.

The car used the Jowett Javelin's flat-four water-cooled engine designed by Gerald Palmer. Unusually, as with the Jowett Javelin, the radiator was located behind the engine which itself sat ahead of the front wheel line. There were early reliability problems with the engine (including crankshaft failures) and gearbox problems too. This ultimately affected sales even though the technical problems were overcome.

In late 1952 Jowett launched the improved Mk1a version of the Jupiter. It had an opening rear boot lid and the recently introduced Series III engine. The engine had many improvements including a sturdier crankshaft which was housed in a stiffer crankcase with a new oil gallery layout for better lubrication. The chassis frame on the Mk1a was also simplified at the rear, the fuel tank was moved and the walnut veneer facia was replaced with a metal panel finished in body colour. Only 94 of these Mk1a cars were made.

The Jupiter had many racing and rallying victories, including 1st in class at Le Mans in 1950, 1951 and 1952, 1st and 2nd in class in the 1951 Monte Carlo Rally, 1st in the 1951 Lisbon International Rally plus outright wins in various races in the US. Jowett constructed three special lightweight Jupiters with modified bodywork, the R1 cars, to compete at Le Mans in 1951 and 1952 though the 1951 class win was by a "standard" Jupiter.

The Jupiter R4 was a planned new lighter version with a revised body in GRP on a shorter chassis, but only three were made before Jowett ceased producing cars, the factory having been sold to International Harvester.

In addition to the 825 factory-built Jupiters, there were four other Jupiters made and c.66 Jupiter chassis sold to coachbuilders to have their own bodies added.

Specific Checks: When considering buying one of these sturdy and well built cars, the main area to check is the steel bodyframe that unites the aluminium panels to the chassis. Secondly, look for corrosion in the aluminium panels, especially where they are folded over steelwork (for example, at the rear of the bonnet).

Prices Today: The Jowett Car Club estimates that possibly over 450 cars survive world-wide (and half are roadworthy or actively being restored). There is no significant difference in value between the two Marks.

Above: **The Mark 1 had no rear boot lid, just access to the spare wheel. Access to its boot was from behind the seat.** Below: **A Mark 1a.**

Dates: 1952-55   **Number Built:** c.100

Body/Chassis: Alloy body with steel chassis, 2-seater open sports.

Engine: Mainly Ford (See text).

Layout: Front engine, rear wheel drive, 3 or 4-speed manual gearbox.

Performance: 1172cc: Top speed c.75-80mph, 0-60mph in c.13sec.

Price Today: £££

The Lotus Mark VI was the first production car from the newly formed Lotus company, founded by Colin Chapman. The car was more advanced and lighter than its rivals. The Lotus designed multi-tubular chassis was not strictly a spaceframe, but it was light (c.55lb/25kg) and rugged. The Mark VI made its public debut at a club race at Silverstone in 1952 and the first customer cars were delivered in 1953. The Mark VI soon became the car to beat in the newly announced 1172 racing formula. About 100 cars were built, the last ones in late 1955.

The Progress Chassis company made the Mark VI frames for Lotus and the aluminium bodies were made by Williams & Pritchard. The aluminium panels were usually left unpainted and when polished look most attractive. Some of the early cars had rear spats.

The front suspension was a low-pivot swing axle using a Ford E93 beam axle cut in half. The rear suspension, steering, cable-operated drum brakes, torque tube transmission, and rear axle were also Ford-based. The rear axle was located by a Panhard rod.

A variety of engines were fitted, but normally they were Ford E93 1172cc, 4-cylinder, side-valve units. There were also cars fitted with 1508cc Ford Consul engines de-stroked to 1499cc (to make them eligible in 1.5-litre class races), 1100cc Coventry Climax and MG TC 1250cc engines (sometimes bored-out to 1500cc). Virtually all Mark VI cars with Ford side-valve engines have had their E93 engines replaced with the stronger 100E unit (also 1172cc) and the cars converted to 12v electrics.

Cars with Ford side-valve engines normally had the Ford 3-speed gearbox (usually with Buckler close ratio gears). The Climax and MG-engined cars used the MG TC 4-speed gearbox.

To avoid Purchase Tax the cars were all sold in component form. Buyers bought a body/chassis unit from Lotus plus any Ford suspension or transmission components that had to be modified, then fitted their own engines, gearboxes, instruments etc. This means that there is no such thing as a standard specification for the Mark VI – they are all slightly different.

Specific Checks: First look at the paperwork then later contact the Historic Lotus Register to check the authenticity of the car you are inspecting as there are replicas and fakes around.

Next move on to check the car itself. There are few specific faults or weaknesses to look for when buying a Mark VI today, but as the cars are all over 50 years old, it is essential to check the chassis for rust and bent chassis members caused by accident damage.

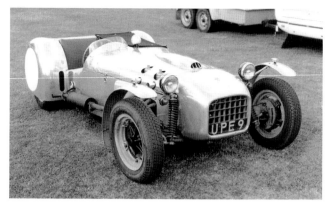

Above: **"UPE 9" is a well-known Lotus Mark VI, with an MG 1250cc engine. Note the rear wheel spats and Turner wheels.**

The Ford steering arms did have a reputation for breaking so it might be wise to have those crack-tested after buying a Mark VI.

Prices Today: The Historic Lotus Register estimates that perhaps 70 or so of these vehicles have survived, their remarkable survival rate in part due to the simplicity and "rightness" of Chapman's original design. Prices depend not only on condition but also racing history.

Above: **A restored Mark VI (seen in 2006).**
Below: **This is a 1957 photo by A.E. (Nobby) Burch. Weather equipment is not often seen these days.**

Dates: 1957-73   **Number Built:** c.2,550

Body/Chassis: S1: Alloy body (S2 & S3: Alloy & GRP; S4: GRP) with steel spaceframe chassis, 2-seater open sports.

Engines:

S1:   Ford 100E 1172cc, 4-cyl in-line, side-valve, 28+bhp;
       BMC A-series 948cc, 4-cyl in-line, ohv, 37-43bhp;
       Coventry Climax FWA 1097cc, 4-cyl in-line, sohc, 75+bhp.

S2:   As per S1 (excluding Coventry Climax) plus
       BMC A-series 1098cc, 4-cyl in-line, ohv, 55-59bhp;
       Ford 105E 997cc, 4-cyl in-line, ohv, 39bhp;
       Ford 109E (Cosworth) 1340cc, 4-cyl in-line, ohv, 85bhp;
       Ford Cortina 116E 1498cc, 4-cyl in-line, ohv, 66+bhp.

S2½: Ford 1599cc, 4-cyl in-line, ohv, 84bhp.

S3:   Ford 1599cc, 4-cyl in-line, ohv, 84bhp (Holbay: 120bhp);
       Ford 1297cc, 4-cyl in-line, ohv, 72bhp;
       Lotus 1558cc, 4-cyl in-line, Twin Cam, 115-125bhp.

S4:   Ford 1599cc, 4-cyl in-line, ohv, 84bhp;
       Lotus 1558cc, 4-cyl in-line, Twin Cam, 115-125bhp.

Layout: Front engine, rear wheel drive, 3/4-speed manual gearbox.

Performance: Dependent on engine fitted (See text).

Prices Today: S1: **££££**   S2/3: **£££**   S4: **££**

Above: **The Lotus 7 in its element. Here is JF Barnes at Wiscombe Park Hill Climb in 1962.**

The enduring Lotus 7 can be thought of as a road-going racing car and is still in production today, half a century on (see the Caterham entry). The Lotus 7 is undoubtedly one of the great classic sports cars and a lasting tribute to the founder of Lotus, Colin Chapman, who died in 1982. Along with the AC Cobra, the Lotus Seven "look" has been copied more often than any other sports car.

The Lotus 7 Series 1, 2 and 3 have similar lines, except the S1 (and some S2 cars) have front cycle wings, though most S2 cars have flared wings. The S2 and S3 also have a revised shape of nose cone. The Ford-engined cars had 3-speed gearboxes until 1961 when the Ford 105E Anglia 997cc engine was introduced with its 4-speed gearbox. The S1 cars were all RHD and had 15-inch wheels with drum brakes. About 240 S1 cars were built 1957-60.

The S2 (1960-68) had smaller 13-inch wheels and there were LHD versions for export. The S1's alloy fuel tank, held on with elastic, was replaced by a steel tank held on by metal straps. The 1.5-litre S2 cars had front disc brakes. About 1,300 S2 cars were made.

These early cars had a large variety of engines in various states of tuning, and used a letter suffix to indicate the engine type (ie A: BMC A-Series; C: Coventry Climax; F: Ford) but in time Ford engines became the standard. Cars destined for the US were called the "Seven America" and had Austin-Healey Sprite A-series engines of either 948cc or 1098cc. The name "Super Seven" was used for higher performance versions. The S1 Super Sevens had the Coventry Climax engine, while the S2 Super Sevens had the larger Ford engines, sometimes tuned by Cosworth. At the end of the S2 production, the

Ford 1600 crossflow engine was fitted and these cars are sometimes referred to as Series 2½ cars. In performance terms, a tuned Ford 100E S1 car could do over 80mph with an 0-60mph time of under 20 seconds, while the S1 and S2 Super Sevens could do over 100mph and sprint to 60mph in under 10 seconds. The exact performance was very dependent on engine tune, gear ratios etc.

The S3 cars (built 1968-70) had mainly Ford 1600cc crossflow engines (plus one known Ford 1300cc car) with front disc brakes and negative earth electrical systems. A dozen or so cars had the Lotus twin cam engine and were known as the SS (Super Sprint) model. About 340 S3 cars were built in total.

The S4 (Type 60), launched in 1970, retained the overall look of its predecessors, but was completely re-engineered and had a longer, sleeker, all-glassfibre body, a different chassis and better weather protection. The S4 was made from 1970-73 by Lotus, then by Caterham to 1974. About 600-650 were made by Lotus and Caterham

Below: **A Series 1 Lotus 7 with cycle wings and proper headlamps (some cars had tiny spotlights as their headlamps).**

made a further 40 or so cars. All S4 cars could do 110mph, (or more in the case of the Twin Cam), and reach 60mph in under 9 seconds.

In the UK, to avoid Purchase Tax, Lotus 7 cars were offered in component form (usually with all new parts, though early cars were also available without an engine).

The cars were marketed with a long list of options and are often modified by owners, so no two Sevens are likely to be identical.

Specific Checks: There are fake Lotus Sevens, so before purchase, note the chassis number and the frame maker's number (which will be different). Then check the car's identity with the Lotus Seven Club.

The body/chassis unit is the most important aspect to check as the steel tubing can rust and can suffer from poorly repaired accident damage. Remove the bonnet and nose cone to facilitate your inspection. The S4's design, with its enveloping GRP body, makes chassis inspection and repair more difficult though new GRP panels can be made to order.

If the car's handling is not perfect it may be due to wear in the suspension, which is relatively cheap to rectify, but it may also be due to chassis distortion or damage, which could be expensive. With luck it might just be because the tyre pressures are incorrect.

The S2 had a badly located weak axle resulting in cracks in the casing leading to oil loss. Even the addition of a strengthening plate on the axle may not overcome this problem if there is excessive engine power and modern sticky tyres are fitted.

Prices Today: Overall, the Lotus Seven Register knows the whereabouts of about half the S1 cars, a third of the S2 & S3 cars, and a fifth of the S4s.

Many Lotus Sevens were exported or have since been taken abroad, and demand for cars in good condition often outstrips supply, therefore values remain high. The S1 is worth considerably more than the S2/S3, while the S4 costs less than half that of an S2/S3 (though an S4 Twin Cam will be not far short of an S2/S3).

Below: **A nice example of a Lotus 7, photographed in 2007.**

Above: **A Lotus 7 with its full weather protection in place .**
Below: **The Lotus 7's distinctive side exhaust is clearly visible.**

Above: **An interesting angle for a 1964 Lotus publicity photo.**
Below: **A Series 4 Lotus 7, when all bodies were glassfibre.**

Dates:	1957-63	Number Built:	c.1,000

Body/Chassis: GRP monocoque, 2-seater fixed-head coupé.

Engine: Coventry Climax 1216cc, 4-cyl in-line, sohc, 75+bhp (See text).

Layout: Front engine, rear wheel drive, 4-speed manual gearbox.

Performance: Top speed c.110-125mph, 0-60mph in 10-11sec.

Price Today: £££££

Above: **Racing principles were employed in the Lotus Elite's design.**

When launched at the 1957 London Motor Show, the Lotus Elite took the show by storm due to its good looks and advanced technical specification. It featured a novel glassfibre monocoque construction with all-independent suspension, disc brakes on all wheels, an all-alloy Coventry Climax FWE 1.2-litre engine and a very low aerodynamic drag factor (the engine was canted at an angle to reduce the bonnet height). An unusual feature was that the side windows could be removed entirely but did not wind up and down. Ventilation was by opening the quarter light windows.

The attractive and timeless bodywork was styled by Peter Kirwan-Taylor, refined by John Frayling, with aerodynamic design input from Frank Costin. Overall management of the project was by Colin Chapman.

It was not until the end of 1958 that the first production car was ready, but lack of space restricted output until Lotus opened a new factory the following year. The manufacture of the bodies was soon contracted out, and from the Series 2 cars they were laminated, painted and trimmed by Bristol's.

The Series 2 cars were launched in 1960 with improved suspension all round and better interior trim. Then there was the SE (Special Equipment) version with more powerful 83 or 90bhp engines and the better ZF gearbox (the standard gearbox was the BMC "B" series). Small numbers of the even more powerful Elite Super were also built, its engine producing 95-105bhp.

Although the Elite was the first closed Lotus road car, it was successful in competition work. The Elite was ultimately replaced by the Elan which was easier (and hence cheaper) to make.

Specific Checks: As the glassfibre body is stressed, the Elite requires careful checking in those areas that take loads. In particular, the bodywork should be inspected around the top of the rear suspension units and differential. There is a steel hoop in the roof and a steel subframe to reinforce the front suspension and engine mountings. These can, of course, rust and should be checked carefully. The suspension itself needs regular maintenance.

In cars which have been neglected, it is important to check that water has not got into the gel coat as the glassfibre then starts to de-laminate. Scrutinise the front area of the engine bay where the front subframe should be completely enclosed. Any damage to the front end can allow air and water to get into the fibreglass and thus slowly destroy the subframe. This is quite expensive to replace.

The GRP bodies varied in strength, the best being the "double dimples" (which were the last bodies to be made). These dimples (one is c.0.5in diameter, the other c.0.3in) are about an inch apart and can be felt under the back of the car in the middle, between the silencers.

The original cooling system was marginal and overheated engines warp heads and blow head gaskets, so it is important to check the system is up to the task.

Prices Today: Club Elite estimates that over 650 of these fabulous cars survive (with possibly 150 in the UK). The Lotus Elite is highly desirable as a collector's car and historic racer, which is reflected in its value.

Above: **Twin silencers despite having a 4-cylinder in-line engine. Wire wheels were the norm. A silver roof normally indicated an SE version.**

Below: **A period photo showing the Elite in its natural habitat – on the track. It won its first race outing (at Silverstone) and later went on to win its class at Le Mans for 6 years running (1959-64).**

Dates: 1962-73

Number Built: 9,500-10,000 (See text).

Body/Chassis: GRP body on steel backbone chassis, 2-seater open sports or fixed-head coupé.

Engine: 1558cc, 4-cyl in-line, Twin Cam, 105bhp; (S/E: 115bhp; Sprint: 126bhp).

Layout: Front engine, rear wheel drive, 4-speed manual gearbox (some of the last cars had a 5-speed manual gearbox).

Performance: Top speed 115-120mph, 0-60mph in c.7-8sec.

Price Today: £££

One of the great early Lotus road cars, the compact Elan, with its all round independent suspension, had excellent road manners and was progressively improved during its production life. Styled mainly by Ron Hickman, the car featured an advanced chassis design using a light but stiff backbone chassis, much admired at the time. It also had all disc brakes and novel vacuum-operated pop-up headlamps. The attractive glassfibre body was created as upper (bodywork) and lower (floor and wheelarches) sections bonded together in the mould, effectively forming a one-piece moulding. The body was then bolted to the steel backbone chassis. Steel frames reinforced the door apertures.

A key element of the Elan was its superb new 4-cylinder Ford-based engine, with a new twin cam head designed by Harry Mundy. The engine was originally equipped with twin Weber 40 DCOE carbs and most Elans also had a slick 4-speed all-synchromesh Ford gearbox.

The first version of the Elan (Type 26) was a drophead open sports car. The S2, in 1964, had restyled rear lights, larger front brake calipers and a new wood veneer facia. The following year saw the S3 (Type 36) fixed-head coupé version added. These early coupés did not have through-flow ventilation but this was solved in later cars by adding extractor vents in the roof quarter panels. A drophead S3 version (Type 45), with improved soft-top, followed in 1966. The S3 had electric windows as standard and fixed side window frames (earlier cars had manually operated sliding windows). The S3's boot lid was extended to eliminate a rain leakage problem.

The S/E (Special Equipment) versions, available 1966-71, featured a more powerful 115bhp engine, servo-assisted brakes and a close-ratio gearbox.

The S4 (made from 1968) had flared wheelarches to accommodate lower profile tyres, a revised facia with rocker switches (for safety in a crash), revised rear lights and trim changes. Most S4 cars had twin Stromberg carburettors, necessitating a bonnet bulge.

The final version, the Elan Sprint, was announced in late 1970 and introduced in early 1971. It was easily identified by its two-tone colour scheme with the words ELAN SPRINT. It had the "Big Valve" engine, with its revised camshaft, porting and higher compression ratio, which raised the engine's power output to 126bhp. The car's carburettors were either Webers or Dellortos (though

Above: **A Lotus Elan S3 S/E (with a non-standard roll bar fitted).**

Below: **An early drophead.**

Below: **This Elan has the two-tone colour scheme of a Sprint version but is in fact an earlier model.**

some export models had Strombergs). A handful of the last Sprints had 5-speed gearboxes.

In the UK, to avoid Purchase Tax, Elans were offered in component form (with all new parts) for customer assembly, but the completed vehicle was then checked by a Lotus dealer to initiate the warranty.

The Type 26R was a racing version and nearly 100 were built. They were raced very successfully by such famous drivers as Jim Clark and Jackie Stewart.

Optional extras for the Elans included a removable hardtop for the drophead and a close-ratio gearbox. Knock-off hubs were an option available on the S2 but became standard from the S3 model.

The exact number of Elans made is unknown, and different sources quote widely varying figures, but probably the most accurate estimate is between 9,500 and 10,000 cars. Production ended in autumn 1973, but the name "Elan" was revived by Lotus in 1989 for a quite different sports car, the M100 Elan (see page 161).

Specific Checks: Start with the paperwork and check the numbers match those on the vehicle.

Moving on to the Elan itself, when checking the engine, start it from cold and listen for timing chain rattle, noisy tappets or knocking big ends. Also check the water pump for wear by trying to move its boss. The Lotus developed engine is highly tuned and requires expertise to work on it. It tends to leak oil and run hot.

With the chassis, check the front pillars where they join the crossmember as they rust from the inside out and rectification is difficult. Check too the rear suspension pillars which can crack. Beware of any welded repairs to the chassis. By now, most surviving Elans will have a new chassis, which should be galvanised.

Overall, today there is good parts availability for the Elans.

Modifications you might find include a stiffer space frame chassis from Spyder Engineering Ltd. Pre-Sprint models originally suffered from an unpleasant lurching motion when opening or closing the throttle. This was due to rubber Rotoflex "doughnuts" on the drive shafts winding up and springing back. Most cars have had this problem rectified by the fitting of uprated doughnuts. It is also possible to completely replace the rubber doughnuts by fitting a solid drive line conversion kit.

Prices Today: Finding a good Elan in the UK can be a challenge, as many were exported or have since gone abroad. The drophead versions are worth more than a fixed-head Elan and the Sprints are worth a bit more than the earlier cars.

Photo Top Right: **The side window frames always remain in place. The S4's rear lights are the same as those on the Elan Plus 2.**
Middle Photos: **This is a fixed-head Elan Sprint, identified by its distinctive two-tone colour scheme and side script.**
Lower Right: **The cockpit of an S3 S/E, with non-standard roll bar.**

Dates: 1966-75

Number Built: c.9,300 (See text).

Body/Chassis: GRP body on steel backbone chassis, 2-seater fixed-head coupé.

Engines: S1 & S2:   Renault 1470cc, 4-cyl in-line, ohv, 78-82bhp (US Spec: 1565cc, 87bhp);
Twin Cam: Lotus 1558cc, 4-cyl in-line, Twin Cam, 105bhp (Special: 126bhp; US Spec: 113bhp).

Layout: Mid-engine (mounted fore & aft), rear wheel drive, 4 or 5-speed manual gearbox.

Performance: Renault: Top speed c.115mph, 0-60mph in c.10sec; Lotus: Top speed c.120mph, 0-60mph in c.7-8sec.

Prices Today: S1, S2: £/££   Twin Cam: £££

Above: **This Lotus Europa S2 has Cosmic alloy wheels and is lowered.**

This head-turning design, styled by John Frayling, brought a new dimension to the sports car scene, being the first British road-going car with a mid-engine layout. The Europa was not only very attractive but it was also very low, standing a mere 42.5 inches high. The S1 examples (all LHD) were a joint venture with Renault and only for export to Europe (hence the appropriate choice of the car's name). The car used the transaxle and a tuned 78bhp version of the Renault 16's engine, but by cleverly turning the engine and transaxle around, it could be mounted amidships giving Lotus the arrangement it required for the Europa. Behind the engine (under the engine cover) was a large plastic tray that acted as a useful rear "boot" though the contents would be warmed by the engine.

To minimise weight, Colin Chapman took some of the rear suspension loads through the gearbox casing, but this requires the engine/gearbox mounts to be kept in good condition and replaced regularly.

The Series 1 (Type 46) cars were very spartan, with fixed side windows and fixed seats (though the steering wheel and pedals were adjustable). Their GRP bodies were bonded to the chassis. The S1A cars, from late 1967, had a stronger gear linkage and other minor improvements. Possibly about 650 S1 and S1A cars were made.

Below: **This S2 has the optional Lotus alloy wheels fitted.**

A racing version, the Type 47, was built 1966-68 with a modified chassis, 1594cc Lotus-Cosworth twin cam engine and a non-synchromesh Hewland 5-speed gearbox. The exact number of cars made is unknown, but c.55-70 is likely. The Type 47 was raced successfully by John Miles and Jackie Oliver. A one-off Type 47 with a Rover V8 engine was reputed to do over 180mph in tests.

The S2 (Type 54) cars from 1968 (UK sales from 1969) were much improved, with electric windows, better trim and adjustable seating. The bodies were no longer bonded to the chassis, but bolted instead, and the engine was now rated at 82bhp.

Sales to US customers commenced in 1969. This Type 65 Europa had a bored-out 1565cc Renault engine and a body modified to meet Federal regulations.

The Lotus Europa Twin Cam (Type 74), launched in 1971, is easily recognisable with its reduced rear three-quarter panels to improve the driver's field of vision. It

Below: **The Europa's distinctive rear three-quarter side panels restricted vision at road junctions and when overtaking cars. They were therefore reduced on the later Twin Cam and Special (as can be clearly seen on the Europa Special on the opposite page).**

also had more cockpit space, created by a lowered floor, wider footwell and reshaped seats. There was also a better gear linkage, stiffer chassis, improved suspension, servo-assisted brakes and twin fuel tanks.

The last version, the Europa Special, had the "Big Valve" engine, which with revised camshafts, porting and higher compression ratio, raised the engine's power output to 126bhp. US-spec cars had the same engine, but with emission controls the power output was reduced to 113bhp. There were many other improvements too, including an optional 5-speed gearbox (this became standard later) and tinted glass was fitted to many. The interior colour could be beige instead of black. A third of all Europas made were these Specials.

In the UK, to avoid Purchase Tax, some Europas were customer assembled, but the completed vehicle was then checked by a Lotus dealer to initiate the warranty.

The exact number of cars made is unknown, but most agree the best estimate is around 9,300 cars.

Specific Checks: Start with the paperwork and check the numbers match those on the vehicle. Moving on to the car itself, the Renault engine is fairly reliable. For a Lotus-engined vehicle, start it from cold and listen for timing chain rattle, noisy tappets or knocking big ends. Also check the water pump for wear by trying to move its boss. The Lotus engine is highly tuned and requires expertise to work on it. It tends to leak oil and run hot.

With the chassis, check carefully for corrosion, especially around the front wishbone mountings. By now, many cars will have a new or repaired chassis. If the car does not run in a straight line it could be the chassis is distorted, or there is wear in the rear suspension/drive, or the front and rear toe-in are incorrectly set. All these can have a significant effect on the Europa's handling.

Modifications that you might find include a stiffer spaceframe chassis from Spyder Engineering or Banks (Europa Engineering), also changes made to the rear suspension to overcome handling issues.

Prices Today: Finding a good Europa in the UK can be a challenge, as many were exported or have since gone abroad. The Lotus-engined examples are valued considerably more than a Renault-engined S1 or S2 and the Special has the edge on price over a Twin Cam. A genuine Type 47 car will be "HiValue".

Below: **The Type 47 (like the example below) was a special racing version.**

Above & Below: **This Europa Special has the attractive JPS racing team colours of black with silver sills and gold striping.**

Above: **The Europa's front bumper came from the Ford Anglia.**
Below: **The car's side profile is both exciting and distinctive.**

Dates: 1967-74

Number Built: c.4,500 (See text).

Body/Chassis: GRP body on steel backbone chassis, 2+2 seater fixed-head coupé.

Engine: 1558cc, 4-cyl in-line, Twin Cam, 118bhp (US Spec: 108bhp); S130: 126bhp (US Spec: 113bhp).

Layout: Front engine, rear wheel drive, 4 or 5-speed manual gearbox.

Performance: Top speed c.120mph, 0-60mph in c.7-8sec.

Price Today: ££+

Above: **The Lotus Plus 2's sleek lines are evident on this 1970 car. Knock-off wheels were standard (on most cars).**

Although the Lotus Plus 2 was developed from the Lotus Elan and was similar mechanically, it had a new body and a revised chassis. The car was originally called the "Elan Plus 2" but later simply "Plus 2" in its own right. Despite any similarity in name, it was very different to the original Elan, being considerably wider (by about 7 inches), longer (by nearly 2 feet) and heavier (by almost 300lb/136kg). This increase in size was partly to accommodate the extra seating and partly to provide more comfort.

The Elan Plus 2 (Type 50) was launched in 1967 in response to customer demand for a 2+2 seater car. It was very much a "classic" in its own time, as it possessed superb styling, elegance and performance, coupled with its useful 2+2 practicality, making it coveted by many drivers.

The Plus 2 came with a luxury interior, electric windows and pop-up headlamps. Many cars had tinted glass, sunroof and leather trim.

Despite its extra weight, thanks to superior aero-dynamics, the car's performance was remarkably similar to that of its smaller sister, the Elan, with the same S/E specification engine. This was the 4-cylinder Ford-based engine with its twin cam head designed by Harry Mundy.

The brakes were servo-assisted and later cars (including US specification cars) had dual circuit brakes. Knock-off hubs were fitted to most cars.

The Plus 2 was only available as a fixed-head coupé, though a few were subsequently converted privately to dropheads (see photo on opposite page).

The Plus 2S (introduced in 1968) had an improved interior, fog lamps and optional alloy wheels (from 1973 alloy wheels became standard).

In the UK, to avoid Purchase Tax, some early Plus 2 cars (ie before the Plus 2S) were offered in component form (with all new parts) for customer assembly, but this was stopped with the Plus 2S.

The S130 version, with a distinctive silver roof, was announced in late 1970 and became available from early 1971. It had the new "Big Valve" engine like the Elan Sprint and was available with an optional 5-speed manual gearbox from 1972, in which case it was designated the Plus 2 S130/5.

Production of the Plus 2 continued for over a year after Lotus had stopped producing the smaller Elan. The

Below: **The car's rear was attractive too. Note the ventilation extraction vent behind the door window.**

Below: **This photo shows the pop-up headlamps raised. They were vacuum-operated.**

exact number of cars made is unknown, and different sources quote widely varying figures, but probably the most accurate estimate is approximately 4,500 cars.

Typical optional extras fitted to these cars included leather trim, tinted glass and a fabric sunroof.

Specific Checks: Start with the paperwork and check the numbers match those on the vehicle.

Moving on to the Plus 2 itself, not surprisingly, these checks are the same as for the Elan. When checking the engine, start it from cold and listen for timing chain rattle, noisy tappets or knocking big ends. Also check the water pump for wear by trying to move its boss. The Lotus developed engine is highly tuned and requires expertise to work on it. It tends to leak oil and run hot.

With the chassis, check the front pillars where they join the crossmember as they rust from the inside out and rectification is difficult. Check too the rear suspension pillars which can crack. Beware of any welded repairs to the chassis. By now, most surviving Plus 2 cars will have a new chassis, which should be galvanised.

Overall, today there is good parts availability for the Elans and Plus 2 cars.

Modifications you might find include a stiffer space frame chassis from Spyder Engineering Ltd, also suspension tweaks. A small number have been altered privately into convertibles.

Prices Today: Finding a good Plus 2 in the UK can be a challenge, as many were exported or have since gone abroad. Perhaps surprisingly, the cars are currently worth less than a fixed-head Elan in similar condition.

Photo Top Right: **The front fog lamps were part of the Plus 2S kit.**
2nd From Top: **This nice side view shows the car's good proportions.**
3rd From Top: **A silver roof normally indicated a S130 version.**
Lower Right: **A rare open top conversion (not a factory option).**
Below: **A Lotus publicity photo reflecting the car's aspirations.**

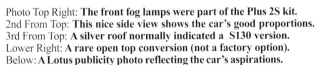

Dates: 1974-83

Number Built: c.2,500

Body/Chassis: GRP semi-unitary body with steel backbone/subframes chassis, 4-seater fixed-head coupé.

Engines:
S1: Lotus 907, 1973cc, 4-cyl in-line, dohc, 155-160bhp (US:140bhp);
S2.2: Lotus 912, 2174cc, 4-cyl in-line, dohc,160bhp.

Layout: Front engine, rear wheel drive, 5-speed manual or 3-speed automatic gearbox.

Performance: Top speed c.125mph, 0-60mph in c.7-8sec.

Price Today: £/££

Above: **The sophisticated and stylish wedge-shaped Lotus Elite represented a major move up-market by Lotus.**

After a long gestation period, Lotus eventually launched the first of their new wedge-shaped cars for the 1970s that would replace the famous trio of the Elan, Plus 2 and Europa. The styling of the new Elite (Type 75) was by Oliver Winterbottom and was a result of the company making a conscious decision that their new models would be considerably more up-market than their predecessors. The new cars (the Elite, and the Eclat and Esprit that followed) were also physically bigger and heavier. The first, the 4-seater Elite, was 8 inches wider (excluding mirrors), 7 inches longer and the unladen weight had risen by over 600lb (270kg) compared with an early Plus 2. This increase in size and weight was partly to accommodate additional equipment, but was also due to strengthening, required to meet increasingly rigorous safety standards.

The Elite had the Lotus 907, all-alloy, 4-cylinder, 16-valve, 1973cc engine. This had been developed by Lotus and had been fitted as original equipment to the earlier Jensen-Healey, then with 140bhp. But many changes had been found necessary – this development being of benefit to the Elite which started out at 155bhp (later 160bhp). The new car also had a 5-speed gearbox and disc brakes at the front with (unusually) inboard drum brakes at the rear (often incorrectly reported as disc brakes all round).

The Elite's interior was designed by Giugiaro and the car was available in several different trim states – the 501 was the entry level model, the 502 included air-conditioning, the 503 also had power-assisted steering and the later 504 model had a 3-speed automatic gearbox (the first in a Lotus car).

In 1980 the Elite acquired the newly developed, longer stroke, Lotus 912, 2174cc engine, becoming the (Type 83) S2.2. Although the power output remained the same at 160bhp, the torque figure of the 2.2-litre unit was significantly better (160lbft rather than the 140lbft of the 2-litre unit) and the car was much easier to drive. By now it had a galvanised chassis (essential for longevity), revised dashboard, and electric pop-up headlamp pods that replaced the earlier, less reliable, vacuum-operated units. The S2.2 also had a deeper, wraparound chin spoiler, revised rear bumper and a stronger Getrag gearbox

Below: **This is a rare 504 model, which had an automatic gearbox.**

Below: **This side view makes an interesting comparison with the Lotus Eclat that appears in the following entry.**

replacing the earlier Maxi-derived unit. By this time, production of the Elite had dropped to a very low level and, despite being better than the 2-litre cars in terms of performance and reliability, only c.130 of these more desirable S2.2 cars were made.

Specific Checks: Start with the paperwork and check the numbers match those on the vehicle.

Moving on to the Elite itself, probably any pre-1980 car with a non-galvanised chassis will have had it replaced by now, but still check very carefully. In particular, you need to check the rear crossmember as it is particularly prone to corrosion and a proper repair usually requires the body to come off. At the front end, check the suspension mounts for corrosion and, as usual, look for any sign of accident damage. Interestingly, one indication of this is headlamp pods that do not sit or function correctly.

With the glassfibre body, the main problem areas are leaking windscreens and sagging doors, both of which are expensive to fix. The situation with the doors is that the internal steel reinforcement can rust badly and the doors drop. Poor shut lines with the door still closed may indicate such a problem. Headlinings are also problematic as they can droop.

The Elite's engines are reasonably reliable provided they are serviced properly and regularly. In particular the cambelt needs replacing on schedule as a broken one will be financially painful. Some owners have replaced the original Lotus engine with a Rover V8 unit. Two gearboxes were used with the Elite, and the Austin Maxi-derived gearbox fitted to the 2-litre car is the least reliable, being prone to wear. The 5-speed manual Getrag gearbox on the 2.2-litre models was the better unit.

The electrics on this car can be troublesome – water can get into the fusebox, the wiring can deteriorate and there can be earthing problems. It pays to check that everything works correctly.

Most spare parts are available as pattern or "used", though stainless steel trim parts are increasingly rare.

To sum up, the Elite is a luxury sports car with fabulous performance but repair costs will reflect its prestige status.

Prices Today: Manual versions and cars with a galvanised chassis are more sought after. Probably it is best to avoid "basket cases" as restoration costs can far exceed the car's likely value. Later cars are probably undervalued.

Photo Top Right: **The rear hatch is clearly visible. Not visible in this photo is the additional (fixed) glass partition behind the rear seats to isolate passengers from the boot space (a thoughtful touch).**
2nd From Top: **Pop-up headlamps were initially vacuum-operated, but became electrically-operated from 1980.**
3rd From Top: **When parking, one needs to remember the Elite is quite a large car, being 14ft 7.5in long and just 0.5in under 6ft wide (excluding door mirrors).**
Lower Right: **A luxury interior. Leather was an optional extra.**

Dates: Eclat: 1975-82   Excel: 1982-92

Numbers Built: Eclat: c.1,500   Excel: c.2,159

Body/Chassis: GRP semi-unitary body with steel backbone/subframes chassis, 4-seater fixed-head coupé.

Engines:
S1: Lotus 907, 1973cc, 4-cyl in-line, dohc, 160bhp (US: 140bhp);
S2.2: Lotus 912, 2174cc, 4-cyl in-line, dohc, 160bhp (SE: 180bhp).

Layout: Front engine, rear wheel drive, 5-speed manual (520:4-speed) or 3 or 4-speed automatic gearbox (rare).

Performance: Top speed c.125mph, 0-60mph in c.7-8sec; (SE: c.130mph, 0-60mph in c.7sec).

Prices Today: Eclat: £/££   Excel: ££

Above: **An official Lotus photo of the Eclat. Compare this side profile with that of the Elite and Excel.**
Below: **A Lotus Eclat 2.2.**

The Lotus Eclat and its derivative, the Excel, had a long, 17 year, production life. Styled by Oliver Winterbottom, the Eclat (Type 76) was launched partly because of US pressure for an Elite with a boot (ie a "trunk"). The Eclat used the Elite's chassis, engine, running gear and front bodyshell, including doors, up to the "B" pillars, but had a fastback rear (and a boot). Rear headroom was about 2 inches less than the Elite.

Mainly in the US market, the Eclat was initially called the Lotus Sprint. It had a higher back axle ratio which gave it slightly better acceleration but a reduced top speed. In the US, it was about three-quarters of the price of the Elite and this gave its sales a considerable boost.

In the UK, the Eclat was also priced under the Elite and appeared in different trim states: the 520 was the entry level model with steel wheels and a Ford 4-speed manual gearbox; the 521 had a different rear axle ratio, 5-speed gearbox and wider wheels; the 522 included air-conditioning and better accessories; the 523 included power steering and the 524 was an automatic. The Riviera special edition (from 1981) had a lift-out glass sunroof, modified bonnet with air outlet slots and a rear spoiler.

The early Eclat was slightly lighter than the Elite due to its different body and fewer fittings hence its performance was marginally better.

Above: **The Eclat's tail with its rear boot lid.**
Below: **Only 76 of these attractive Eclat Rivieras were built.**

In 1980, along with the Elite and the Esprit, the Eclat (Type 84) gained the larger 2.2-litre Lotus 912 engine and a Getrag 5-speed gearbox. By this time, the trim specification (and price) was very similar to the Elite's.

In 1982, Lotus launched the Eclat Excel (Type 89), but later dropped the word "Eclat" from its title. It had a revised body, galvanised chassis, improved suspension, Toyota 5-speed gearbox, ventilated disc brakes all round, a revised interior and other changes – all in all, a much improved car. It replaced the Elite and Eclat.

In 1986 there were subtle changes to the Excel's bodywork while the interior had a make-over including new instruments from VDO and restyled front seats. That year also saw the SE launched. Its engine had a higher compression ratio to give 180bhp and this could propel the car to c.130mph and reach 60mph in under 7 seconds. The SA followed in 1986, with a 4-speed ZF auto gearbox, then in 1989 came new road wheels, bonnet louvres and restyled door mirrors. The suspension was also upgraded.

In 1991 the limited edition Celebration was introduced, before production finally ended in 1992. The last Excel was given to Colin Chapman's widow, Hazel.

Specific Checks: Start with the paperwork and check the numbers match those on the vehicle.

Moving on to the car itself, probably any pre-1980 car with a non-galvanised chassis will have had it replaced by now, but still check very carefully. In particular, you need to check the rear crossmember as it is particularly prone to corrosion and a proper repair usually requires the body to come off. At the front end, check the suspension mounts for corrosion and, as usual, look for any sign of accident damage. Interestingly, one indication of this is headlamp pods that do not sit or function correctly.

With the glassfibre body, like the Elite, the main problem areas are leaking windscreens and sagging doors, both of which are expensive to fix. The situation with the doors is the internal steel reinforcement can rust badly and the doors drop. Poor shut lines with the door still closed may indicate such a problem. Headlinings are also problematic as they can droop.

The engines are reasonably reliable provided they are serviced properly and regularly. In particular the cambelt needs replacing on schedule as a broken one will be financially painful. Various gearboxes were used with the Eclat/Excel, the latter's Toyota Supra box being the most reliable.

The electrics on the later cars improved but it still pays to check that everything works correctly.

To sum up, these cars became ever more reliable as production continued, the best cars being the later ones (though less than 200 cars were made from 1990-92).

Prices Today: The Excels are worth more than the Eclats. The Riviera version is worth perhaps 10% more than a standard car. The Excels, in particular the later cars, are probably undervalued today.

Above & Below: **The attractive Excel SE. Compare its side profile with the earlier Eclat.**

Above: **Later Excels always sported these small tail spoilers.**
Below: **Another bonnet design. The sunroof is an after-market fit.**

Below: **The 2.2-litre Lotus 912 engine in an Eclat. It is canted over at 45 degrees (towards the camera) to permit a lower bonnet line.**
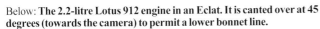

Dates: 1976-2004

Number Built: c.10,675 (all models to 2004).

Body/Chassis: GRP body on steel backbone chassis, 2-seater fixed-head coupé.

Engines:
S1-S2: Lotus 907, 1973cc, 4-cyl in-line, dohc, 160bhp (US:140bhp);
S2.2 & S3: Lotus 912, 2174cc, 4-cyl in-line, dohc,160bhp;
Turbo Esprit: Lotus 910, 2174cc, 4-cyl in-line, dohc, 210-215bhp.

Layout: Mid-engine (mounted fore & aft), rear wheel drive, 5-speed manual gearbox.

Performance: S1-S2: Top speed c.125mph, 0-60mph in c.8sec;
S3: Top speed c.135mph, 0-60mph in c.6-7sec;
Turbo Esprit: Top speed c.150mph, 0-60mph in c.6sec.

Price Today: ££+ (Early Models).

Above: **A Lotus Esprit S1.**
Below: **A new S2 version on show.**

At the 1972 Turin Motor Show, Lotus unveiled a striking new design by Giugiaro of Ital Design. This silver concept car was based on a lengthened and adapted Lotus Europa chassis and used the Lotus Twin Cam engine. The Esprit (Type 79), which finally went on sale in 1976, looked very similar to the 1972 concept car, but it now had the all-new 16-valve Lotus 907 engine, mated to a Citroen SM derived gearbox and a completely new backbone chassis.

The car achieved early fame as it appeared in the James Bond (007) film *The Spy Who Loved Me* (1977) in which the Esprit could turn into a submarine!

After some 718 examples of the S1 had been produced, in 1978 came the S2 with door mirrors, improved interior (including wider seats), Rover tail lights, Speedline wheels that replaced the Wolfrace ones and air scoops behind the side windows. With a larger capacity radiator, the new model tried to address the earlier car's tendency to overheat. Just over 1,050 were made and there were about 147 black and gold special edition cars, made to commemorate the JPS sponsorship of the successful Lotus F1 racing cars.

Above: **The shadow at the rear of the side three-quarter window indicates the location of the cleverly concealed air scoop in this S2 version.**
Below: **A Turbo Esprit in Essex Petroleum colours.**

1980 saw the launch of the interim S2.2 with the larger 2.2-litre Lotus 912 engine. This gave the same power output but with more torque. Only 88 of these cars were made, but the really exciting launch of that year was the first Turbo Esprit (Type 82). Lotus engineers did not simply bolt on a Garrett turbocharger to the engine (called the 910 in this guise, this larger capacity engine having been developed in line with the 912), they made considerable changes to the chassis (which was galvanised by now), the suspension and the brakes. The cars also had larger front and rear spoilers and the rear screen was replaced with a slatted tailgate.

With 210bhp on tap, the Turbo Esprit was a real flyer. The first 45 cars were in the colours of Essex Petroleum, the then sponsors of Lotus F1 racing. They had a high trim specification and are very desirable today (as are all the turbo cars).

The S3 (Type 85) cars, launched in 1981, had a new interior and were normally aspirated but retained the

Turbo Esprit's revised suspension and chassis. About 760 were made. In 1986 the Turbo HC (High Compression) version was launched which boosted power output slightly, to 215bhp. In 1987 came the new Esprit with softer lines, restyled by Peter Stevens, but these and later models are outside this book's timeframe.

Just over 2,900 non-turbo S1 to S3 cars were made plus over 1,900 Turbos. In addition to the total of c.9,200 4-cylinder Esprits made until 1999, there were just over 1,400 V8 cars too, made from 1996 to 2004.

The main optional extras on the early Esprits included air-conditioning, leather trim and a glass sunroof (from the S3 model). Power steering did not appear until the later S4, in 1993.

Specific Checks: Inspecting an early Esprit really needs the services of a qualified Lotus expert as repairs can be very expensive.

Start with the paperwork and check the numbers match those on the vehicle. Moving on to the car itself, the glassfibre bodywork is strong and should not present any problems unless badly repaired after an accident – check the nose section and shut lines in particular. The early chassis can rust and repairs or replacement can be expensive. If the front or rear screen (on the S1 and S2) need resealing, this can be both tricky and expensive.

The Lotus engines are good for at least 100,000 miles before major overhaul, provided they are serviced properly and the cambelts replaced as per schedule. If an engine misfires on acceleration, check for oil in the spark plug wells. If oil is present it could mean a blown cam cover gasket. Exhaust manifolds can crack (you can hear them "chuffing" when the engine is warm) and they are difficult and expensive to repair. Overheating can be a problem (especially on the S1 & S2), leading to cylinder head gasket failure, warped heads and/or failure of other engine compartment components. With the Turbo models, wastegates can seize. To check this, when you lift your foot off the accelerator, you should hear a little gasp of air as the wastegate opens to depressurise. Also, the turbo's boost pressure should not rise above normal.

The Citroen SM gearbox is usually reliable – a worn one will whine. Some gearbox parts are becoming scarce. If the gear changes are not quick and clean, the likely problem will be in the linkage run to the gearbox.

On early cars, check the condition of the clutch hydraulic pipework, which passes close to the exhaust and may cause a fire if it leaks or bursts.

Steering racks can wear quite quickly. The electrics (particularly on later cars) are generally reliable, but (as with any GRP bodied car with its earthing problems) the rule is to do a full functional check on everything!

Prices Today (Early Models): The S1 is quite rare today. The Esprits got progressively better, from S1 to S3, and this is reflected in their desirability, so today an S3 car is usually worth more than an S1. The Turbo versions are the most valuable.

Above: **An early Turbo Esprit.**
Below: **An Esprit S3.**

Above & Below: **The Peter Stevens' restyled Esprit, from 1987.**

Dates: 1964-71 (& from 1981)   **Number Built:** c.1,000 to 1971.

Body/Chassis: GRP body with plywood chassis (from late 1969: tubular steel chassis), 2-seater fixed-head coupé.

Engines:
1964-66:	Volvo 1783cc, 4-cyl in-line, ohv, 114bhp (or 96bhp);
1965-69:	Ford 1498cc or 1599cc, 4-cyl in-line, ohv, 85-88bhp;
1968-71:	Ford 2994cc, V6, ohv, 136bhp;
1970-71:	Volvo 2978cc, 6-cyl in-line, ohv, 145bhp;
From 1981:	Ford 1.6-litre to 3-litre. Later: Rover 3.5-litre V8.

Layout: Front engine, rear wheel drive, 4-speed manual gearbox.

Performance (early models):
1.6-litre: Top speed c.110mph, 0-60mph in c.10sec;
3-litre: Top speed c.125mph, 0-60mph in under 9sec.

Price Today: ££+ (Early Models).

Above & Below: **An early wooden chassis 1800 model (with Marcos alloy wheels), photographed in 2005.**

The name Marcos comes from Jem MARsh and Frank COStin, the company's founders, but Costin had in fact left the company before this stunning classic was launched at the 1964 Racing Car Show in London.

The Adams designed car had many different engines in addition to those listed above. There were also some Ford (Lawrence Tune) 1650cc, Ford 2-litre V4 and Triumph 2.5-litre versions, but the majority were fitted with the Ford Cortina GT or Ford/Volvo 3-litre engines.

Initially the cars had pull up/down windows but later ones had electric windows. Another design oddity was that the seats were fixed while the steering wheel and pedals were adjustable. Although the early plywood chassis was very strong, it was also labour intensive to make, so a tubular steel chassis replaced it in 1969.

Production ended with the (temporary) demise of Marcos Cars in 1972 but Jem Marsh restarted production a decade later, initially with the Marcos in kit form. There followed many derivatives, including the Mantula, Martina and Mantara (see also page 167). These are outside the main period covered by this book.

Typical optional extras included overdrive, fabric sunroof and Marcos alloy wheels.

Specific Checks: When checking a "big" Marcos, look carefully for signs of poorly repaired accident damage. In addition, for those rare cars with a wooden chassis, check for wood rot, exhaust burns and inspect the bulkheads where the front and rear suspension are attached. With steel chassis cars, check for corrosion, especially if the tube sealing bungs are missing. New galvanised tubular chassis are available and desirable.

On 3-litre models, worn differentials and overheating are potential problems. With all models, damp cockpits are common and exhausts are low and vulnerable. Poor handling might be due to "tired" coil springs coupled to leaky dampers in cars that have not been looked after. Today, parts are available from Marcos Heritage Spares Ltd, who also hold all the build records.

Prices Today: Most valuable is the original Volvo 1800, then the 3-litre cars and finally the 1.5/1.6-litre models.

Above: **A Marcos 3-litre with Cosmic alloy wheels. Note the condensation inside the headlamp fairings - a common problem.**

Below: **A metal chassis car (compare its highly visible sill with the car in the top photo). The Adams' flowing lines are evident in this photo.**

Left: **The Marcos Mantis at the 1971 Amsterdam Show.**

Right: **The alloy bonnet grille is the extractor for the ducted radiator.**

Left: **Mini Marcos at the 1968 Earls Court Motor Show.**

Right: **Re-launched by Marcos Heritage in 2005 as a MkVI, and available today.**

Dates: 1970-71	Number Built: 32

Body/Chassis: GRP body on steel chassis, 4-seater FHC.

Engine: Triumph 2498cc, 6-cyl in-line, ohv, fuel injection, 150bhp gross.

Layout: Front engine, RWD, 4-speed manual gearbox with overdrive.

Performance: c.120mph, 0-60 in c.8sec.   **Price Today:** Contact Club.

Dates: Since 1965	Number Built: c.1,300

Body/Chassis: GRP monocoque on steel subframes, 2-seater FHC.

Engines: Mini 848-1275+cc, 4-cyl in-line, ohv, 33+bhp.

Layout: Front transverse engine, FWD, 4-speed manual gearbox.

Performance: Dependent on engine.   **Price Today:** £

The name Mantis had been used by Marcos before for a one-off racer in the late 1960s. The new Mantis was very different. Its futuristic styling was done initially by Dennis Adams, the car then being developed by Brian Cunnington. The Mantis styling was controversial, with its wedge shape being ahead of its time.

The prototype Mantis had a Ford 3-litre V6 engine, but production units had the Triumph TR6 engine. The latter had the important advantage of being available with carburettors and suitable for the US market.

The Mantis used a 1.5-inch square-section steel chassis to which the one-piece GRP body was attached with about 20 bolts and many screws. The front coil spring suspension was a mix of Triumph and Marcos parts, while the Ford live rear axle was located by trailing arms and A-brackets combined with coil springs.

The interior of the car was to a luxury standard as the company was aiming up-market, but only 32 cars were made before the temporary demise of Marcos Cars.

It is popularly thought that the closure of the company was due mainly to the development costs of the Mantis but it was in fact a combination of factors, especially the heavy losses in America.

In the mid 1980s, the Mantis moulds were acquired by Autotune in Lancashire who used them to build a kit car called the Mirage. It used their own chassis and mainly Ford Cortina parts though different engines could be fitted. Only a handful of Mirages were made.

Specific Checks: First, from the paperwork, ensure the car is a genuine Mantis. Contact Marcos Heritage for further information and verification. Secondly, check for corrosion of the chassis, especially the rear outriggers and the side rails.

Prices Today: Probably less than 10 Mantis cars survive world-wide. They are difficult to value due to their rarity.

The Mini Marcos first appeared in 1965 and the next year a Cooper S powered example was the only British car to finish at Le Mans (at an average speed of nearly 90mph). In the 1970s, a car driven by Steve Roberts set four British land speed class records for cars to 1600cc.

The Mini Marcos was usually sold as a bodyshell to which a buyer would fit their own Mini parts. Although Marcos supplied full interior trim as an option, owners completed their cars to very variable standards.

By 1966, the car had opening door windows and the following year saw a revised body. The MkIV, from about 1974, had wind-up windows, a 4-inch longer wheelbase to accommodate a rear bench and a rear-hatch as standard (it had been an option before). From 1975 the car was produced by D&H Fibreglass Techniques, though production was phased out in the early 1980s. Over 400 MkIV cars were made. During 1990-96, Marcos resumed production as the MkV. This new model could take 12-inch wheels (or 13-inch with low profile tyres). Of the 65 made, 10 were fully built and exported to Japan.

In addition to the cars made in the UK, about 40 Mini Marcos were made under licence in Ireland and a smaller number made in South Africa and Australia.

Specific Checks: First, remember that most of the mechanical parts will probably be older than the vehicle's registration. Secondly, check for corrosion of both Mini subframes. Finally, due to the monocoque glassfibre construction of the main body unit, there is no corrosion problem as such but check for accident damage and delamination of the plywood reinforcement. Damage to the sill area may require major repairs or a new bodyshell.

Prices Today: The Mini Marcos Owners' Club estimates that less than 50 cars are currently "road legal" in the UK, but many have gone abroad. Prices are very dependent on condition.

Dates: 1945-55

Numbers Built: TC: 10,000   TD: 29,664   TF: 9,600

Body/Chassis: Steel panels on ash frame with separate steel chassis, 2-seater open sports.

Engines: 1250cc, 4-cyl in-line, ohv, 54-57bhp (gross, untuned); 1466cc, 4-cyl in-line, ohv, 63bhp (gross).

Layout: Front engine, rear wheel drive, 4-speed manual gearbox.

Performance: TC: Top speed over 75mph, 0-60mph in c.20sec; TF1500: Top speed over 80mph, 0-60mph in c.16sec.

Prices Today: £££   Arnolt-MG: Contact Club.

Above: **An MG TC (the radiator cap temperature gauge is non-standard).**
Below: **An MG TC with sidescreens in place.**

The charming and well known MG T-series cars started before WW2. The MG TC Midget was the postwar successor to the TB Midget, which had a rather short-lived existence with only 379 made in 1939 before war intervened. The TC was very similar (both visually and mechanically) though the body was 4 inches wider behind the seats. It was a traditional sports car with 1930s construction and styling, exemplified by its swept wings, running boards, front-opening cutaway doors, fold-down windscreen, louvred bonnet and wire wheels (not chromed). A nice styling touch was that the radiator grille slats were painted to match the colour of the leather upholstery. The car did sound sporty even if its performance was modest. A large number of TC Midgets were exported (despite all being made in RHD form) and it represented MG's first major success in the important US market.

In late 1949 came the improved TD Midget. It used the same 1250cc XPAG engine and twin SU carburettors, but it had a completely new, more rigid chassis – a shortened and modified version of that used in the MG Y-type saloon. This gave the TD independent front suspension and rack and pinion steering. Its longer front wings extending over 15-inch wheels (the TC had 19-inch wheels) and chrome bumpers distinguished it from the earlier TC. To the alarm of some enthusiasts at the time, the car also had pressed steel wheels rather than wire wheels (though many cars have now had wire wheels retrofitted). The TD was more comfortable and had better handling than the TC. A heater and radio were available as optional extras. Sales rose, with most cars going to the US in LHD form.

In late 1951 there were improvements to the engine and drive train. These cars are known as TD2 models. Various tuning kits were available to boost the car's performance and these cars are sometimes known as TD Competition models (ie TDC) or TD MkII.

The Arnolt-MG is a very rare (c.100 built) American-sponsored car that combined an MG TD chassis and running gear with an attractive Bertone body, available in convertible and coupé styles. There are only a handful of these cars in the UK.

There was no TE production model, but at the 1953 London Motor Show, MG launched the TF Midget, which was to be the last of the T-series. The new car was essentially a re-bodied TD but there were some

Above: **An MG TD, with standard (ventilated) pressed steel wheels.**
Below: **An attractive Arnolt-MG, which was based on the MG TD.**

concessions to modernity – a sloping radiator grille (now chromed rather than painted) and a lower bonnet line with headlamps faired into the front wings. Inside the car there was a revised facia, and twin bucket seats rather than a bench. Brakes were still hydraulic drum brakes all round and wire wheels were an optional extra. The windscreen wipers were mounted at the bottom of the screen to improve visibility. The engine of the TF was initially that of the TD MkII with 57bhp but in mid-1954 came the TF1500 with the 63bhp XPEG engine. One third of all TF cars had this bigger engine and it gave the car a slight improvement in performance.

Specific Checks: First check the paperwork, ensuring the numbers match those on the vehicle, then later verify the car's authenticity by contacting the Heritage Motor Centre Archives, Gaydon (unless the car already has a Heritage Certificate).

Restoring a T-series car can prove expensive due to their traditional construction, so a careful inspection before purchase is essential. First check the paint finish and the condition of the steel panels for corrosion and signs of accident damage. Using a magnet, ensure the wings are not glassfibre as this affects value. Inspect the scuttle area carefully as it can rust badly, especially where the windscreen is supported. Check how the bonnet and doors fit – the door hinges are prone to wear.

The ash frame rots. This is difficult to check but if you can move the body in relation to the rest of the vehicle, this is a bad sign! Look under the car to check the condition of the chassis, which rusts and can crack. Also check the chassis for poorly done repairs and accident damage.

Prices Today: The MG Octagon Car Club estimates that perhaps as many as 10-15,000 of these cars still exist worldwide. The TF1500 is possibly the most valuable, the TD the least, but there is little between them. Authenticity (backed up with a Heritage Certificate) and originality are as important as a car's condition.

Above and Below: **Both cars are the MG TD model. The lower car has the optional luggage rack and retrofitted wire wheels.**

Below: **An MG TF1500.**

Below: **An MG TF1500, in production until 1955.**

Dates: 1955-62

Numbers Built: 1500: 58,750   Twin Cam: 2,111
                    1600: 31,501   1600MkII: 8,719

Body/Chassis: Steel body (with alloy panels) on separate chassis, 2-seater open sports or fixed-head coupé.

Engines: 1500: 1489cc, 4-cyl in-line, ohv, 68-72bhp;
            Twin Cam: 1588cc, 4-cyl in-line, dohc, 108bhp;
            1600: 1588cc, 4-cyl in-line, ohv, 80bhp;
            1600MkII: 1622cc, 4-cyl in-line, ohv, 90bhp.

Layout: Front engine, rear wheel drive, 4-speed manual gearbox.

Performance: 1500 Coupé: Top speed c.100mph, 0-60mph in c.15sec;
              Twin Cam: Top speed c.115mph, 0-60mph in c.13sec.

Prices Today: Twin Cam Roadster: ££££   All Others: £££

Above: **An MGA 1500 Coupé – faster than the roadster version due to the better aerodynamics of the Coupé.**

Below: **An MGA Twin Cam, with its distinctive centre-lock ventilated steel wheels (but note these were also used on the De Luxe cars).**

Below: **An MGA 1600 roadster with the optional wire wheels.**

Announced in 1955, the attractive and streamlined MGA, mainly designed by Syd Enever (MG's Chief Engineer), was a radical departure from the traditional MG T-series. The MGA is regarded as the first modern MG sports car and was also the first MG that was only assembled at the MG Plant at Abingdon.

The new car had a pressed steel body and a hefty box-section chassis with aluminium doors, bonnet and boot lid. It used the proven BMC (Austin) B-series 1500 engine and cars were fitted with either ventilated steel wheels or wire wheels. Typical of its period, even the heater/demister was an optional extra. In 1956 came the fixed-head coupé version, which was about 5mph faster than the roadster due to the better aerodynamics of the roof. The coupé also had a more curved windscreen, wind-up windows with swivelling quarter lights, a large rear window and unique door handles.

In 1958 came the much more powerful Twin Cam derivative of the B-series engine. This version was distinguishable only by its badges and centre-lock ventilated steel wheels. It had disc brakes on all wheels, which was advanced for the time. At the 1960 Le Mans, a Twin Cam won its class, but concerns about reliability resulted in only 2,111 cars being built (1958-60).

In 1959 came the MGA 1600 with a larger (pushrod ohv) version of the B-series engine, and front disc brakes. It was nearly identical to the earlier cars except for its badging, redesigned front indicator/side lights, and a separate indicator lamp added above the original tail lamp. The coupés had a revised spare wheel position. In 1961 came the 1600 MkII, which had a larger capacity engine (with many improvements) and can be identified by its recessed front grille and horizontal (rather than vertical) shaped tail lamps.

The De Luxe model used leftover Twin Cam chassis with disc brakes on all wheels, but instead of the twin cam engine it had the normal pushrod 1600 or 1600MkII engine. The exact number made of these desirable De Luxe cars is thought to be just under 400.

Although over 101,000 MGAs were made, 94% were exported, mainly to North America in LHD form. Note that most MGAs were roadsters with less than 10% being coupés.

Specific Checks: Externally there is little to distinguish between the various MGA models and past owners may have exchanged parts between models. To discover which model you are inspecting, examine the engine and chassis numbers, which give useful information about the car's specification. Also check the numbers match the paperwork, then later verify the car's authenticity by contacting the Heritage Motor Centre Archives at Gaydon (unless the car already has a Heritage Certificate).

Next check the bodywork for corrosion, accident damage and a poorly done restoration. In addition to the usual checks, pay particular attention to the sills and main chassis frames, especially around the rear spring mounts. If the doors open and close properly, this is a good sign. Also check carefully for corrosion around the boot floor and inner wheelarches. The twin 6v batteries, behind the seats, sit in boxes that can rust through.

Although most body panels and chassis sections are available, replacement is not easy, mainly because of achieving alignment on re-assembly. One sign of a good rebuild is that the panels fit well.

Check also the main floor that is wood and rots, but is easily repaired. Note too that the aluminium bonnet can twist and may not fit well.

Other than the Twin Cam version, the MGA engines have a reputation for reliability, but check the engine is in fact the correct MGA B-series unit.

The car's electrical systems are not particularly reliable but are usually simple to fix. Check for damage to the exposed underfloor wiring runs at the rear.

Most body panels and complete reconditioned chassis are available today, though some engine parts (especially for the Twin Cam) are becoming difficult to source. Trim parts are generally available. The seats were originally leather covered but this may have been replaced with vinyl.

As with some other sports cars of this era, the lack of locks on the roadster is a security issue that would-be buyers need to consider.

Typical modifications include 5-speed Ford gearboxes (highly rated by owners), MGB engines, unleaded conversions and power tuning.

Prices Today: The MGA Register estimates that there are about 12,000 cars left world-wide, of which around 2,000 are in the UK (many of which have been re-imported). In general, the value of an MGA is determined by its condition, particularly the panel fit, paintwork and attention to detail with trim and brightwork. Coupés are valued less than roadsters; the Twin Cam roadsters are valued the highest (at about double that of a pushrod ohv-engined coupé); the Twin Cam coupés are valued slightly more than a standard coupé and the De Luxe cars carry a small premium.

Photo Top Right: **An MGA 1600 Coupé, with standard steel wheels.**
Middle photos: **An MGA 1600 with handy rear luggage rack.**
Lower Right: **Syd Enever (MG's Chief Engineer) in 1962 with the 100,000th MGA, a 1600 MkII.**

Dates: 1961-79   **Number Built:** 226,553

Body/Chassis: Steel unitary, 2-seater open sports.

Engines:
    1961-66: 948cc then 1098cc, 4-cyl in-line, ohv, 46.5-59bhp (net);
    1966-74: 1275cc, 4-cyl in-line, ohv, 65bhp (net) (US: 65-55bhp);
    1974-79: 1493cc, 4-cyl in-line, ohv, 65bhp (net) (US: 55-50bhp).

Layout: Front engine, rear wheel drive, 4-speed manual gearbox.

Performance:
    MkI: Top speed c.85mph, 0-60mph in c.20sec;
    MkII: Top speed c.95mph, 0-60mph in c.15sec;
    MkIII: Top speed over 95mph, 0-60mph in c.13sec;
    1500:   Top speed near 100mph, 0-60mph in c.12sec (US: slower).

Price Today: £+

Above & Below: **The MG Midget (G-AN2 version) had the larger 1098cc engine and front disc brakes. It looked identical to the first MkI Midgets. Note the grille and the strips on the bonnet and sides that distinguish the early Midgets from the Sprites. They also had different paint schemes.**

The original Austin-Healey Sprite MkI ("Frogeye") was superseded in 1961 by the Sprite MkII. This was closely followed by the announcement of an MG version, the Midget, thereby resurrecting a famous MG name from the past. Although the new Midget was essentially a badge-engineered version of the Sprite MkII, the Midget had a more elaborate radiator grille, plus waistline and central bonnet trim strips and a slightly improved interior to make it more up-market. It carried a higher price tag. Both the Sprite and Midget were assembled at Abingdon and became collectively known as "Spridgets".

In 1962, the 948cc (46.5bhp) engine was replaced by a 1098cc unit giving 55bhp. Front disc brakes and an improved rib-cased gearbox and interior were sufficient to advance the chassis prefix from G-AN1 to G-AN2. It was unofficially called the MkI½. These early Midgets had sidescreens, no external door handles and steel wheels (with optional wire wheels). About 16,080 G-AN1 and 9,600 G-AN2 cars were made.

In 1964 came the Midget MkII (G-AN3) with wind-up windows, openable quarter lights, a more curved wind-screen, external door handles, semi-elliptical rear springs (replacing quarter elliptics) and the interior was updated with a black crinkle finish facia. The A-series engine (now uprated to 59bhp) had its crankshaft and main bearings strengthened. About 26,600 MkII cars were made.

The Midget MkIII (G-AN4) appeared in 1966. It had the bigger 1275cc engine and a soft-top roof that was permanently fixed to the rear bodywork (and was therefore much easier to put up and down). In 1967, 476 MkIII cars were also built at Cowley. In 1969 the G-AN5 version of the car appeared. It was attractively restyled with a matt black grille, black sills (with the word MIDGET prominent), Rostyle steel wheels and slimmer bumpers. The chrome strips that had run down the bonnet and sides of the Midgets disappeared, thereby making it more difficult to distinguish a Midget from a Sprite.

From his notes made in 1979, the author records with some affection that his own MkIII was "easy to drive and park, with an excellent gearbox" but added he found his particular car "noisy at motorway speeds". Just over 100,000 MkIII cars were made.

Below: **The basic but functional cockpit of the MkI car. This is a G-AN1 car, the G-AN2 gaining a padded roll to the lower edge of the dashboard and trim liners to cover the exposed door frames.**

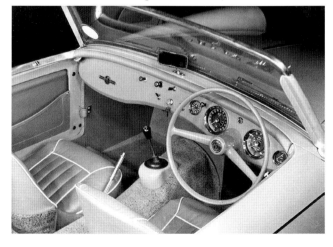

Between 1966 and 1971, nearly 1,200 cars were sent as CKD (Completely Knocked Down) kits to Australia. These cars were then assembled using some locally sourced items, eg tyres, trim and various electrical parts.

The Midget remained essentially unaltered until 1974, apart from minor changes, such as the attractive rounded rear wheelarches (1971-74) and latter US models temporarily sprouted large black rubber over-riders on their chrome bumpers.

The final version came in 1974. This was the Midget 1500 (G-AN6) using the Triumph Spitfire engine coupled to an adapted Morris Marina gearbox. Today this model is sometimes unofficially referred to as the MkIV Midget, though more often it is known as the "rubber bumper" version, while the earlier models are known as "chrome bumper" cars. The new 5mph black impact protection bumpers were not actually made of rubber but were a complex polyurethane moulding with steel box sections (which can rust). The G-AN6 body was strengthened too. Other effects of Federal regulations were the need to raise the ride height and change the rounded rear wheelarches back to a squared profile as this strengthened the rear bodywork.

In 1971, US-spec cars had triple windscreen wipers and amber side marker lights. Then in 1976 the wire wheel option was dropped and in 1977 there was a final (minor) revision of the facia. Emission regulations ensured that cars exported to the US had a single Zenith Stromberg carburettor rather than twin SU carbs and their engines were rated at 50-55bhp.

A third of all MG Midgets made were the final 1500 (G-AN6) version and the last 500 of them built for the home market were, perhaps appropriately, all painted black and had a commemorative plaque.

In good condition, the Midget is very reliable when serviced properly, the front suspension requiring regular greasing to avoid an expensive overhaul.

Typical options were a hardtop, radio, heater (standard only from 1969) and wire wheels.

Specific Checks: First check the paperwork, ensuring the numbers match those on the vehicle, then later verify the car's authenticity by contacting the Heritage Motor Centre Archives, Gaydon (unless the car already has a Heritage Certificate).

Next check the car itself. The most important item is body corrosion and in particular rusting of the sills, which are structurally critical and often expensive to rectify. Take out the rubber bungs in the sills to look behind them for rust or dirt. Watch out for new oversills hiding rusty inners behind them. The early design of unitary construction is complex and though it creates a very stiff structure, it makes repair more difficult due to "hidden" sections. If rust is visible, assume there is much more which you cannot see. For instance, if the outer wheelarch is rusted, the inner will probably be rusty too. In the Midget, structural areas that are often affected by rust include the complex sill sections, "chassis" rails, outriggers, rear spring attachments, the floor and the door pillars. Open the doors and inspect the bottom of the A-posts (a particular rust trap which is usually worse than what can be seen). Continued....

Above: **An early LHD MkIII (GAN-4) car with its US-spec side reflectors, head restraints, sun visors and whitewall tyres. The engine gained an air pump to reduce emission levels.**

Below: **A later MkIII (GAN-5) car with its distinctive black sills, Rostyle steel wheels and slimmer bumpers. The fuel tank was enlarged by one (useful) gallon.**

Below: **The author's MkIII (GAN-5) in 1979. The MIDGET sill badge is missing, probably due to a sill replacement.**

If the car looks a bit down at the rear, the rear spring mounting has probably rusted badly and/or the springs have sagged. Look also for broken leaves. Check for rusty floor pans (under the carpeting) just behind the seats as this is where the leaf spring front mountings are located. While in this area, check also for corrosion of the cross-members just in front of the seats. The leaf spring rear mounting can be inspected from inside the boot.

Check the gap at the front and rear edges of the doors. The gap should be even, but if narrower at the top it may indicate the bodyshell is sagging, which is a bad sign! Check too for rust by the bonnet hinges, battery tray and around the brake and clutch master cylinders. Note that new Heritage bodyshells are available for some versions of the Midget.

The early Midget engine is the trusty A-series, which is relatively easy and cheap to work on, but leaks oil and the tappets can be noisy, as can a worn timing chain. The 948cc engines can run very hot, the 1275cc versions less so. An oil cooler can assist matters.

The 1500 (Triumph) engine also suffers from tappet noise and runs hot. It is not noted for its longevity – and it needs an oil cooler too. These 1500 engines can destroy their crankshaft thrust washers – to check this, push the crankshaft bottom fanbelt pulley rearward as hard as you can, then ask someone to depress the clutch pedal. If you see and maybe even hear the pulley move forwards, the engine may need major repairs. These engines also suffer from premature bottom end wear – to check, while the engine is idling, listen for a low rumbling noise when the clutch is pressed in.

The pre-1500 gearboxes tend to 'whine', especially in 1st gear, and the gearlevers make a 'sizzling' noise but this is usually not serious. The 1500 gearboxes are regarded as weaker and can fail at relatively low mileages.

The rack and pinion steering should be light and precise. If not, it probably means things are worn or seized. A common occurrence is king-pins becoming worn and seized due to lack of regular greasing and this often necessitates the replacement of the complete suspension unit. Note that springs may creak in hot dry weather. Handbrakes are sometimes ineffective due to worn clevis pins on the linkage and seized reaction arms in the brake drums.

Modifications you might find include Rover K-series engines with 5-speed Ford or Toyota gearboxes, or overdrive fitted on the 1500 model (overdrive was never an MG factory option).

There were a number of adaptations or specials based on the Spridget, such as the Arkley and Lenham (refer to the Other Models section from page 156).

Prices Today: About three-quarters of the cars were exported. Today, there is a small variation in price between the different models but condition is the key factor, though colour can also affect the price.

Photo Top Right: **The cockpit of a MkIII (GAN-5), with rocker switches.**
2nd From Top: **A 1976 Midget 1500 (GAN-6) "rubber bumper" car.**
3rd From Top: **A US-spec 1979 car, awaiting despatch from Abingdon.**
Lower Right: **The production line, photographed by the author in 1979.**

Dates: 1962-80 (GT: 1965-80)

Numbers Built: Tourer/Roadster: 386,961   GT: 125,282

Body/Chassis: Steel unitary, 2-seater open sports (GT: rear-hatch fixed-head coupé).

Engine: 1798cc, 4-cyl in-line, ohv, 95bhp (See text).

Layout: Front engine, rear wheel drive, 4-speed manual gearbox (optional overdrive) or 3-speed automatic gearbox.

Performance:
Early cars: Top speed c.105mph, 0-60mph in c.12sec;
Later cars: Top speed in the mid 90s, 0-60mph in over 14sec.

Prices Today: Tourer/Roadster: ££+   GT: £+   (See text).

Above: **A 1964 MGB MkI Tourer (later cars were called "Roadsters").**
Below: **A 1971 Roadster with non-standard, but period, alloy wheels.**

Below: **A 1965 publicity photo of an MGB GT taken beside an Argosy aircraft at RAF Abingdon (near the MG Plant). The author was based here in the 1970s and had this view of the airfield from his office.**

The MGB is MG's greatest success story, with over half a million cars sold, making it the largest selling British sports car ever. Today the evergreen "B" is still a very popular sports car, offering many owners what they regard as the ideal combination of performance, comfort, reliability, image and value.

The original MGB Tourer was launched in 1962 as the replacement to the MGA and was mechanically similar. The MGB Tourer was designed mainly by Syd Enever (MG's Chief Engineer), ably assisted by Roy Brocklehurst, Don Hayter and Jim O'Neil. It used a larger capacity B-series engine than the MGA's, and was of early unitary construction with large longitudinal chassis rails welded to the bodyshell to form a single structure, which was very sturdy.

In 1964 the original 3-bearing engine was replaced by a stronger 5-bearing unit, rated at 95bhp. The following year saw the introduction of a rear-hatch coupé, the MGB GT, which had detail styling by Farina. The MGB GT had the same mechanical components as the open top MGB, and though it had a small rear bench it was not a true 2+2 seater.

From the introduction of the GT, all model changes were made to both the Roadster and GT.

The MkII version, from late 1967, had an all-synchromesh gearbox and many other improvements such as a negative earth electrical system with an alternator (rather than dynamo), two-speed wipers and a pre-engaged starter motor. An automatic gearbox was available as an option from 1967-73, but it is rare, with only about 1,700 made.

Over the next few years there was a stream of improvements and trim changes. Home market highlights included new reclining seats (1968), the late 1969 face-lift with a recessed matt black grille and stylish Rostyle steel wheels, then a steering lock (end of 1970).

Late 1971 saw further changes including a new facia with rocker switches and air vents. By this time the bonnet was steel rather than aluminium (the rest of the bodywork had always been made of steel). A revised black honeycomb radiator grille was introduced before the end of 1972 and a brake servo became standard equipment from autumn 1973.

Late 1974 saw a major change to the bodyshells with the introduction of black "rubber bumpers" (previous models are known as "chrome bumper" cars). The new 5mph black impact protection bumpers were not actually made of rubber but were a complex polyurethane moulding with steel box sections (which can rust). There were also other changes, including the use of one 12v battery rather than two 6v units.

Federal safety legislation also led to the car's ride height being increased to the detriment of its handling. The handling issue was, however, addressed in the major 1976 face-lift which gave the roadster back a front anti-roll bar (it had been removed in 1974), increased the thickness of the GT's, and introduced a rear anti-roll bar. The 1976 face-lift also brought the car up-to-date with some long-needed modifications which included a new facia, halogen headlights, electric engine cooling fan and the overdrive switch was incorporated in the gear knob (by this time overdrive was standard). Note that overdrive is a sought-after option by buyers today. The seating was also changed to a striped nylon fabric.

In 1975, to commemorate MG's 50th Anniversary, 750 MGB GT Jubilee cars were made. They were well equipped, including MGB GT V8-style wheels (but in a gold finish), and had a distinctive broad gold side stripe on a British Racing Green paint finish.

During its long production life, the MGB used the increasingly venerable, but reliable, B-series engine with the same 1798cc capacity, but the power output varied. The normally quoted figure for UK specification cars is 94-95bhp for early cars, then 95bhp, but in the 1970s this was re-calibrated and MG brochures quoted 84bhp (DIN) for twin carb versions. Federal versions, due to emission regulations, gave ever-decreasing power, down to 65-67bhp (DIN) by the late 1970s. However, with tuning, the "B" could be competitive – in fact it came second in its class at Le Mans in 1964 and 1965, and went on to win many races and rallies thereafter.

The MGB Tourer/Roadster and GT were assembled at the MG Plant at Abingdon, near Oxford, and over half a million of these cars were made. Many were exported, in fact 87% of the Tourers/Roadsters and 48% of the GTs went abroad, so in the UK, GT sales exceeded those of the Roadster. Exports were fairly consistent over the long life of these cars except for the "rubber bumper" GTs of which only 1,500 were exported in the car's last 6 years of production. The last 1,000 Roadsters and GTs built were the "Limited Edition" models, available only in metallic pewter (for the 580 GTs) and bronze (for the 420 Roadsters) with special distinguishing livery and front air dam. The very last cars to be made at the MG Plant at Abingdon were completed in October 1980.

Typical optional extras that you might find include wire wheels, hardtop (on the Roadster), overdrive (fitted as standard from 1975), and on the GT, tinted glass (standard from late 1976) and dealer-fitted sunroof. An automatic transmission was available from 1967-73, but is rare today.

Above: A "chrome bumper" Roadster with non-standard alloy wheels.

Below: A "chrome bumper" MGB GT with optional wire wheels.

Below: A "chrome bumper" MGB GT with standard Rostyle wheels.

Federal Versions: Pre-1967 cars exported to the US were essentially the same as UK ones, except for being LHD and having different lights. But from late 1967 there were many changes due to safety and emission regulations. For instance, Roadsters sent to the US were fitted with triple wipers to comply with safety regulations regarding the swept area of the screen (the taller screen of the GT was not affected). Dual-circuit brakes were also fitted, becoming standard on UK cars much later. Federal cars also gained head restraints and side reflectors (later changed to side marker lights). They also had thick safety padding on the passenger side of the dashboard.

For 1974 only, US cars had large black rubber over-riders on their chrome bumpers (never seen on UK cars), this being prior to the "rubber bumper" cars the following year. The end of 1974 also saw the twin SU carbs being replaced by a single Zenith Stromberg unit. By early 1976, US cars had a catalytic converter. Later all exports of the GT to North America stopped. In 1979 came the final "Limited Edition" export model – these Roadsters were appropriately black cars with silver stripes, front air dam and Triumph Stag-style wheels.

Specific Checks: First check the paperwork, ensuring the numbers match those on the vehicle, then later verify the car's authenticity by contacting the Heritage Motor Centre Archives, Gaydon (unless the car already has a Heritage Certificate).

When checking the car, the most important item is body corrosion and in particular rusting of the sills which are structurally critical and often expensive to rectify. Look for bodged sill repairs or new oversills hiding rusty inners behind them (if possible, prise up the door seal and count the number of pieces of metal under the seal – it should be three). The early design of unitary construction is complex and though it creates a very stiff structure, it makes repair more difficult due to "hidden" sections. If rust is visible, assume there is much more in the hidden areas. In the "B", structural areas which are often affected by rust include the complex sill sections, "chassis" rails, outriggers, rear spring attachments, floor and door pillars.

The wings are also prone to rusting and though the front wings are bolted on, removing corroded nuts to replace a wing is a long, hard task. Check also the wheelarches for rust. One good test with a Roadster (and with the seller's permission) is to jack it up using the original jacking points and observe the door gaps. If they open at the top, this is a bad sign!

When checking "rubber bumper" cars for accident damage, be warned that a bumper can appear unmarked though the bodywork beyond it is in fact damaged.

The engine is relatively robust and reliable but it still requires regular maintenance at the correct service intervals. The twin SU carburettors should be carefully tuned periodically. Some tappet noise is normal with this engine, and the tappets need adjusting regularly. Pre-1975 cars use two 6v batteries in series (located behind the seats) and the two battery wells are prone to rust due to leaked battery acid. Continued....

Above: **A nice MG publicity photo of the mid-1970s.**

Below: **One of 750 special MG 50th Anniversary Jubilee cars.**

Below: **Part of the MGB production line at Abingdon, photographed by the author in 1979.**

The front suspension needs greasing every 3,000 miles so is often neglected which results in major wear and replacement of components. The "B" tends to sag on its suspension with old age.

With the Roadster, check the condition of the soft-top roof carefully and try putting it up and down, as a replacement is expensive. All open sports cars are vulnerable to rainwater ingress so check the carpets and if they show any signs of dampness, lift them to see if corrosion has started on the floor below. Also check for water damage to seating and trim as replacing items or re-trimming can be expensive.

Parts availability for the "B" is excellent, from complete new Heritage bodyshells upwards. But note that it is very time consuming to rebody a car.

Modifications you might find include tuned engines (eg with Weber carb, larger 1.75-inch SU carbs, unleaded conversions, hot camshafts, and bored out cylinders). Some Roadsters have had a V8 engine fitted (see the MGB GT V8 entry). The car's handling may be improved by using uprated bushes and telescopic dampers.

Prices Today: In terms of values, the MkI Tourer (if in "as original" condition) commands the highest price. All the GTs are less than the equivalent Roadsters by maybe as much as a third. The "rubber bumper" versions of both the Roadster and GT are valued less than the "chrome bumper" cars, though authenticity, body colour and condition are, as always, key factors in a valuation.

Above: **A sectioned MGB engine and gearbox.**
Below: **A "rubber bumper" MGB Roadster with optional wire wheels.**

Above: **A "rubber bumper" MGB with standard Rostyle steel wheels.**
Below: **The comfortable interior of a 1976 MGB GT.**

Below: **One of the UK "Limited Edition" MGBs of 1980. 1,000 were made of which 580 were the GT version.**

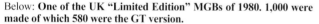

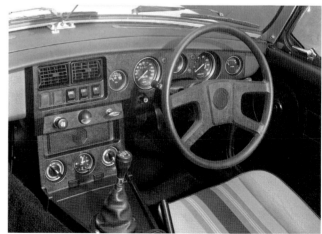

Dates: 1967-69

Numbers Built: Roadster: 4,544   GT: 4,458

Body/Chassis: Steel unitary, 2-seater open sports (GT: rear-hatch fixed-head coupé).

Engine: 2912cc, 6-cyl in-line, ohv, 150bhp (gross)/145bhp (net).

Layout: Front engine, rear wheel drive, 4-speed manual gearbox (optional overdrive) or 3-speed automatic gearbox.

Performance: Top speed c.120mph, 0-60mph in c.10sec.

Prices Today: Roadster: ££+   GT: ££

Above: **An MGC Roadster with optional wire wheels.**

The MGC was not an MGB replacement, but intended to supersede the Austin-Healey 3000 – though the Healeys distanced themselves from the project and it was never sold as an Austin-Healey. The MGC looked identical to the MGB except for a prominent bonnet bulge, 15-inch wheels rather than 14-inch, and it stood about 1-inch higher than a standard "B".

The MGC GT was launched at the same time as the mechanically identical Roadster. The main difference between them and the MGBs was that they used the C-Series six-cylinder engine. The earlier "Big Healey" had also used a C-Series engine with the same capacity (2912cc), but the one used in the MGCs was different due to a major redesign of the engine. The new version had seven rather than four main bearings and a new cylinder block which made the engine shorter by about 1.75 inches, and lighter by about 44lb (20kg), but it still weighed over 200lb (90kg) more than the MGB's four-cylinder B-Series engine. Overall, an MGC weighed about one sixth more than an equivalent MGB and its weight distribution was very slightly more nose-heavy.

Because the C-Series engine was much bigger than the B-Series engine, many changes were required to accommodate it. The radiator was moved as far forward as possible, a new welded-in crossmember was required and the front suspension was altered to incorporate torsion bars and telescopic dampers. The car had larger front disc brakes than the then current MGB and they were servo-assisted (which was not the case with the "B" at that time). The rear suspension was altered, having seven rather than five leaf springs. There was also a new all-synchromesh gearbox and stronger rear axle. From late 1967 the MGC was available with an automatic gearbox, using the Borg-Warner Type 35 unit.

As for the bodywork, apart from the bonnet, inner wings and internally strengthened areas such as the bulkhead and the floor panels, the body panels for the "C" were the same as the "B". The interior trim and equipment was initially identical, except the "C" had its speedo calibrated to 140mph (rather than 120mph) and there were other minor differences. From late 1968, there were improvements including lever-adjustable seat backs and different ratios in the gearbox and rear axle.

Almost half the cars produced were exported to America. These cars had thick safety padding on the passenger side of the dashboard, dual-circuit brakes and

the Roadsters were fitted with triple wipers to comply with safety regulations regarding the swept area of the windscreen (the taller screen of the GT was not affected). Later, the cars also had head restraints and side reflectors (changed later still to side marker lights).

Though it was a fast, stable and effortless cruiser, the MGC was not well received by the motoring press, in part due to a tendency to understeer. The criticism was not entirely justified as it was subsequently found that the demo cars were fitted with incorrect tyres and with tyre pressures that were too low. Interestingly, the automatic version impressed many of the journalists.

Production of the MGC was discontinued in August 1969. At the end, University Motors in London bought the last 141 cars, comprising 23 Roadsters and 118 GTs. They specially modified about 20 and these are quite valuable today but note there are some standard cars that have been modified by owners to look like one of the University Motors' Specials.   Continued....

Below: **From this angle, only the larger wheels and rear badge indicate that this is an MGC rather than an MGB.**

Typical optional extras you might find include overdrive, wire wheels, hardtop (on the Roadster) and fabric sunroof (on the GT).

Specific Checks: First check the paperwork, ensuring the numbers match those on the vehicle, then later verify the car's authenticity by contacting the Heritage Motor Centre Archives, Gaydon (unless the car already has a Heritage Certificate).

When checking the car, the most important item is body corrosion and in particular rusting of the sills which are structurally critical and often expensive to rectify. Look for bodged sill repairs or new oversills hiding rusty inners behind them (if possible, prise up the door seal and count the number of pieces of metal under the seal – it should be three). The early design of unitary construction is complex and though it creates a very stiff structure, it makes repair more difficult due to "hidden" sections. If rust is visible, assume there is much more in the hidden areas. In the "C" (as with the "B"), structural areas which are often affected by rust include the complex sill sections, "chassis" rails, outriggers, rear spring attachments, floor and door pillars.

An area specific to the "C" to check for corrosion is the crossmember supporting the torsion bar ends, the adjacent floorpan and the front chassis, as no repair panels are available. The wings are also prone to rusting and though the front wings are bolted on, removing corroded nuts to replace a wing is a long, hard task. Check also the wheelarches for rust. One good test with a Roadster (and with the seller's permission) is to jack it up using the original jacking points and observe the door gaps. If they open at the top, this is a bad sign!

The bonnet is aluminium (which can dent) and any creases or buckling at the front probably indicates the car has had a front end accident at some time.

Check too the rear leaf springs for cracks and for deterioration of the spring mountings.

The large, almost lazy, engine in the "C" means it is not over-stressed (especially in automatic models). Together with the gearbox and rear axle, the engine is not particularly prone to problems and if serviced properly, they are long-lived items. The engines also do not usually suffer from overheating or loss of oil. The C-Series engine was shared only with the Austin 3-Litre saloon (1967-71) but note that the Austin used a version with a lower compression ratio.

Today MGC spares are generally not difficult to find, though the situation is not as easy as with the MGB and there is currently no Heritage replacement bodyshell (as there is for the MGB Roadster, MGB GT and V8).

Prices Today: The MGC Roadster is worth slightly more than the GT.

Photo Top Right: **The GT was launched at the same time as the roadster.**
2nd From Top: **There was no "rubber bumper" version of the "C".**
3rd From Top: **This restored car has non-standard Compomotive wheels.**
Lower Right: **A Downton Stage 3 specification engine installed in the car illustrated above, with triple SU carbs and other tuning modifications.**

Dates:	1973-76	Number Built:	2,601

Body/Chassis: Steel unitary, 2-seater rear-hatch fixed-head coupé.

Engine: Rover 3528cc, V8, ohv, 137bhp (DIN).

Layout: Front engine, rear wheel drive, 4-speed manual gearbox with overdrive.

Performance: Top speed c.125mph and 0-60mph under c.8sec.

Price Today: ££

Above: **An MGB GT V8. Externally, V8 badges and Dunlop wheels distinguish it from a standard MGB GT.**

Not available as a roadster or with automatic transmission, the exciting MGB GT V8 was visually identical to the standard MGB GT except for the small, unpretentious "V8" badges and the smart Dunlop wheels that had alloy centres and chrome-plated steel rims. These wheels were unique to the V8 at the time, though they were used later for the MG 50th Anniversary MGB GT Jubilee cars. Even the V8's interior was the same as the MGB GT apart from a smaller speedometer and rev counter to accommodate the collapsible steering column (note that over time, broken nylon pins in the column may have been replaced by steel pins, and hence the column is no longer collapsible). Luxury equipment, such as tinted glass and overdrive, was fitted as standard, the overdrive giving an impressive 28mph/1000rpm.

Similarity to the MGB GT was only skin deep for under the bonnet was the large, reliable and proven Rover (née Buick) V8 all-alloy engine which used a modified gearbox and rear axle and transformed the standard MGB GT's performance. The Rover V8 was a popular choice for several sports car manufacturers, including Marcos, Morgan, Triumph and TVR. In the MG the V8 engine was lighter than the standard B-series but with ancillaries it ended up weighing a bit more. To fit the V8 under the bonnet without bulges required a neat and novel solution which was to locate the two SU carburettors at the very rear of the engine.

In addition, there were also modifications to the bulkhead, inner wheelarches and front crossmember to squeeze in the new engine. The suspension springs and brakes were beefed up and a larger radiator with twin electric fans plus an oil cooler were fitted.

In late 1974 the car, like its sisters, got the Federal-look with large black "rubber bumpers", though exports of these cars to the US did not, in fact, materialise. Hence, unlike all other MG sports cars, only a handful of the MGB GT V8s were exported. The car never achieved the success hoped for and production ceased in 1976 with just 2,601 examples made, of which 1,856 were the "chrome bumper" version.

Mention should be made of the MGB V8 conversions carried out privately by Ken Costello from 1970-73. Unlike the MG Factory which produced only the MGB GT V8 model, Costello converted both roadsters and GTs. Perhaps as many as 200 were modified by Costello – some, but not all, have distinctive bonnet bulges.

More recently too, there has been a trend to convert standard "B"s by fitting V8 engines. The "rubber bumper"

version of the "B" even has the appropriate engine mountings for the V8. With these conversions it is vital to check the full details of how the conversion has been carried out and whether it was carried out professionally. Ideally there should be a full and illustrated build record. In most cases it may be wise to have a V8 conversion inspected professionally. To find a factory-built RHD MGB GT V8, the chassis number should start with GD2D1.

The Rover V8 engine was to reappear once more in a later MG, the MG RV8 of 1992-95. 1,983 of these desirable cars were made, of which only 300 or so were for the UK, the rest being exported (mainly to Japan, though some of these have since returned to the UK). The RV8 used a 3.9-litre, 190bhp, fuel-injected version of the V8 and was available only as a roadster, using an adapted MGB Heritage bodyshell. The RV8 falls outside the period covered by this book but is mentioned here for completeness.

Specific Checks: Start with the paperwork, and contact the Heritage Motor Centre Archives at Gaydon to verify the car's authenticity (unless the car already has a Heritage Certificate), also the V8 Register. Continued....

Below: **A rare Costello with distinctive bonnet bulge, egg-crate grille, V8 badges and vinyl roof. This example also has period accessories.**

Moving on to check the car, the most important item is body corrosion and in particular rusting of the sills which are structurally critical and often expensive to rectify. Look for bodged sill repairs or new oversills hiding rusty inners behind them (if possible, prise up the door seal and count the number of pieces of metal under the seal – it should be three).

The early design of unitary construction is complex and though it creates a very stiff structure, it makes repair more difficult due to "hidden" sections. If rust is visible, assume there is much more in the hidden areas. In the V8 (as with the standard "B"), structural areas which are often affected by rust include the complex sill sections, "chassis" rails, outriggers, rear spring attachments, floor and door pillars. The wings are also prone to rusting and though the front wings are bolted on, removing corroded nuts to replace a wing is a long task. Check also the wheelarches for rust.

When inspecting "rubber bumper" cars for accident damage, be warned that a bumper can appear unmarked though the bodywork beyond it is in fact damaged.

The V8 engine is generally a reliable unit, but it needs frequent oil changes to minimise wear. Common problems include worn hydraulic cam followers (indicated by tappet noise when idling) and water pump failure (indicated by a rumbling sound). Normal engine oil pressure is low when idling and when driving hard the running pressure level should remain constant. A good engine will not normally lose oil. The cast iron exhaust manifolds have a tendency to crack.

Check the gearbox is quiet and the synchromesh still works, as it has to cope with a lot of torque (and many gearboxes have failed). Note the SU fuel pump can be troublesome on cars that are not run regularly.

The front suspension needs greasing every 3,000 miles, so is often neglected which results in major wear and replacement of components. As with the standard MGB GT, the V8 tends to sag on its suspension with old age – when new you could see the top of the rear tyres.

Parts availability is good, from a complete new Heritage bodyshell upwards. But note that it is very time consuming to rebody a car.

Modifications include the stronger Rover 5-speed gearbox and fitting a 3.9-litre or even larger V8 engine.

Prices Today: The MGB GT V8 is highly regarded and sought after. The V8 Register calculates that just under 70% of the factory produced cars survive. In terms of value, the "rubber bumper" cars are worth slightly less than the "chrome bumper" versions but condition (and colour) are the key factors. The MGB GT V8 is generally valued at more than a comparable MGB GT but is possibly undervalued as it is relatively scarce.

Photo Top Right: **The V8 badge is just visible on the front wing. MG did not fit a similar badge to the offside wing (to economise, apparently).**
2nd From Top: **Later cars had "rubber bumpers". There is a small V8 badge on the left side of the rear-hatch.**
3rd From Top: **The superb Rover V8 engine with its twin SU carbs cleverly located behind the engine to accommodate their height.**
Lower Right: **An MG RV8 - the spiritual successor to the MGB GT V8.**

Dates: Since 1936 (See text).

Numbers Built: Plus 4 (1950-69): c.4,500   4/4 (1955-82): c.4,900

Body/Chassis: Steel and aluminium panels on ash frame with separate steel chassis, 2 or 4-seat open sports or drophead coupé.

Engines:

Plus 4 (1950-58): Vanguard 2088cc, 4-cyl in-line, ohv, 68bhp; (1953-69): Triumph 1991-2138cc, 4-cyl in-line, ohv, 90-104bhp.

4/4 (1955-60): Ford 100E 1172cc, 4-cyl in-line, side-valve, 36bhp; (1960-61): Ford 105E 997cc, 4-cyl in-line, ohv, 39bhp; (1961-63): Ford 109E 1340cc, 4-cyl in-line, ohv, 54bhp; (1963-68): Ford 116E 1498cc, 4-cyl in-line, ohv, 65-84bhp.

4/4 1600 (1968-82): Ford 1599cc, 4-cyl in-line, ohv, 70-96bhp; (1981-85) Fiat 1584cc, 4-cyl in-line, dohc, 98bhp.

Layout: Front engine, rear wheel drive with 3-speed (4-speed from 1960, 5-speed from 1980s) manual gearbox.

Performance:

Plus 4 (TR): Top speed over 100mph, 0-60mph in under 10sec; 4/4 Series II: Top speed about 75mph, 0-60mph in under 30sec; 4/4 Series V & 1600: Top speed over 100mph, 0-60mph in c.10sec.

Prices Today: £££

Above: **This rare prewar drophead Morgan 4-4 Series I car (together with the roadster version) were the start of a long line of Morgan sports cars that are still in production over 70 years later.**

This quintessentially traditional British sports car's lineage dates back to 1936 when Morgan launched the 4-4. Its model name reflected the car's 4 cylinders and 4 wheels, as up to that time the company had been better known for their 3-wheelers.

In 1950 the Plus 4 ("plus" meaning more power) was launched, with deliveries from 1951 (the 4-4 Series I being phased out). The Plus 4 had a bigger engine (a 2-litre Standard Vanguard unit), stronger chassis and hydraulic brakes. In late 1953 came the first of the Triumph TR-engined cars that started a long relationship with Triumph stretching to 1969, passing through the TR3, TR4 and finally TR4A.

The Morgans all used a Z-section chassis with longitudinal side rails. Unusually, the chassis was designed to flex rather than be rigid. All the cars had independent front suspension utilising Morgan's own patent design of a sliding front vertical pillar with coil springs and telescopic dampers, which together made for hard, but precise, handling. The Plus 4 introduced the Morgan "one shot chassis lubrication system" whereby the driver had to regularly lubricate the front suspension king-pins with engine oil by pressing a button in the cockpit.

The gearbox in the Plus 4 was a Moss unit and it sat immediately under the gear lever but this required it to be connected by a short torque tube to the engine. Braking was by drum brakes but front discs became optional from 1959 and standard on the Plus 4 from 1960.

The cars were available as two or four-seater roadsters or (until 1969) as a drophead coupé. The drophead coupé version had larger, higher doors (with no cutaway) and it was generally fitted out more luxuriously. The four-seater roadster had its spare wheel

mounted vertically at the rear to create more room for the extra row of seats.

During the mid-1950s, Morgan changed the look of their cars. First, during 1953-54, the flat radiator and separately-mounted headlights were replaced by the "high cowl" sloped grille, and the headlights were faired into more enveloping bodywork. This was much to the horror of the traditionalists at the time! Next to change was the rear, and from that time Morgans have remained essentially unchanged visually, though there have been many minor changes, both in dimensions and details – but probably only noticeable by the *cognoscenti*.

In 1955 Morgan re-introduced the 4-4 (but renamed as the 4/4) to be a lower-powered sister to the then current Plus 4. At the time, the 4/4 was the cheapest open two-seater sports car on the market. This new 4/4 Series II was Ford powered, and the 4/4 went through four different Series (II to V) using new Ford engines as they became available; the initial Ford Anglia 100E for the Series II, then the 105E engine in the Series III (only

Below: **A 1950 "flat rad" Morgan 4/4, as seen in 2006.**

59 made), the 109E in the Series IV and finally the 116E engine in the Series V (646 cars made). Note these Series numbers did not appear on any badges on the Morgan cars themselves.

The Series II cars had 3-speed Ford gearboxes, while the later Series were 4-speed. The Series II to IV cars had rather unusual pendant gear levers acting through a convoluted remote linkage, while the Series V was more direct. Braking was by drum brakes until the Series IV when front disc brakes became standard. A competition model with mild tuning was also available.

The Series II to V cars were made up to 1968 and (with one or two exceptions) were only available as two-seater roadsters. Nearly 1,300 were made before the advent of the 4/4 1600 in 1968.

This new 4/4 1600 used the Ford "Kent" crossflow engine in standard 70bhp form or the Cortina GT 96bhp version in the 4/4 Competition model (to 1971). The GT engine became standard on all 4/4s from 1971. From 1981-85, 92 cars were fitted with a Fiat Twin Cam engine, when Ford stopped making the Kent unit. With the demise of the Plus 4, the 4/4 was available as a two or four-seater.

Although deliveries of the initial Plus 4 cars ceased in 1968-69 (due to the arrival of the Plus 8), the model was re-introduced in 1985 with engines from Fiat, then Rover and then later, Ford, but that falls outside the period covered in this book.

The Plus 4 Super Sports (from 1961) was a highly tuned version (by Chris Lawrence of Lawrence Tune), with aluminium panels. A modified version, driven by Chris Lawrence and Richard Shepherd-Barron, had a historic class win at Le Mans in 1962. Only 101 of the Super Sports were made. The Plus 4 Competition model (from 1965-66, only 42 made) does not have the aluminium panelling and the engine is only lightly tuned.

From 1970 a collapsible steering column (with lock) was fitted and a dual braking system followed the next year. The dash top was also padded for safety. From 1974 there was a screen demister. 1977 saw the change to triple windscreen wipers, aluminium rather than chrome bumpers and the option of aluminium body and wings. That year also saw a major redesign of the dashboard.

The 4/4 1600 was a very successful model range for Morgan, with some 3,600 sold to 1982, when the new Ford CVH engine came in to use. In the following decades the car continued to be developed and improved. In particular, attention was given to increasing longevity by treating the ash frame, painting each panel separately before assembly and giving corrosion protection to the chassis (including optional galvanising).

Today the four-cylinder Morgans continue in production. Current models meet full Type Approval and the latest crash test standards.

The cars are still lovingly hand built by the Morgan Motor Company, who are apparently the oldest independently owned car manufacturer in the world.

Specific Checks: Start with the paperwork and check the numbers match those on the car.

Until 1986, the ash frame was untreated when the cars were built, so when examining a used Morgan, start

Above & Below: **The rare 4-seater DHC (only 51 made, 1954-56).**

Above: **A 1954 Morgan Plus 4. Note the two spare wheels.**
Below: **A 1968-69 car.**

by checking the wooden floor and ash frame for rot, woodworm and cracking (though the frame is mostly covered so this is difficult to check without dismantling). Open the doors wide and see if lifting them moves the body frame (not a good sign). Check also the wood at the bottom of the back panel (with the seller's permission, remove the spare wheel to gain access). Next, check the chassis for rust, repair welds and cracks (especially near the engine, steering box and suspension mountings). Pre-1986 cars are prone to rot in the corner where the front wing and the bulkhead meet. Water is trapped here and then the wood rots and the metal rusts.

The pre-1986 chassis was not rust-proofed so it tends to rust along the side rails (especially behind the rear wheels) and where the crossmembers meet the side rails.

With the bodywork, the front wings are prone to rust particularly where they are attached near the doors. Corrosion also occurs around the front wings' lips (if steel) and at most panel joints. The bulkhead is difficult to replace and can rust, so lift the floor covering to check it. In early cars with the full width toolbox on the bulkhead, look inside to check for corrosion.

Until the introduction of moulded wings in 1998, alloy wing edges were rolled over mild steel wire, leading to corrosion. Some owners have fitted GRP wings, which are lighter and do not rust but reduce the car's value.

A good Morgan requires regular oiling and greasing, particularly the sliding pillar front suspension. Neglect of this will show up as a lack of oil coating. Also, king-pin wear will be revealed in a road test if the car wanders and a clunking sound is heard on hitting a pot hole. Note that some of these cars will have been raced.

A modification you might find is a change of engine on some early 4/4 cars, where the owners have upgraded to later Ford 1.6-litre units.

Prices Today: As these cars are still in production there is a natural cap on prices, equivalent to a new Morgan. A Plus 4 is slightly more valuable than a 4/4, and a 1600 is worth more than an early 4/4, but much depends on a car's condition. An original Plus 4 Super Sports can be worth 2-3 times the value of a standard car.

Below: **A new Morgan is born! In the sunlight outside the Morgan factory at Malvern Link in Worcestershire.**

Above & Below: **A 1968 4-seater Plus 4. The spare wheel has to be more vertical than on a 2-seater, to provide room for the rear seat. A typical 2-seater Morgan rear (albeit on a Plus 8) can be seen on page 115.**

Above: **A 4/4 1600. Steel wheels are less common than wire wheels.**
Below: **The large soft-top required for a 4-seater is evident here.**

Dates:	1968-2003	Number Built:	6,233

Body/Chassis: Steel and aluminium panels on ash frame with separate steel chassis, 2-seater open sports.

Engines: Rover 3528cc (later 3.9L, 4.0L & optional 4.6L), V8 (See text).

Layout: Front engine, rear wheel drive with 4-speed (5-speed from 1976) manual gearbox.

Performance: Top speed over 120mph, 0-60mph in under 7sec.

Price Today: £££+

The mating of the traditional Morgan sports car design with the Rover (née Buick) 3.5-litre V8 engine was an inspired move by Peter Morgan. It came about because the Plus 4's use of the Triumph TR engines came to an end with the introduction of the TR5 as its 6-cylinder engine was simply too long and too high to fit under the Morgan's bonnet. An alternative had to be found and the new light-alloy Rover V8 engine appeared to meet the requirements. The development of the new car, to be called the Plus 8, was carried out by Maurice Owen and was finally launched at the 1968 London Motor Show.

The V8 had to be shoe-horned into the car, but with chassis changes it fitted. Early engines produced 160bhp (151bhp net) but over the years this power output varied, with different compression ratios (and a change of carburettors from SU to Strombergs in 1981). With the optional fuel injection (deliveries from 1984), the power output increased to a thundering 190bhp and by 1987 all Plus 8 cars were fuel injected.

When the Plus 8 was launched, Rover could not offer a suitable manual gearbox so a remote Moss gearbox was used for the first batch of cars (nearly 500). However, from 1972 Morgan was able to use the new 4-speed Rover gearbox, which became 5-speed from 1976.

The Plus 8 chassis was based on that of the Plus 4 but it had to be strengthened, lengthened (by 2 inches) and widened to suit. In fact, during the car's long production life it continued to get wider and wider, the overall car width going up from 4ft 9in to 5ft 3in by 1982. This expansion was mainly to enclose ever wider wheels, but the Plus 8's cockpit was also wider than the Plus 4's.

The Plus 8 can be readily identified by its unique alloy wheels, nose badge, wider frontage and triple wipers (though the 4/4 also had triple wipers from 1977). From the rear, two exhaust pipes are also an indication of a Plus 8 (though the first 50 or so cars had single exhausts as did cars in the late 1980s and post-1990 cars with catalytic converters).

Production Plus 8s were initially not fitted with wire wheels due to concerns about their strength. Instead they had specially cast, silver-painted, 15-inch alloy wheels. In 1977 these changed to Milrace 14-inch alloy wheels (of a different design and 0.5-inch wider) but still painted silver. From 1982 the wheels changed back to the original design (15-inch diameter again but now 6.5-inch wide) and the casting was smoother, with the Morgan company name embossed on it. (This same year, the brake servo, which had been standard from the

Above: **The launch of the Morgan Plus 8 at the 1968 London Motor Show. Note the special and distinctive alloy wheels.**

beginning, was removed). From 1993, wire wheels were available as an (expensive) option, and later there were optional 16-inch centre lock alloy wheels.

The Plus 8 had the same cockpit trim changes as the 4/4 so from 1971 the dashboard top was padded for safety and in 1977 the dash was redesigned.

From 1975-77, there were 19 special Sports Lightweight cars made with alloy bodies. But all Plus 8s are very fast cars and it is no surprise that the model has a great racing tradition.

During the 1980s and 1990s, the Plus 8 continued to be developed and improved. For instance, from 1986, rack and pinion steering became standard (it had been optional from 1984), the ash frame was treated, each panel was painted separately before assembly and the chassis was rust-proofed. In 1990, the V8 engine's capacity was increased to 3946cc (producing 190bhp), with an optional 4.6-litres (220bhp) from 1997. In 2000, a 4.0-litre V8 was introduced which produced 200bhp and featured a new ECU for cleaner emissions that allowed the car to be sold in the US.

Production of the Plus 8 eventually came to an end in 2003 due to the Rover engine being phased out as not meeting new emission regulations. By chance, the car's production ended the same year that Peter Morgan died.

Below: **A later Plus 8 with head restraints and optional centre lock wheels. Many Morgans have "MOG" registration numbers.**

Specific Checks: Start with the paperwork and check the numbers match those on the car.

As with the Plus 4 and 4/4, until 1986 the ash frame was untreated when the cars were built, so when examining a Plus 8, start by checking the wooden floor and ash frame for rot, woodworm and cracking (though the frame is mostly covered so this is difficult to check without dismantling). Open the doors wide and see if lifting them moves the body frame (not a good sign). Check also the wood at the bottom of the back panel (with the seller's permission, remove the spare wheel to gain access). Next, check the chassis for rust, repair welds and cracks (especially near the engine, steering box and suspension mountings). Pre-1986 cars are prone to rot in the corner where the front wing and the bulkhead meet. Water is trapped here and then the wood rots and the metal rusts.

The pre-1986 chassis was not rust-proofed so it tends to rust along the side rails (especially behind the rear wheels) and where the crossmembers meet the side rails.

With the bodywork, the front wings are prone to rust particularly where they are attached near the doors. Corrosion also occurs around the front wings' lips (if steel) and at most panel joints. The bulkhead is difficult to replace and can rust, so lift the floor covering to check.

Until the introduction of moulded wings in 1998, alloy wing edges were rolled over mild steel wire, leading to corrosion. Some owners have fitted GRP wings, which are lighter and do not rust but reduce the car's value.

The V8 is generally a reliable unit, but needs frequent changes to minimise wear. Common problems include worn hydraulic cam followers (indicated by tappet noise when idling) and water pump failure (indicated by a rumbling sound). When idling, the engine oil pressure is low and when driving hard it should remain constant. It should not normally lose oil.

A good Morgan requires regular oiling and greasing, particularly the sliding pillar front suspension. Neglect of this will show up as a lack of oil coating. Also, king-pin wear will be revealed in a road test if the car wanders and a clunking sound is heard on hitting a pot hole. Note that some of these cars will have been raced.

Prices Today: Post-1986 cars are better than the earlier ones while the later ones are the best, but as always, a car's value depends mainly on its condition.

Below: **Just visible is the slightly open bonnet due to extenders to assist with under-bonnet cooling. This car has the large 4.6L engine fitted.**

Above: **A Plus 8 wearing its weather equipment.**
Below: **This car has an alloy body and centre lock alloy wheels.**

Above & Below: **A 1998 car with optional 4.6L engine and optional 16in centre lock alloy wheels. Rear luggage carriers are popular.**

Dates: 1972-81 (See text).	**Number Built:** c.368

Body/Chassis: Aluminium body on steel chassis, 2-seater open sports.

Engines: Jaguar 3781-4235cc, 6-cyl in-line, dohc, 190bhp (net);
Jaguar 5343cc, V12, ohc, 272bhp (net).

Layout: Front engine, rear wheel drive, 4-speed manual (with overdrive) or 3-speed automatic gearbox.

Performance: 6-cyl: Top speed c.115mph, 0-60mph in 6-7sec;
V12: Top speed over 125mph, 0-60mph in c.6sec.

Prices Today: 6-cyl: £££/££££ V12: Contact Club.

Robert Jankel started Panther (so named by a family member) and the J72 was the first of their production cars. Its styling was reminiscent of the famous 1930s Jaguar SS100 sports car. It was therefore entirely appropriate that the J72 was Jaguar powered (and it had many other Jaguar parts too).

The early Jaguar 3.8-litre 6-cylinder engine was soon replaced by the 4.2-litre version. From 1974 there was an optional Jaguar V12 unit and an automatic gearbox could also be specified, though most cars had the 6-cylinder engines. The manual gearbox came with overdrive as standard. Fitting air cleaners on the 6-cylinder cars required a large bonnet side bulge on the driver's side, while the V12 cars required bulges on both sides for the carburettors.

These beautifully hand-made cars, expensive when new, had luxurious leather interiors with Wilton carpets. Wire wheels were standard. The large chromed headlamp units cleverly disguised smaller, modern headlamps inside (just visible in the photos on the right). Although the car looked vintage, it had modern underpinnings including all-disc brakes that were servo-assisted.

There were various improvements during the car's production life, such as increased ground clearance and in particular, in 1977, the handling was improved by fitting independent front suspension (replacing the earlier beam axle, which gave a large turning circle).

The J72 out-accelerated most of its rivals, though its non-aerodynamic shape affected its overall top speed.

In its final production year the car was renamed the "Brooklands" after the famous racing circuit nearby. Although 1981 is usually considered as the last year of production, one-offs were made into the early 1980s.

A long list of options included air-conditioning and power steering.

Specific Checks: The main areas to check are the body panels and the chassis. Check all the panels for damage, as they are no longer available. With the chassis, check for corrosion and poorly repaired accident damage. Examine all chrome work as it can deteriorate and replacements are not readily available.

Fortunately the major mechanical components – engine, gearbox and rear axle are all robust, but engine overheating can be a problem if a previous owner has

Above: **A later J72, with front-hinged doors and bonnet side bulge.**

not used sufficient antifreeze, allowing the internal waterways to corrode. The Jaguar V12 engine is so smooth that any untoward noises can indicate bad news. Some oil consumption is not abnormal on all these engines. The cost of an engine rebuild, especially the V12, is very expensive. Check also that the Jaguar rear brakes are working fully.

Prices Today: It is estimated that at least 300 of these exquisite J72 cars probably survive world-wide. The V12 version is valued more than the 6-cylinder models, as only a dozen were produced.

Above & Below: **An early Panther J72, with rear-hinged doors.**

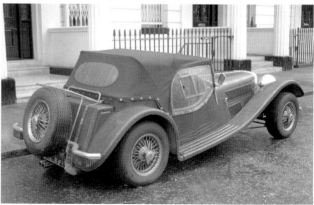

Dates:	1976-82	Number Built: c.900

Body/Chassis: GRP body on steel chassis, 2-seater open sports.

Engine: Vauxhall 2279cc, 4-cyl in-line, ohc, 108bhp (DIN).

Layout: Front engine, rear wheel drive, 4-speed manual (See text).

Performance: Top speed c.100mph, 0-60mph in c.10sec.

Price Today: £/££

Above: **A Series 1 Panther Lima with the optional bolt-on wire wheels.**

Following Panther's winning formula of creating sports cars that had a traditional look but utilised modern mechanical parts, the Lima had echoes of sports cars of the 1930s but was based on the 1970s Vauxhall Magnum car. The S1 (ie Series 1) Lima used the Magnum's 2.3-litre engine, transmission, floor pan, suspension and brakes. The Lima's floor pan was strengthened by steel box sections that also provided support for the engine, scuttle and door posts. By using the steel doors from the MG Midget, Panther cleverly overcame the usual specialist car manufacturer's problem of creating good functional doors. The shut lines were disguised by the attractive and distinctive two-tone colour scheme that was standard on the Lima.

The Lima was created with the full agreement and assistance of Vauxhall, whose dealers then sold and serviced the cars.

Although the Limas were generally well constructed and had luxury features such as leather trim, the heater was basic and there was no boot (but there was useful storage space behind the seats).

After about 600 cars had been made, came the S2 cars (ie Series 2), using a completely new, stiffer chassis, created by Panther just for the Lima. The S2 also had a revised dashboard layout, new seats (that sat lower), smaller fuel tank and plain tubular bumpers (rather than the S1's Austin Maxi units). To improve accessibility to the alternator, it was repositioned using a special bracket (that in time can shear its mounting bolts). The exhaust system on the S2 was improved by being stainless steel rather than the S1's mild steel unit.

The S1 had a distinctive "egg box" grille (as seen in the photo top right), as did some S2s (see photo lower right). Other S2s had grilles with vertical chrome bars, more reminiscent of a 1960s Jaguar grille.

Special models were also produced, including the rare "Turbo" and "Jubilee".

Although 1980 is usually considered the last year of Lima production, further cars were assembled after that date from in-stock parts. The car was eventually replaced by the Kallista in 1982. The Lima has become synonymous with Panther, a credible alternative classic.

Optional extras included wire-spoked wheels, ZF 5-speed manual gearbox or 3-speed automatic gearbox and various states of engine tuning. The distinctive front spoiler (as seen on the example right), though optional, was fitted to most Limas.

Specific Checks: On the S1, check for chassis/floor corrosion. This is generally repairable unless the centre section is corroded so badly that the doors do not open and close properly due to body sag. The S2 chassis is stronger but should be checked carefully too. With the bodywork, any glassfibre defects can be repaired by a competent GRP fabricator but on the mechanical front, some Vauxhall engine parts and running gear are becoming difficult to source.

Prices Today: It is estimated that around 400 of these cars survive in the UK and a similar number abroad. Values are very dependent on a car's condition.

Above & Below: **A Series 2 Lima with the optional front spoiler.**

Dates: 1982-91	**Number Built:** c.1,700

Body/Chassis: Aluminium body on steel chassis, 2-seater open sports.

Engines: Ford 1597cc, 4-cyl in-line, ohc, 96bhp (DIN);
Ford 2792-2933cc, V6, ohv, 135-150bhp (DIN).

Layout: Front engine, rear wheel drive, 4 or 5-speed manual gearbox, (V6: optional automatic gearbox).

Performance: 1.6: Top speed over 90mph, 0-60mph in c.12sec;
V6: Top speed c.110mph, 0-60mph in c.8sec.

Price Today: ££+

Above: **A Panther Kallista with optional "full" front spoiler.**

In 1979, the original Panther company went into receivership and was immediately purchased by the South Korean company, Jindo.

In 1982 the new Panther Car company launched the Kallista. Although it looked very similar to the earlier Lima, it was in fact a very different car and few parts were interchangeable. Whereas the Lima was Vauxhall-based, the Kallista was Ford-based and whereas the Lima used a glassfibre body with MG Midget doors, the Kallista used an aluminium body with longer steel doors (though MG door furniture was retained). Otherwise, Ford parts were used throughout.

There were two standard engine options, a Ford 1.6-litre 4-cylinder or Ford V6. The latter changed from 2.8-litre to 2.9-litre (during 1989/90) and with fuel injection gave 150bhp. Some US export models were fitted with Ford (US) 2.3-litre 4-cylinder engines.

The 1.6-litre car came initially with a 4-speed manual gearbox (and black brightwork), but later with a 5-speed gearbox. The V6 cars had 5-speed gearboxes as standard and an automatic gearbox was available as an option. The V6 cars' brightwork was all chrome.

Distribution of these cars was direct from the factory with no dealers in the UK. A handful of special models were produced, including the "Anniversary", the rare "Turbo", plus the popular "Brooklands" with its full leather interior.

The Kallista usually did not have the distinctive two-tone colour schemes of the Lima. There were also many trim differences between the two cars. Improvements included a longer cockpit (about 3 inches) and handling was helped by using longer-travel, stiffer springs and dampers. From 1987-88 a new dashboard was introduced.

Although production of this popular model ended in 1990, apparently one more car was made in 1991. A further 80 or so GRP "widebody" cars were made in Korea in the early 1990s (but these were not exported to the UK).

Optional extras included special alloy or wire wheels, two-tone paintwork, electric windows, tinted glass, air-conditioning, walnut veneer facia and leather upholstery. The Panther option list was a long one.

Specific Checks: First check the aluminium bodywork, which can dent (and is usually expensive to rectify). New body panels are hard to find. Check the paintwork carefully (eg no blistering) as a respray can be expensive.

Next check the chassis for corrosion and for any poorly repaired accident damage.

Trim items are bespoke, but most Ford spare parts are still readily available. Overall, the Kallista has become known for being a robust and reliable sports classic.

Prices Today: It is estimated that around 500 cars exist today in the UK and up to twice that number world-wide (it is especially popular in Germany, but there are also large numbers elsewhere). The 1.6-litre Kallista is slightly more valuable than a Lima and the V6 Kallista can be worth considerably more.

Robert Jankel, the founder of Panther, died in 2005.

Above & Below: **Later Kallistas have the grille design shown here. This car also has the useful optional rear luggage carrier.**

Dates: 1961-64

Numbers Built: Sabra: c.260   Sabre 4: 55   Sabre 6: 77

Body/Chassis: GRP body on steel chassis, 2-seater open sports or fixed-head coupé.

Engines: Sabra & Sabre 4: Ford 1703cc, 4-cyl in-line, ohv, 73bhp; Sabre 6: Ford 2553cc, 6-cyl in-line, ohv, 109bhp.

Layout: Front engine, rear wheel drive, 4-speed gearbox (See text).

Performance: Sabra & Sabre 4: Top c.90mph, 0-60mph in c.16sec; Sabre 6: Top speed c.110mph, 0-60mph in c.12sec.

Prices Today: Contact Club.

Above & Below: **A Reliant Sabre 4 with the later design of front end.**

In the mid-1950s, Reliant had an agreement with Autocars of Israel to supply them with vehicle kits for local assembly. In 1960 Autocars asked Reliant to develop a sports car for them, based on an attractive body by Ashley Laminates and a Leslie Ballamy-designed chassis that Autocars had seen at the 1960 London Racing Car Show. Autocars intended to build the car in Israel and export it to the US. It was to be called the Sabra, and Reliant's task was to match the body to the chassis, develop it and make the glassfibre moulds for Autocars. In fact, Reliant ended up making 208 of the cars (all for export, three-quarters to the US) plus a further 50 kits for assembly in Israel.

Reliant realised that, with modification, the car could be marketed in the UK. They developed a right-hand drive version and this was launched, as the Sabre, at the London Motor Show in 1961. The production Sabres did not have the perspex headlamp fairings of the Sabras but retained their controversial front "horn" bumpers, required apparently to meet US regulations.

The Sabre was more expensive and slower than its rivals, so Reliant produced a revised version, the SE2, with a Ford 6-cylinder engine and (after the first 17 of these cars) they also changed the front suspension to one based on the Triumph TR4. The SE2 was later called the "Sabre 6" as opposed to the 4-cylinder "Sabre 4".

In 1963 Reliant changed the front profile of the car with the "short bonnet" version, removing the horn bumpers and introducing a new wider grille. The styling was again by Eddie Pepall and the car by now had most pleasing lines. Some earlier cars were later modified by owners to take the new nose and there are no "long nose" Sabre 6 cars. The Sabras and Sabre 4 cars used the excellent ZF gearbox, while most Sabre 6 cars used a Ford gearbox with overdrive (the ZF was optional).

The first Sabras were convertibles but a fixed-head version was added later and the last ones had re-profiled wheelarches which were more attractive. Almost all Sabre 4 cars were convertibles, whereas all (except 3) Sabre 6 cars were coupés, and nominally 2+2 seaters. The Sabres enjoyed some rally successes, notably class wins in the Alpine Rally of 1963. Optional extras included a hardtop (for the Sabre 4) and wire wheels.

Specific Checks: After inspecting the paperwork, the key item to check is the condition of the chassis. Note too

that spares are becoming a problem – consult the Reliant Sabre & Scimitar Owners' Club before buying a car.

Prices Today: The Club estimates there may be as many as 50 Sabre 6 cars still in existence, but fewer Sabre 4s. The Sabre 6 is valued more than the Sabre 4, but they are difficult to value due to their rarity.

Above & Below: **A Sabre 6. Note the distinctive roof top moulding.**

Dates: 1964-70   **Number Built:** 1,005

Body/Chassis: GRP body on steel chassis, 2+2 seater coupé.

Engines: SE4: Ford 2553cc, 6-cyl in-line, ohv, 120bhp;
SE4A/B: Ford 2994cc, V6, ohv, 136bhp;
SE4C: Ford 2495cc, V6, ohv, 112bhp.

Layout: Front engine, rear wheel drive, 4-speed gearbox (See text).

Performance: SE4: Top speed over 115mph, 0-60mph in c.11sec;
SE4A/B: Top speed c.120mph, 0-60mph in c.10sec.

Price Today: Contact Club.

Above: **The Scimitar GT (above) was based closely on the Ogle SX250.**

Sales of Reliant's first sports car, the Sabre, were slower than the company had expected and so they began to think of a replacement. Fortuitously, at the London Motor Show, the Reliant management came across the Ogle SX250. This had a handsome glassfibre body by Ogle Design and used a Daimler SP250 chassis and V8 engine. The SX250 had been commissioned by a cosmetics firm, but only two cars were made, and Ogle were happy to find another customer for their design.

By good fortune, it was discovered that the body would fit the Reliant Sabre chassis with few changes. Hence the Scimitar GT Coupé was born, its body based on the SX250 and its chassis developed from the Sabre 6.

Although the Ogle SX250 and Scimitar GT look almost identical, Reliant made many subtle changes to the original car's shape – at the front the headlamp and bumpers were altered, a grille added and a Ford windscreen was used. Along the sides of the car, the crease line was altered and the rear wheelarches were rounded. At the rear, more subtle changes were made and the fuel filler cap was moved.

After about 60 Scimitars had been made, the rear suspension was changed (for the better) by introducing twin trailing arms and a transverse Watt linkage.

The original SE4 version was fitted with a ZF gearbox and 297 cars were made. The SE4 was replaced in 1966 by the SE4A, with Ford's new 3-litre V6 "Essex" engine and a Ford gearbox with optional overdrive. 539 of these SE4A cars were built. Wire wheels, originally standard, were now only an option.

The SE4B (51 built) was a 4A with minor adjustments. In 1967 the 2.5-litre version of the engine was fitted to the cheaper "economy" SE4C (only 118 made). Production of it and the SE4B were both phased out in favour of the Scimitar GTE in 1970.

Specific Checks: After the paperwork, start with the chassis and check for rust in the outriggers and where the front and rear suspension are attached – look also for cracks here. It is difficult to see key parts of the chassis but you could ask the seller if they are prepared to remove each road wheel in turn. If the main chassis (spine) rails are rusty, that is bad news. In contrast, most of the outrigger sections of the chassis can be repaired or replaced by an expert, with the body still on the chassis.

With the glassfibre body, cracks and crazing are common and require specialist repair and respray. Beware a very recent respray, for it may conceal defects which could soon resurface.

The suspension has grease nipples so check they look as if they have been greased regularly. Poor handling or oddly worn tyres may indicate suspension problems. The springs sag too – measure the space from the tyre top to the wheelarch and compare one car with another. Look also for bodged wiring, cracked electrical insulation and corroded contacts – these can lead to electrical failures and possibly a fire!

Prices Today: Currently the Scimitar GT is valued more than the later Scimitar GTE (excluding the Middlebridge GTE cars), but contact the club for more information.

Above & Below: **The Scimitar GT Coupé looks good from any angle. The design was mainly by Tom Karen of Ogle Design.**

Dates: 1968-86 and 1988-90

Numbers Built: SE5: 9,415   SE6: 4,858   Middlebridge: 77

Body/Chassis: GRP body on steel chassis, 4-seater sports estate.

Engines:
SE5/5A/6: Ford 2994cc, V6, ohv, 128bhp (138bhp from 1972);
SE6B: Ford 2792cc, V6, ohv, 135bhp;
Middlebridge: Ford 2933cc, V6, ohv, fuel injection, 150bhp.

Layout: Front engine, rear wheel drive, 4-speed manual (some with overdrive) or 3-speed automatic gearbox;
Middlebridge: 5-speed manual or 4-speed auto gearbox.

Performance: Top speed c.115-120mph, 0-60mph in under 10sec.

Prices Today: SE5-6: £+   Middlebridge: ££

Above: **A Reliant Scimitar GTE SE5A.**

Launched at the 1968 London Motor Show, the Scimitar GTE (Grand Touring Estate) was styled by Tom Karen of Ogle Design and was developed from the earlier Scimitar GT Coupé. It was not only good looking but also a remarkably practical design of sports car, incorporating innovative split rear seats and (after the first 500 cars) a rear wash/wipe. The GTE was a great success for Reliant.

Over its long production life the car was improved and updated. In late 1971 the initial SE5 model was replaced with the SE5A. This had a new facia, revised trim, raised headlamps, Dunlop steel/alloy wheels and other minor changes. In 1972 the engine was uprated and then in 1975 there was a big change with the SE6.

This new SE6 model had squarer styling, black bumpers (replacing chrome ones) and many trim and mechanical changes. It was also wider, longer and heavier than the SE5 or 5A and could be easily identified by its larger outer headlamps (in the SE5 and 5A, the headlamp pair matches). The SE6A, launched in 1976, had improved suspension and brakes and in 1980 came the SE6B with the smaller 2.8-litre Ford "Cologne" engine.

Two years after Reliant stopped making the GTE, production restarted under Middlebridge Scimitar Ltd, a new company that had acquired the manufacturing rights and tooling. The new cars incorporated several hundred changes due to the need to replace components that were no longer available, to meet Type Approval and to make various improvements. The Middlebridge Scimitar GTE came with a 5-speed manual gearbox as standard though a 4-speed auto gearbox was an optional extra. The car also had a galvanised chassis, a new design of alloy wheels, improved suspension, revised rear light clusters and it came with a high equipment specification as standard. Its bumpers were colour matched to the car's paintwork. Unfortunately only 77 cars were built before the company ceased trading.

Typical optional extras included Wolfrace alloy wheels, overdrive (standard from 1971), power steering, tinted glass, electric windows, Webasto sunroof and leather trim.

The Scimitar GTE has been popular with HRH The Princess Royal, who has owned a number of examples.

Specific Checks: After paperwork checks, examine the chassis, particularly with non-galvanised chassis cars (ie before 1984). If the main chassis (spine) rails or the tubular crossmember in front of the rear wheels is rusty, that is bad news. In contrast, most of the outrigger sections of the chassis can be repaired or replaced by an expert, with the body still on the chassis. It is difficult to see some parts but you could ask the seller if you could remove the spare wheel in order to check the nose cone support frame behind the headlights. Even galvanised chassis cars can have rust problems, often caused by poorly repaired accident damage, so check these cars carefully too.

With the glassfibre body, cracks and crazing are common and require specialist repair and then respraying. Beware a very recent respray for it may conceal defects which could soon resurface. Check too that the hinges of the rear-hatch are not rusted.

Some GTE engines tend to overheat (especially in the SE6 and 6A). Avoid cars with faulty cooling fans as the engine may have already been overheated. With all engines check for leaks.   Continued....

Below: **A Reliant Scimitar GTE SE6A, with its larger outer headlamps.**

Manual gearboxes are usually reliable but often the first sign of trouble is having it jump out of gear. Overdrives should engage without a jolt. Both Borg Warner and Ford auto boxes were used. Manual gearboxes should not leak, though automatics may do slightly.

The suspension and propshaft (on most cars) have grease nipples so check they look as if they have been greased regularly. The front suspension (which is Triumph based) is prone to wear if it has not been properly maintained and close examination of the trunnions and stub axles is recommended. Poor handling or oddly worn tyres may indicate suspension problems. The springs sag too – measure the space from the tyre top to the wheelarch and compare one car with another. There have been some problems with rear axles rusting and failing at the trailing arm/damper attachment brackets.

On older cars check for bodged wiring, cracked electrical insulation and corroded contacts – these can lead to electrical failures and possibly a fire! In addition, as with most GRP bodied cars, earthing can be a problem, so check all systems function correctly.

Note that interiors can suffer from water ingress leading to rotten carpets. Finally, check all 5 wheels actually match and are the correct size for the car.

The GTE is essentially a relatively reliable vehicle, provided it is maintained properly.

Modifications you might find include a Weber carburettor on the 2.8-litre engine, replacing the less reliable Solex units and the use of non-standard (larger) batteries.

Prices Today: Most GTEs remained in the UK but LHD versions were available. These mainly went to Europe with only a handful going to North America. Today the Middlebridge cars are valued considerably more than the earlier cars, which are probably undervalued.

Photo Top Right: **The characteristic rear-hatch of the GTE.**
2nd From Top: **A Middlebridge GTE.**
3rd From Top: **This nice side view shows the timeless lines of the GTE.**
Lower Right: **The cockpit of a Middlebridge GTE.**
Below: **The two-tone colour schemes were popular as were the optional Wolfrace alloy wheels.**

Dates:	1980-86	Number Built:	442

Body/Chassis: GRP body on steel chassis, 4-seater open sports.

Engine: Ford 2792cc, V6, ohv, 135bhp.

Layout: Front engine, rear wheel drive, 4-speed manual (with overdrive) or 3-speed automatic gearbox.

Performance: Top speed c.115mph, 0-60mph in under 10sec.

Price Today: ££

Above: **From the front, the Reliant Scimitar GTC's connection with the GTE is obvious as the body was the same from the B-pillar forward.**

The Scimitar GTC (Grand Touring Convertible) was styled by Ogle Design and was developed from the earlier Scimitar GTE. To create the GTC, Ogle removed the roof from a GTE, retained the front of the car (to the B-pillar behind the doors) then added a new rear end, incorporating a large boot. The boot could take a useful 6.5 cubic feet of luggage, and the car retained the GTE's facility to fold down the rear seat backs which, when the divider between the boot and the car's interior was removed, greatly increased the boot's capacity. The prominent T-bar provided structural stiffness and acted as a roll-over bar. There was also structural strengthening around the scuttle area and behind the rear seats.

Known by Reliant as the SE8B (the prototype was the one and only SE8 car), the GTC was available with either a 4-speed manual gearbox (with overdrive as standard) or 3-speed automatic. Production of the GTC cars ran concurrently with the GTE.

With the earlier demise of the Triumph Stag, there was a ready market niche for the new car, and it had good press reviews. Unfortunately it was launched at the time of an economic recession and, sadly, only 442 cars were made. When Middlebridge Scimitar Ltd bought the rights to the Scimitar, they intended to reintroduce the GTC but that plan did not materialise before Middlebridge ceased trading.

Typical optional extras included electric windows, tinted glass, power steering and hardtop.

Specific Checks: As the GTC is mechanically similar to its contemporary, the GTE SE6B model, please refer to that entry for specific checks. However, note the interior trim aft of the B-pillar is unique to the GTC, as is the boot area trim. There is limited availability of these items so check it is all there and in an acceptable condition.

In addition, with the GTC, check the soft-top roof for condition and fit, in particular where the front rail of the roof frame closes onto the top of the windscreen frame. The clamps should be in sound condition and should achieve a firm fit. If it is not secure there is the possibility of the roof detaching from the body. A poor seal here will let in rainwater and cause significant wind noise. The fit of the soft-top roof to the B-pillars should also be checked as worn Velcro here can lead to the roof material blowing away from the car. Dulled plastic in the rear and side windows of the soft-top roof will be instantly obvious. The roof frame and canvas straps between frame sections should be checked for wear and also possible cracks in the frame. If the car has the optional hardtop this should be inspected for condition and the fit of the

rear glass screen. If it is in sound condition ensure that the full fitting kit is available and also check if the heated rear screen still works. Being a convertible, interiors can suffer from water ingress leading to rotten carpets and damage to seats and trim.

For modifications you might find today, refer to the Scimitar GTE entry.

Prices Today: GTCs are valued higher than comparable GTEs. Possibly around 200 GTCs survive today. Note that some GTEs have been made into convertibles – check the chassis number and then contact the Reliant Sabre & Scimitar Owners' Club for verification.

Above: **A Triumph Stag-style roof T-bar was used with the GTC.**
Below: **The GTC's luxury interior.**

Left: **The Singer Roadster featured cutaway doors, sidescreens and a fold-flat windscreen. This is a 4AD.**

Right: **The lovely sweeping rear of the Roadster. This is a 4AB.**

Left: **The Sunbeam Alpine styling was developed by Loewy Studios from the 90 saloon. This is a MkI car.**

Right: **The spare wheel had its own access panel behind the number plate.**

Dates: 1939-55   **Number Built:** c.11,940
Body/Chassis: Alloy and steel panels on ash frame with separate steel chassis, 4-seater open sports.
Engines: 1074cc, 4-cyl in-line, ohc, 36bhp;
1497cc, 4-cyl in-line, ohc, 48-58bhp.
Layout: Front engine, RWD, 3-speed (later 4-speed) manual.
Performance: 65-80mph, 0-60 in c.25-20sec. **Price Today:** ££

Dates: 1953-55   **Number Built:** c.3,000
Body/Chassis: Steel body & separate chassis, 2-seater open sports.
Engine: 2267cc, 4-cyl in-line, ohv, 80bhp.
Layout: Front engine, RWD, 4-speed manual (some with overdrive).
Performance: Over 95mph, 0-60 in c.18sec. **Price Today:** £££

The Singer Nine Roadster was launched in 1939 but production was stopped during WW2. In 1946 it was reintroduced with various improvements.

The Series 4A cars (from 1949) had 4-speed gearboxes but looked the same as the earlier model. Then in late 1950 came the 4AB with a number of technical improvements including independent front suspension (by coil spring and wishbone), and a hydro-mechanical braking system with 9-inch drums, greatly improving stopping power. The turning circle was reduced to 33ft. The 4AB, with its shorter radiator grille, cutaway wings and slotted disc wheels, updated the Roadster's styling and 1,000 of this series were made 1951-52. About half were exported.

Only 13 of the following 4AC development cars were built (with 1.2-litre engines) before the Series 4AD cars were launched in 1951. The 4AD is officially known as the Singer SM Roadster as it had the 1.5-litre short-stroke engine from Singer's SM 1500 saloon car. Externally the 4AD was indistinguishable from the last 250 4ABs which ran in parallel production. The 4AD was originally only for export, but in 1953 UK sales started. There were 3,440 4ADs made, of which perhaps about one third were a twin carbs version known as the 4ADT. Some 4AD cars were dealer upgraded to 4ADT specification.

Specific Checks: First check the paperwork and ensure the car's numbers match. The chassis was made from heavy-gauge steel and generally resists corrosion well. The ash frame rots but replacement frames are available.

Prices Today: Over 1,000 cars are thought to survive world-wide, mostly in the UK but also in Australia, New Zealand, the Netherlands and the US. The 4AD is worth around 20-25% more than a 4AB, while earlier cars are worth perhaps a similar amount less than a 4AB.

The Alpine was developed from the Sunbeam-Talbot 90 saloon, which had been styled by Ted White. The new car was named after the company's recent Alpine Rally successes. While similar to the 90 at the front, the good-looking Alpine had a louvred bonnet, a large rear "deck" and a graceful tail. Sidescreens were required.

A stiffened version of the 90 saloon's chassis was used, together with a stiffer front suspension, more direct steering, a new cylinder head to give more power and altered gearbox ratios. As the car was aimed at the North American market, it had a steering-column gearchange (though some cars have since been modified with a floor change). Drum brakes were fitted all round. The optional overdrive became standard from late 1954.

In 1953, a specially tuned version attained a speed of just over 120mph at Jabbeke in Belgium.

There were two Marks of car, the MkI and the MkIII (there was no MkII) and a rare, factory-tuned, Alpine Special, which looked identical but had an "S" suffix in its chassis number. The differences between the two Marks are minor, for example, indicators (not trafficators) on the MkIII, different bumpers and standard rev counter. The Alpine is visually similar to the 90 drophead coupé (but that has a quite different rear and is a 4-seater).

Specific Checks: First, check the bodywork and chassis very carefully, especially the bottom of the bulkhead, the A and B-posts, sills, double-skin rear wheelarches and rear spring hangers. Next inspect the soft-top and its frame carefully then (with the owner's help) raise and lower the soft-top to check it operates correctly. The engines are sturdy but original gearboxes are weak.

Prices Today: The Sunbeam Talbot Alpine Register estimates that around 300 Alpines survive world-wide. There is no price difference between a MkI and a MkIII, but a Special may command about 25-30% more.

Dates:	1959-68	Number Built:	c.69,250

Body/Chassis: Steel unitary, 2-seater open sports (See text).

Engines:
Series I: 1494cc, 4-cyl in-line, ohv, 78bhp (84bhp gross);
Series II: 1592cc, 4-cyl in-line, ohv, 80bhp (86bhp gross);
Series III-IV: 1592cc, 4-cyl in-line, ohv, 82bhp (88bhp gross);
Series V: 1725cc, 4-cyl in-line, ohv, 92bhp net.

Layout: Front engine, rear wheel drive, 4-speed manual (optional overdrive) or 3-speed automatic gearbox (Series IV only).

Performance: Top speed 95-100mph, 0-60mph in 13-15sec.

Price Today: ££

Above: **The good-looking Sunbeam Alpine. This is a Series III car, with non-standard, but period, alloy wheels.**

This was the second "Sunbeam Alpine", the first being the 1953 model (see opposite). To create the new Alpine, parts were cleverly combined from other models, with an attractive open sports body styled by Kenneth Howes. The early design of unitary construction employed in the Alpine had the bodywork stiffened by a substantial cruciform box section, together with chassis legs extending to both front and rear.

The 1.5-litre engine had a new aluminium cylinder head designed for this application.

The Alpine was a comfortable and practical vehicle, which had been well developed. It had a soft ride, good interior and used wind-up windows (ahead of its main rivals).

There were five Series of these Alpines. After c.11,900 Series I cars had been made, there came the Series II in late 1960. These had a larger engine, also improved suspension and c.19,950 were built. The Series III (from 1963) improved the suspension further, including telescopic rear dampers. They also had twin fuel tanks in the tail fins (thereby increasing both fuel capacity and boot space), an adjustable steering column, reclining seats, a revised windscreen, fixed quarter light door windows and servo-assisted brakes became standard. Later cars had the twin Zenith carbs replaced by a single Solex. There were c.5,900 Series III cars made.

Visually the Series IV (1964-65) and later Series V Alpines are easy to distinguish from earlier cars due to the cropping of the tail fins and a single bar front grille. From late 1964, Alpines had an all-synchromesh gearbox (and are sometimes known as Series IVa vehicles). Including the IVa, c.12,400 Series IV cars were made.

In 1965 came the Series V with a 1725cc engine with five bearing crankshaft, twin Stromberg carbs and alternator. Body panel corners were squared off. The Series V also had footwell ventilation. The very last cars carried Chrysler badges and their headlamp cowls were not "hooded". Production ended in January 1968 with c.19,100 of the Series V cars built, marking the end of Sunbeam sports car manufacture.

The Series I-IV cars had steel bins to store the soft-top roof. The Series V had instead a fixed rear panel and small tonneau for the soft-top roof stowage.

Options included overdrive (desirable today), wire wheels, heater, detachable hardtop (aluminium in early cars, then a squarer steel design from the Series III onwards) and on the Series IV only, a 3-speed Borg-Warner automatic gearbox (only a handful being left in the UK today). From the Series III, two models were available, the Sports Tourer and the GT. The latter was in effect an options package that included a steel hardtop but no soft-top, a wood veneer dashboard, heater, carpets and slightly more room in the back (as there was no soft-top to store there). The Series III GT also had a quieter, cast iron, exhaust manifold, detuning the engine to 77bhp.

The Harrington Alpines (1961-64) are rare and sought after variants created by Thomas Harrington Ltd, specialist coachbuilders. The cars had a new permanent glassfibre roof added to the car. The first Harrington Alpines were based on the Series II cars and featured a nicely styled permanent fastback roof, fixed rear window and a small boot lid. About 110 were made. The more numerous Harrington Le Mans (about 250 made) were mainly exported to the US. These cars featured a completely different design of roof and restyled rear complete with opening tailgate and were again based on Series II cars. Finally, a further dozen or so were made using Series III/IV cars, again with opening tailgates. Most Harringtons were available with different states of Hartwell engine tuning. Continued....

Below: **The fins show this car to be pre-Series IV, and the fixed quarter-lights denote a Series III. Wire wheels were an extra.**

Specific Checks: After examining the paperwork, move on to check the car.

The condition of the body/chassis unit is critical. Rust is the main enemy as are poorly done accident repairs or bodged renovation. First examine the gap between the doors and the surrounding panels. A door that has sagged could simply require new hinges, but a door that is tight at the top of its opening edge may indicate a sagging body. Ask the seller to jack up the car using its original jacking points and watch the shut lines around the door – they should not change and the doors should open and shut readily. This is a good test.

The complex 3-section sills provide significant strength to the overall structure. Check them carefully and inspect the seal at the rear of the front wheelarches as that is where water gets into the sills. Sill replacement can cost £1,000 or more per side as it usually involves repairs to the A-post, front bulkhead and floors. This work requires removal of lower portions of the front and rear wings.

Other areas particularly prone to rust include the scuttle in front of the windscreen, the floorpan, the battery area, doors, around the headlights, the boot floor and the rear spring attachment areas. Replacement panels are generally still available.

The Alpine's engine, gearbox and rear axle are all relatively robust, but the engine can blow a head gasket due to problems with the alloy cylinder head. Most mechanical parts are available, though some may be challenging to locate, as are some trim items.

Series I to III cars have grease nipples on their front suspension that require greasing every 1,000 miles (plus lots of grease nipples elsewhere too). Failure to do this results in premature wear and some components are difficult to find today. Later cars had Metalastik bushes. On a test drive the steering should be light and precise and the car should be relatively free from rattles.

Prices Today: The Sunbeam Alpine Owners' Club knows of approximately 1,300 Alpines in the UK which are either in use or under restoration. In terms of value, the Harringtons command a small premium, while the GTs are less desirable and sell for slightly less than the open top cars. Note that many GTs have been converted to open top cars with soft-top roofs, but these modifications should be done correctly, ideally using components possibly from a scrapped car. Contact the club for help in ascertaining just what you are buying!

Below: **The comfortable cockpit of an Alpine.**

Above: **A 1962 C-Type Harrington.**
Below: **Rear fins were a feature of the Series I to III cars.**

Above: **A Series V car with standard wheels.**
Below: **The Series IV and V cars had cropped rear fins.**

Dates: 1964-67

Numbers Built: MkI: c.6,550   MkII: 535

Body/Chassis: Steel unitary, 2-seater open sports.

Engines: Mk I: Ford 4.2-litre (260 cubic inch), V8, ohv, 164bhp;
MkII: Ford 4.7-litre (289 cubic inch), V8, ohv, 200bhp.

Layout: Front engine, rear wheel drive, 4-speed manual gearbox.

Performance: Top speed c.120mph, 0-60mph in 9sec (MkII: 7.5sec).

Prices Today: MkI: £££   MkII: Contact Club.

Above: **A Mark I Sunbeam Tiger with steel hardtop and steel wheels.**
Below: **A Mark I Sunbeam Tiger with soft-top (and non-standard alloys).**

Take one Sunbeam Alpine body, add one big American Ford V8 engine and gearbox, make some changes to steering and suspension .... and you have a remarkably potent sports car – the Sunbeam Tiger. The idea came from Ian Garrad, Rootes' US West Coast manager and the first prototype was built by Carroll Shelby (of Cobra fame), then tested in secret by racing driver Ken Miles. Once Lord Rootes (who was head of the Rootes Group that included Sunbeam) approved the new car, its production was subcontracted to Jensen Motors. The Tiger was finally unveiled to the public at the 1964 International Auto Show in New York.

The Mark I Tiger was based on the Series IV Alpine, the only external differences being the discrete badges and a thin stainless steel side strip – a real "Q-car"! Beneath the skin, changes included rack and pinion steering (necessary to accommodate the new engine), stiffer suspension and a tougher Salisbury rear axle with a Panhard rod to help locate it. Surprisingly, the brakes remained unchanged.

During 1965 Rootes rationalised and computerised their systems of chassis numbering. In the case of the Tiger this coincided with some minor changes to the body and interior as the car was now based on the Series V Alpine body tub. These Tigers are sometimes referred to as Mark IA cars and feature footwell ventilation, and their soft-top hood stowage is different to the earlier cars.

After c.6,550 Mark I (and IA) cars were made, Rootes introduced the Mark II in January 1967. This had a larger 289 cubic inch Ford Mustang engine, a distinctive crosshatch grille, prominent side stripes (rather than stainless side strips), and their headlight cowls were not "hooded". 535 of these desirable cars were made. The Mark II was not marketed in the UK, though six production RHD cars were sold to the Police and four more slipped out into the hands of favoured dealers.

Optional extras available for the Tiger included a detachable steel hardtop. Hardtops were in body colour when ordered with a car but supplied in black when purchased separately.

Jensen also evaluated an advanced prototype Tiger with disc brakes all round and larger 5-stud 14in wheels. A 3-speed Ford automatic was also tested, but none of this went into production, mainly due to likely costs making the car too expensive.

Production of the Tiger ended in June 1967 after the Rootes Group were fully taken over by Chrysler, who

Above: **From this angle, little distinguishes a Tiger from an Alpine.**
Below: **This particular car is the final pre-production prototype and was used to test knock-on wire wheels (which were not put into production).**

among other things did not like a car that used a rival's powerplant. Chrysler did, however, try to install their 4.5-litre Valiant engine but the rear siting of its distributor fouled the scuttle.

In total, only about 875 Tigers were sold in the UK, the rest being exported, mainly to the US and Canada.

Specific Checks: First inspect the paperwork, then later contact the Sunbeam Tiger Owners' Club to establish the car's authenticity.

In terms of checking the vehicle itself, as the Tiger shares the same body/chassis as the later Alpines, not surprisingly the initial checks are the same.

The condition of the body/chassis unit is critical. Rust is the main enemy as are poorly done accident repairs or bodged renovation. First examine the gap between the doors and the surrounding panels. A door that has sagged could simply require new hinges, but a door that is tight at the top of its opening edge may indicate a sagging body. Ask the seller to jack up the car using its original jacking points and watch the shut lines around the door – they should not change and the doors should open and shut readily. This is a good test.

The complex 3-section sills provide significant strength to the overall structure. Check them carefully and inspect the seal at the rear of the front wheelarches as that is where water gets into the sills. Sill replacement can cost £1,000 or more per side as it usually involves repairs to the A-post, front bulkhead and floors. This work requires removal of lower portions of the front and rear wings.

Other areas particularly prone to rust include the scuttle in front of the windscreen, the floorpan, the battery area, doors, around the headlights, the boot floor and the rear spring attachment areas. Replacement panels are generally still available.

The compact Ford V8 engines are used in a relatively low state of tune which helps their reliability. However, overheating can be a problem in the Tiger's installation, so check the temperatures carefully during a test drive. An electric cooling fan can help. Gearboxes and rear axles are relatively robust.

Modifications you are likely to find include the transplant of the 289 unit into MkI cars due to the far greater availability of that engine. Many enthusiasts have also uprated braking and suspension components. Some have fitted 5 or 6-speed gearboxes and lower axle ratios, but ideally all modifications are done on the basis that the car should look outwardly standard. Modern tyre technology combined with modest suspension tweaks can make for more stable handling.

Prices Today: The Sunbeam Tiger Owners' Club estimates there are just over 600 MkI Tigers in the UK today, including re-imports. The worldwide survival rate is possibly over 60%. Factory specification "standard" Tigers are now more sought after than modified hot rod versions. The rare MkII cars, with less than 25 in the UK, can cost almost double the MkI cars.

Above & Below: **More Mark I Tigers. Minilite alloy wheels are common.**

Above: **All Tigers have cropped tail fins. This car also has a hardtop.**
Below: **A very rare RHD Mark II (in fact this is the last one made).**

Dates:	1953-55	Number Built:	c.8,600

Body/Chassis: Steel body with separate steel chassis, 2-seater open sports.

Engine: 1991cc, 4-cyl in-line, ohv, 90bhp.

Layout: Front engine, rear wheel drive, 4-speed manual gearbox (with optional overdrive).

Performance: Top speed c.105mph, 0-60mph in c.12sec.

Price Today: £££

Above: **A "long-door" early Triumph TR2 with soft-top and side screens in place. Wire wheels were a popular option.**

The unofficial title "TR1" ("TR" for "Triumph Roadster") is sometimes given to the Triumph sports car prototype, designed by Walter Belgrove, which appeared at the 1952 London Motor Show. However, the first actual production TR, the TR2, was launched at the Geneva Motor Show in 1953.

The TR2 was developed from the earlier show car, and Ken Richardson is the man usually credited with being responsible for its development. Other engineers were also involved, such as Harry Webster, who was a chassis design engineer, and Lewis Dawtrey, who later designed the engines for the Triumph Stag, Dolomite and TR7.

The new car had a distinctive recessed grille with prominent headlamps and flowing lines with traditional deeply cutaway doors, utilising sidescreens rather than wind-up side windows. The TR2 not only looked good, but it was also affordable, pleasant to drive, frugal and fast. In fact, in 1953 Ken Richardson took a prototype TR2 down the Jabbeke highway in Belgium at an astonishing 124mph. This car had various aerodynamic aids, such as a full length undershield, metal tonneau cover, rear wheel spats and a small racing screen.

The TR2 was also rallied, including coming 1st and 2nd in the 1954 RAC Rally, the first of many successes which helped to publicise the new car. Not surprisingly, sales far exceeded the company's expectations. Around two-thirds of the cars that were made were exported to North America.

In 1954 came the "short-door" cars which had the bottom of the doors raised to prevent them hitting kerbs when opened and the new sills helped to strengthen the body. In the last year of production (1955) the rear drum brakes were increased in size.

Optional extras included wire wheels and overdrive (initially only on top gear, but later on 2nd, 3rd and top giving seven usable forward speeds).

Specific Checks: Some early TRs have had identity changes with different TR model bodies being fitted, so the first check is to ensure that the car you are inspecting is indeed a genuine TR2. The key to answering this important question is to check the commission and engine numbers. The car's commission number (which is equivalent to a VIN) for the TR2/3/3A starts TS (although cars assembled abroad may differ). This

Below: **The distinctive recessed grille identifies a TR2. Note the engine starting handle guide hole in the intake recess.**

Below: **A later "short-door" car with the standard steel wheels.**

number is found on a plate on the front bulkhead in the engine compartment. There are also two other numbers found above the battery box, and which relate to the body itself. Check the commission and engine numbers on the vehicle match the paperwork, then later (if there is no Heritage Certificate) contact the Heritage Motor Centre Archives at Gaydon to verify the car's authenticity. This information will also reveal if the vehicle has been converted from LHD to RHD.

As with most cars of this period, rust is the big problem. In the case of early TRs this is compounded by a rainwater drainage design which takes water from the bulkhead/scuttle area down between panels and out through a drainhole. These get blocked and corrosion results. A similar drainage problem exists with the boot. Most cars should have been modified with plumbing that drains the rainwater more reliably. In general, with the TR2, typical body rust areas include the sills, floor pan, wheelarches and spare wheel well, but remember the inner panels which are difficult to see. Check also for poor restoration or accident repairs.

Due to the separate chassis design, check the chassis condition for corrosion and badly repaired accident damage. In particular, inspect the jacking points (or anywhere else where a car may have been jacked up incorrectly), suspension attachments and chassis outriggers.

Mechanically these cars are fundamentally sturdy and reliable, but check the engine for oil leaks from the timing cover and from the rear of the crankshaft (they all have a tendency to do this but it should not be excessive). The lack of synchromesh on 1st gear can lead to gear teeth failure so check that during the test drive. Watch out for oil leaks from the gearbox, for if it runs dry – it's bad news!

Typical modifications include the steering replaced by a rack and pinion unit, the addition of front disc brakes, suspension improvements and the fitting of an auxiliary fan to aid engine cooling. The last item is particularly relevant if unleaded fuel is used as this causes the engine to run hotter. Many cars have also had a new unleaded conversion cylinder head fitted. Finally, some cars have been fitted with the later TR3 two box silencer system to quieten the exhaust note.

Prices Today: About 500 cars are known to the DVLA in the UK but there may be more that were laid up before 1998. In terms of value, a TR2 is one of the more valuable TRs, assuming it is in near original condition. Cars converted from LHD are valued slightly less and those which are still LHD are worth less still.

Photo Top Right: **Sidescreens in place - a useful touring configuration.**
2nd From Top: **This side view illustrates the deeply cutaway doors and the car's nice sweeping lines.**
3rd From Top: **This view shows the small rear bumpers.**
Lower Right: **The interior of a TR2.**

Dates: 1955-62

Numbers Built: TR3: c.13,400   TR3A: c.58,200   TR3B: c.3,300

Body/Chassis: Steel body with separate steel chassis, 2-seater open sports.

Engine: 1991cc, 4-cyl in-line, ohv, 95-100bhp; From 1959 (optional): 2138cc, 4-cyl in-line, ohv, 100bhp.

Layout: Front engine, rear wheel drive, 4-speed manual gearbox (with optional overdrive).

Performance: Top speed c.105mph, 0-60mph in c.12sec.

Price Today: £££

Above: **The grille on the Triumph TR3 was located at the front of the air intake, unlike the grille on the earlier TR2 that was at the intake's rear.**

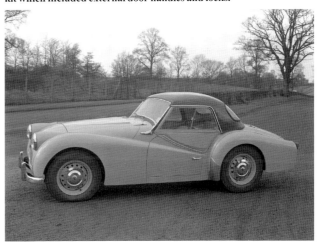

Below: **A TR3 with steel hardtop, part of the "Grand Touring" conversion kit which included external door handles and locks.**

Starting a tradition that went on until the TR6, Triumph created a new TR model by cleverly adapting an earlier one. In the case of the TR3, it was basically a TR2 with a new "egg-crate" grille and larger carburettors to give a bit more power. The next year saw disc brakes fitted to the front – an innovation on a mass-produced sports car. A second silencer was also fitted (for quietness) and the rear axle was strengthened.

In 1957 came a revised model unofficially, though widely, referred to as the TR3A. It had a full width grille and those big headlamps were slightly recessed, rather than protruding. In addition, there were external door handles as standard for the first time on a TR. In 1959 the body panel tooling was altered and there were many minor changes (of particular relevance when restoring a car). From mid-1959 buyers could specify the optional 2138cc engine.

In 1962, the TR3B (again, an unofficial title) was built specifically for export to North America at the request of dealers there who were concerned that deliveries of the new TR4 were too slow. They also thought that there was still a market for a more traditional sports car. Initially the cars had the same specification as the TR3A but later ones had the optional 2138cc engine and the same all-synchromesh gearbox as fitted to the new TR4.

Optional extras included wire wheels, overdrive, hardtop and leather trim.

Over 90% of the TR3/3A cars were exported, as were all the TR3B cars. In addition, cars were assembled in Australia (approximately 120 cars), Belgium, Ireland, the Philippines, Rhodesia (now Zimbabwe) and South Africa.

Specific Checks: Some early TRs have had identity changes with different TR model bodies being fitted, so the first check is to ensure that the car is indeed a genuine TR3, TR3A or TR3B. The key to answering this important question is the commission and engine numbers. The car's commission number (equivalent to a VIN) for the TR2/3/3A starts TS (although cars assembled abroad may differ and the TR3B starts TSF for the 1991cc engine or TCF for the 2138cc version). This number is found on a plate on the front bulkhead in the engine compartment. There are also two other numbers found above the

Below: **The grille on the TR3A is full width, the headlamps are slightly recessed and there are external door handles. This car also has the optional hardtop fitted and extra driving lights.**

battery box and which relate to the body itself. Engine numbers for the TR3 and TR3A should normally start TS and end in E, but if a 2138cc engine has been fitted it will start CT. Any other prefix should be regarded with suspicion as it may have come from another model. Check the commission and engine numbers on the vehicle match the paperwork, then later (if there is no Heritage Certificate) contact the Heritage Motor Centre Archives at Gaydon to verify the car's authenticity. This data will also reveal if the vehicle has been converted from LHD to RHD.

As with most cars of this period, rust is the big problem. In the case of early TRs this is compounded by a rainwater drainage design which takes water from the bulkhead/scuttle area down between panels and out through a drainhole. These get blocked and corrosion results. A similar drainage problem exists with the boot. Most cars should have been modified with plumbing that drains the rainwater more reliably. In general, with the TR3 series, typical body rust areas include the sills, floor pan, wheelarches and spare wheel well, but remember the inner panels which are difficult to see. Check also for poor restoration or accident repairs.

Due to the separate chassis design, check the chassis condition for corrosion and badly repaired accident damage. In particular, inspect the jacking points (or anywhere else where a car may have been jacked up incorrectly), suspension attachments and chassis outriggers.

Mechanically these cars are fundamentally sturdy and reliable, but check the engine for oil leaks from the timing cover and from the rear of the crankshaft (they all have a tendency to do this but it should not be excessive). The lack of synchromesh on 1st gear can lead to gear teeth failure so check that during the test drive. Watch out for oil leaks from the gearbox, for if it runs dry – it's bad news!

Typical modifications found today include the steering replaced by a rack and pinion unit, the addition of front disc brakes on the early cars, suspension improvements and the fitting of an auxiliary fan to aid engine cooling. The last item is particularly relevant if unleaded fuel is used as this causes the engine to run hotter. Many cars have also had a new unleaded conversion cylinder head fitted.

Prices Today: About 900 cars are known to the DVLA in the UK but there may be more that were laid up before 1998. In terms of value, a TR3/3A is one of the more valuable TRs, assuming it is in near original condition. Cars converted from LHD are valued slightly less and those which are still LHD are worth less still.

Top Right: **A TR3A with sidescreens in place.**
2nd From Top: **A TR3A with sidescreens removed.**
3rd From Top: **A US-spec car with full weather equipment in place.**
Lower Right: **The interior of a TR3 (with non-standard steering wheel).**

Dates: 1961-67

Numbers Built: TR4: c.40,250   TR4A: c.28,500

Body/Chassis: Steel body with separate steel chassis, 2-seater open sports (in 2 versions - See text).

Engine: 2138cc, 4-cyl in-line, ohv, 100-104bhp (TR4A: 104bhp).

Layout: Front engine, rear wheel drive, 4-speed manual gearbox (with optional overdrive).

Performance: Top speed c.105-110mph, 0-60mph in c.11sec.

Price Today: £££

Above: **A Triumph TR4 with the optional wire wheels.**

After much deliberation, Triumph launched their replacement for the earlier "sidescreen" TR sports cars at the 1961 London Motor Show. The new Michelotti styled body was very modern and both longer and wider than its predecessor. Though outwardly the new TR4 looked completely different, mechanically the car owed much to the TR3A. But there were important improvements – the steering had become more precise with rack and pinion, there was a collapsible steering column and the new gearbox was all-synchromesh. The interior was several inches wider and more spacious, as was the boot. There was also innovative face-level ventilation and wind-up windows (to the horror of many traditional TR owners who preferred sidescreens).

The car was available in two versions – a roadster with folding soft-top roof, or a coupé with a permanent rear screen and a removable hard roof. This hard roof (which did not fit in the boot) could be replaced by a vinyl piece that rolled up and could be stowed in the boot. The vinyl piece was called a "Surrey Top", though the whole roof is sometimes called that today.

Initially the engines were fitted with SU carburettors but later ones had Strombergs plus reworked cylinder heads and improved inlet manifolds that pushed the power up to 104bhp. SU carbs reappeared about half way through the TR4A production. Although the 2138cc engine was now standard, the earlier 1991cc engine was used on a few cars, especially those exported to Japan.

During the car's production, there were many detail changes and improvements involving items such as seats, steering, suspension, radiator and bonnet design.

In 1965, in response to some adverse comments regarding the ride and difficulty in putting up the soft-top roof, came the TR4A. Its new soft-top, with a scissor-frame, was easy to put up but took more space when folded down. The car also had a completely new chassis with independent rear suspension (IRS) which was softer. In addition it had a modified grille and the front sidelights were faired into a chrome trim strip on each wing. The interior was revised and the white painted dashboard was replaced by a polished mahogany veneer unit (as seen on late US-spec TR4 cars). There were other minor improvements too, and at the insistence of their American distributors, cars for the US could have an alternative live rear-axle rather than IRS.   Continued....

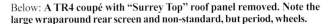

Below: **A TR4 coupé with "Surrey Top" roof panel removed. Note the large wraparound rear screen and non-standard, but period, wheels.**

Below: **A TR4 with soft-top roof in place. This photo nicely illustrates Michelotti's elegant lines.**

Options included wire wheels, overdrive, hardtop, leather seat facings and brake servo.

As with earlier TRs, over 90% of these cars were exported. In addition, CKD (Completely Knocked Down) kits were assembled abroad (including Belgium and Ireland).

Specific Checks: First be sure that the car is a genuine TR4 or TR4A. The commission numbers for the TR4 and TR4A (live axle model) start CT, while the TR4A (IRS model) starts CTC and will include an "L" for LHD and "O" for overdrive. Check the commission and engine numbers on the vehicle match the paperwork, then later (if there is no Heritage Certificate) contact the Heritage Motor Centre Archives at Gaydon to verify the car's authenticity.

As with most steel cars of this period, rust is the big problem. In general, with the TR4 & TR4A, typical body rust areas include the sills, floor pan, wheelarches and spare wheel well, but remember the inner panels which are difficult to see. Check the panels also for poor restoration or accident repairs.

Due to the separate chassis design, check the chassis condition for corrosion and badly repaired accident damage (eg open the bonnet and look for buckling of the chassis rails). In particular, inspect the suspension attachments, differential mountings and the chassis outriggers. Also look for damage caused by clumsy jacking. On the TR4A, the IRS suspension attachment area is a known rust area. Check also the integrity of the front suspension.

Mechanically these cars are fundamentally sturdy and reliable, but check the engine for oil leaks from the timing cover and from the rear of the crankshaft (they all have a tendency to this but it should not be excessive).

Typical modifications include an unleaded cylinder head conversion, wooden dashboards on early TR4 cars and a replacement electric fan to aid engine cooling. The last item is particularly relevant if unleaded fuel is used as this causes the engine to run hotter.

Prices Today: Re-imported LHD cars are valued slightly less than original RHD versions. The Dove carries a small premium in value.

Photo Top Right: **A left-hand drive Triumph TR4.**
2nd From Top: **A TR4A. Note the front sidelights were faired into the front of the wing chrome strips, and the grille is slightly different.**
3rd From Top: **A very rare derivative was the 2+2 seater Dove GTR4 fixed-head coupé. The conversion was by Thomas Harrington Ltd and about 40 or so were made. The car shown is the last known TR4-based one, though there were a few TR4A-based cars too.**
Lower Right: **The interior of an export TR4.**

Dates: 1967-68

Numbers Built: TR5: c.3,000   TR250: c.8,500

Body/Chassis: Steel body with separate steel chassis, 2-seater open sports (in 2 versions - See text).

Engine: 2498cc, 6-cyl in-line, ohv, fuel injection, 150bhp gross; TR250: twin carbs, 104-105bhp.

Layout: Front engine, rear wheel drive, 4-speed manual gearbox (with optional overdrive).

Performance: TR5: Top speed c.120mph, 0-60mph in c.9sec; TR250: Top speed 105+mph, 0-60mph under 11sec.

Price Today: TR5: £££+   TR250: ££+

Above: **The Triumph TR5 had a completely different engine to the TR4A but the car looked confusingly similar. The wire wheels were an option - the standard fit was steel wheels with Rostyle trims.**

The TR5 was the first 6-cylinder TR and the first to have fuel injection. The need for the new engine was partly to achieve the higher performance requested by European customers who wanted to make the most of the new motorway network on the Continent.

The TR5 was a short-run interim model using the body and chassis of the earlier TR4A (with some detail changes) but incorporating the lusty and smooth 6-cylinder engine due to be used in the later TR6. In fact, the car was originally going to be called the TR4B. The TR5 was the first mass-produced sports car to use fuel injection (or PI – Petrol Injection, as it was then known). In contrast, the TR250 (the US market version) had twin Stromberg carburettors, producing a third less power. This was because the fuel injected version could not meet US emission standards. The TR250 could usually be easily identified by bold racing stripes that ran across the front of the car's bonnet and wings.

The rear axle was stronger than the TR4A and to stop these one-ton high-speed projectiles, the brakes (disc/drum) were now servo-assisted, but the steering was not powered.

The car was available in two versions – a roadster with folding soft-top roof, or a coupé with a permanent rear screen and a removable hard roof (sometimes called a "Surrey Top" – see TR4/4A for a description of this top).

The TR5/TR250 interior incorporated the latest in safety ideas at the time, for example they had a padded centre to the steering wheel, a padded dashboard top and rocker switches. The passenger grab handle of earlier TRs was no more, while the facia included "eyeball" fresh air vents.

Of the relatively small number of fuel injected TR5 cars made, only just over a third were for the home market, the rest being exported. This scarcity in the UK market has a bearing on its value today. Typical optional extras included wire wheels and overdrive.

Specific Checks: First be sure that the car you are inspecting is a genuine TR5 or TR250. The commission number for the TR5 starts CP (as does the TR6 PI) and CD for the TR250 and will, as usual, include an "L" for LHD and "O" for overdrive. Those export TR5s that were

Below: **A Dutch-registered TR250, minus the usual racing stripes.**

Below: **A TR5 with a tonneau cover and the optional wire wheels.**

assembled in Belgium usually have a "1" prefix. Check that the commission and engine numbers on the vehicle match the paperwork, then later contact the Heritage Motor Centre Archives at Gaydon, to verify the car's authenticity (unless there is a Heritage Certificate).

Moving on to check the car, as with most steel cars of this period, rust is the big problem. Check every panel carefully, but especially the sills, floor pan, wheelarches and spare wheel well, but remember the inner panels which are difficult to see. While checking the panels, look also for poor restoration or accident repairs.

Check all visible parts of the chassis carefully for corrosion and badly repaired accident damage (eg open the bonnet and look for buckling of the chassis rails). In particular, check suspension attachments, steering rack mountings, differential mountings and the chassis outriggers. Also look for damage caused by clumsy jacking. The IRS attachment points are known rust areas.

The mechanical fuel injection system can be troublesome – lumpy idling can be normal, but a misfire is not. Some owners have replaced the Lucas fuel pump with the better Bosch unit. Overall, the engines are reasonably solid and reliable, but may leak oil and can destroy their crankshaft thrust washers. To check the latter, push the crankshaft bottom fanbelt pulley rearward as hard as you can, then ask someone to depress the clutch pedal. If you see, and maybe even hear, the pulley move forwards, the engine may need major repairs. Coolant leaks can be another issue with this engine.

The gearbox and transmission are reliable but with a lot of torque from this engine, the transmission can suffer. A clonking sound on accelerating or decelerating is almost inevitable with so many universal joints in the drive train plus driveshaft splines, but listen for more unusual sounds.

Prices Today: The TR Register estimates that world-wide perhaps about 700 TR5 cars survive, of which there are over 400 in the TR Register. It is more difficult to estimate how many TR250 cars have survived. Although only a minority are in the UK, the survivors world-wide considerably outnumber the TR5. The relative rarity of the TR5 in relation to other TRs gives this model the edge in value terms today making it one of the most valuable of the TR family, provided it is in near original condition. A TR250 is less valuable than a TR5.

Photo Top Right: **This TR250 has its vinyl "Surrey Top" in place.**
2nd From Top: **A nice side profile of a TR5.**
3rd From Top: **A period Triumph publicity photo.**
Lower Right: **The car's interior had an attractive wooden facia.**

Dates: 1968-75 (US model to 1976).

Number Built: c.91,850

Body/Chassis: Steel body with separate steel chassis, 2-seater open sports.

Engine: 2498cc, 6-cyl in-line, ohv, fuel injection, 142bhp (150bhp gross); (125bhp DIN from end 1972); US: twin carbs, 103-105bhp (101bhp from 1973).

Layout: Front engine, rear wheel drive, 4-speed manual gearbox (with optional overdrive).

Performance: Early PI: Top speed c.120mph, 0-60mph in c.8-9sec; US: Top speed c.110mph, 0-60mph in c.11-12sec.

Price Today: ££+

Above: **The Karmann restyling of the TR5 was most successful, creating the much-loved Triumph TR6 (above).**

The Triumph TR6 was internally an updated TR5 as it retained the former's engine, main structure, chassis, most mechanical parts and even the doors and windscreen, but the Karmann restyling job was both clever and attractive, the new outer panels giving the car a completely different look. Other minor changes (eg a front anti-roll bar) improved the car's handling.

Today the TR6 is regarded by some as the last of the "he-man" British sports cars with its heavy clutch and brakes but a gutsy and exhilarating performance from its smooth 6-cylinder engine. The home market car had fuel injection (PI – Petrol Injection, as it was known), whereas cars exported to the US had twin Stromberg carburettors due to emission regulations.

In 1970 the windscreen surround became matt black (rather than body colour) and reclining seats were fitted. The following year saw a steering lock introduced. The late 1972 changes included a new front spoiler, optional headrests and a new facia (where the minor instruments' needles pointed upwards). The engines were all detuned for emission purposes using a different camshaft – such engines can be recognised by the prefix CR on the commission and engine numbers. Note: the earlier PI engine prefix is CP (like the TR5), while carb versions were CC then CF from late 1972. The overdrive unit was changed from an "A" type to a stronger "J" type from late 1972, and became standard on home market cars from late 1973.

From 1974, the US models were fitted with large black bumper overriders, as can be seen in the photo on the following page.

Some 13,900 TR6 cars were fuel injected, the remainder (which were all exported) having twin Stromberg carburettors. Production of the fuel injected model ended in early 1975 but the US model continued until mid-1976. In Belgium, 3,600 LHD cars were assembled, all were fuel injected and they usually have an additional "1" prefix in their commission number, so can be readily distinguished from cars assembled at Canley. Of all the TR6 cars made, approximately 9% were for the UK market (c. 8,370 cars in total). Continued....

Below: **The TR6's handsome lines and flatish rear deck are evident.**

Below: **This TR6 has the optional wire wheels fitted.**

Optional extras included overdrive (standard from late 1972), headrests, steel hardtop (rare today) and wire wheels (up to late 1972).

Specific Checks: Start with the paperwork. Note that the engine number prefix should match the commission number prefix. LHD cars are identified by an "L" suffix on the commission number, while a "U" signifies a North American specification. For verification of the car's authenticity, contact the Heritage Motor Centre Archives, Gaydon (unless the car already has a Heritage Certificate).

Moving on to check the car, as with most steel cars of this period, rust is the big problem. Check every panel carefully, but especially the sills, floor pan, wheelarches and spare wheel well, but remember the inner panels which are difficult to see. While checking the panels, look also for poor restoration or accident repairs.

Check all visible parts of the chassis carefully for corrosion and badly repaired accident damage (eg open the bonnet and look for buckling of the chassis rails). In particular, check suspension attachments, steering rack mountings, differential mountings and the chassis outriggers. Also look for damage caused by clumsy jacking. The IRS attachment points are known rust areas. Another specific area to check is the integrity of the front lower wishbone mounting point.

As with the TR5PI, the mechanical fuel injection system can be troublesome – lumpy idling can be normal, but a misfire is not. Some owners have replaced the Lucas fuel pump with the better Bosch unit. Overall, the engines are reasonably solid and reliable, but may leak oil and can destroy their crankshaft thrust washers. To check the latter, push the crankshaft bottom fanbelt pulley rearward as hard as you can, then ask someone to depress the clutch pedal. If you see, and maybe even hear, the pulley move forwards, the engine may need major repairs. Coolant leaks can be another issue with this engine.

The gearbox and transmission are reliable but with a lot of torque from this engine, the transmission can suffer. A clonking sound on accelerating or decelerating is almost inevitable with so many universal joints in the drivetrain plus driveshaft splines, but listen for more unusual sounds.

Prices Today: The TR Register says that according to the DVLA there are c.3,700 TR6 cars registered for the road in the UK. Including cars waiting for restoration, the total figure is probably nearer 5-6,000 cars still in existence in the UK, though nobody can be sure. In value terms, a LHD car is worth slightly less than a RHD car, assuming comparable condition.

Photo Top Right: **A TR6 with optional hardtop and non-standard wheels.**
2nd From Top: **The standard, attractive, perforated steel wheels, as seen on this TR6, are more common than wire wheels.**
3rd From Top: **This late left-hand drive car has large bumper overriders required by US safety regulations.**
Lower Right: **A TR6 cockpit (fitted with a replacement facia).**

Dates: 1975-81 (See text).

Number Built: c.115,000

Body/Chassis: Steel unitary, 2-seat fixed-head coupé or open sports.

Engines: TR7: 1998cc, 4-cyl in-line, ohc, 105bhp (US: See text);
TR7 V8: See text.

Layout: Front engine, rear wheel drive, 4 or 5-speed manual
or 3-speed automatic gearbox.

Performance: TR7: Top speed c.110mph, 0-60mph in c.10sec;
TR7 V8: Top speed c.120mph, 0-60mph in c.8-9sec.

Prices Today: FHC: **£** DHC: **£+** TR7 V8: See Text.

Above: **The author's Triumph TR7 in 1980. This photo clearly shows the prominent rising swage line on the car's side.**
Below: **The headlamps could be raised quickly. The bonnet decal indicates a Speke-built car. The salt encrustation is from winter driving in Scotland.**

Whereas previous TR sports cars were usually created by cleverly updating an earlier TR, the TR7 was virtually all new. Its avant-garde wedge shape, penned by Harris Mann, was controversial at the time. Initially the car was only available as a fixed-head coupé as Triumph believed that Federal safety regulations were about to ban soft-top cars. Thankfully this never materialised and a pretty convertible was at last added in 1979, though British buyers had to wait until 1980.

The TR7 was easy and relaxing to drive, it was comfortable, its interior was nicely designed and the car's overall performance was more than adequate. In addition, the car was stylish and so it was not surprising that it eventually outsold every other TR sports car.

Federal TR7 cars had twin Stromberg carburettors (rather than twin SU carbs) and produced 90bhp. Californian customers initially had a single carb (and 76bhp) but later had twin carbs and then fuel injection from 1980. Fuel injection was eventually used on all US cars, but not those exported to Canada.

Early cars had 4-speed gearboxes, then the Rover 5-speed became available as an option and finally it was standard. There was also a 3-speed automatic gearbox option which is quite rare. In 1977 the suspension was lowered and a smart tartan plaid trim introduced. There was also an optional fabric sunroof. In 1980 there were further minor changes to the interior, including the facia colour becoming dark grey rather than black.

The cars were initially assembled at Speke. These cars can be identified as they have a "TR7" decal on the bonnet. Build quality improved when assembly was moved in 1978 to Canley, near Coventry. These cars have bonnet decals with a Triumph logo and laurel leaves. When production moved again in 1980 to Solihull, these final cars had a "Triumph" badge on their bonnets.

There were also about sixty TR7 Sprint coupés made by Triumph in 1977, with the 16-valve Dolomite Sprint engine. They have commission numbers beginning ACH.

The "TR7 V8" is not an official Triumph designation but is the name usually given today to the many TR7 cars that owners have converted to Rover V8 power. Note that it is quite common for these TR7 V8 modified cars to carry TR8 decals.

Typical optional extras on the TR7 included alloy wheels, front air dam and fabric sunroof. Continued....

Above: **The TR7's bluff rear was distinctive.**
Below: **A TR7 V8 Grinnall body conversion. Note winning trophies!**

Specific Checks: Start with the paperwork, and to verify the car's authenticity, contact the Heritage Motor Centre Archives, Gaydon (if there is no Heritage Certificate).

In common with many cars of the time, the TR7 bodies were not adequately rust-proofed and so corrosion is a real problem today. First, lift the carpets to check the rear floorpan, especially where each rear suspension trailing arm pivots. Similarly, check the footwell, which is difficult to repair. Next, inspect all four wings and the inner wings for rust.

The front suspension turrets may have already been repaired, but see that it has been done correctly. The bulkhead, bonnet and boot lid also need inspecting for corrosion.

Check the important inner sills from inside the car (where carpeting permits), and on a convertible, give the car's rear a sharp push downwards to ensure that the gap between the doors and body does not change.

With an aluminium head and cast-iron block the engine can suffer from a warped cylinder head, head gasket problems and overheating. The cause is often neglect of the antifreeze and its corrosion inhibitor. There can also be electrical problems too, so check everything works correctly, especially the headlamp pods which should both pop up instantly together.

About one third of surviving TR7s have been modified to use other engines, notably the Rover V8 3.5-litre engine (though larger capacity V8 engines are fitted too). All these conversions should be done properly, the engine mounted on the correct subframe and the brakes should be uprated. There are proprietary kits available to do this.

Other typical modifications include upgraded front brakes, uprated suspension springs and anti-dive blocks. Some 4-speed gearbox cars have had the later 5-speed unit fitted. Many cars no longer have the original tartan plaid trim interiors, leather being a popular replacement.

Prices Today: The TR Register says that recent DVLA statistics indicate that there are about 2,500 surviving cars in the UK, but this excludes long-term off-road projects. Although only a quarter of all the TR7 cars made were convertibles, today they outnumber fixed-head cars in the UK and are more valuable, costing typically about 50% or more than the fixed-head versions. Cars with a professional V8 conversion cost perhaps about £1,000-£2,000 more. Overall, the TR7 is currently thought to be undervalued.

Photo Top Right: **The laurel leaves bonnet decal indicates this is a Canley-built car, reputedly better built than the earlier Speke cars.**
2nd From Top: **The bonnet badge indicates this is a Solihull-built car. It has the optional alloy wheels fitted.**
3rd From Top: **Another late Solihull car, this time fitted with the standard steel wheels with wheel trims.**
Lower Right: **A 1980 TR7 Convertible's comfortable cockpit.**

Dates: 1978-81 (See text).   **Number Built:** c.2,600

Body/Chassis: Steel unitary, 2-seater fixed-head coupé or open sports.

Engine: Rover 3528cc, V8, ohv, 133bhp (fuel injection: 137-148bhp).

Layout: Front engine, rear wheel drive, 5-speed manual or 3-speed automatic gearbox.

Performance: Top speed c.120mph, 0-60mph in c.8-9sec.

Price Today: Contact Club.

Above: **A rare right-hand drive (genuine) Triumph TR8.**

This was arguably the car that TR purists would have liked to have succeeded the much-loved TR6. Sadly the TR8 was not offered to the British market, though a small number (probably fewer than 50) were made in right-hand drive form, mostly for testing or for conversion to rally cars. Almost all TR8s were exported, mainly to North America (plus 39 European spec LHD cars).

The TR8 looks just like another TR7. The features that distinguish it include the "TR8" decals and twin exhausts. Under the skin, the brakes, suspension and engine cooling were all uprated and power-assisted steering was common. The gearboxes were the same as those used in the later TR7s, but the final drive was higher. Fuel injection was used initially on Californian cars and later on all cars.

Triumph had planned this V8-engined car from an early stage and in 1977-78 about 145 pre-production fixed-head TR7 V8 cars were shipped to the US as promotional vehicles for Triumph dealers. These cars have a commission number starting ACN. Many of the cars were automatics. Although these TR8 sports cars were not for consumer sale, ultimately they found their way into the market. After a further 200 or so fixed-head cars were made, subsequent cars were all convertibles. Together with the TR7, production ended in 1981.

Specific Checks: Many TR7s have been converted by their owners into "TR8" cars, even carrying TR8 decals (refer to the TR7 entry). With any TR8, note the car's "commission" number then later contact the Heritage Motor Centre Archives, Gaydon, to verify the car's authenticity (if there is no Heritage Certificate).

In common with many cars of the time, the bodies were not adequately rust-proofed and so corrosion is a real problem today. As with the TR7, first lift the carpets to check the rear floorpan, especially where each rear suspension trailing arm pivots. Similarly, check the footwell, which is difficult to repair. Next, inspect all four wings and the inner wings for rust. The front suspension turrets may have already been repaired, but see that it has been done correctly. The bulkhead, bonnet and boot lid also need inspecting for corrosion. Check the important inner sills from inside the car (where carpeting permits), and on a convertible, give the car's rear a sharp push downwards to ensure that the gap between the doors and body does not change.

The V8 engine is generally a solid and reliable unit, but needs regular oil changes to minimise wear. Common problems include worn hydraulic cam followers (indicated by tappet noise when idling) and water pump failure (indicated by a rumbling sound). Normal engine oil pressure is low when idling and when driving hard the running pressure level should remain constant. A good engine will not normally lose oil.

Check all electrics fully too, especially the headlamp pods, which should both pop up instantly together.

Prices Today: The TR Register says that DVLA statistics indicate there are less than 50 genuine TR8s registered in the UK (excluding long-term off-road cars). Note that original RHD cars are worth about twice that of LHD cars.

Above: **A RHD TR8.**   Below: **A carburettor version V8 in a TR8.**

Dates: 1962-80

Numbers Built: Mk1: c.45,750 Mk2: c.37,400 Mk3: c.65,320
MkIV: c.70,020 1500: c.95,830

Body/Chassis: Steel body on separate steel chassis,
2-seater open sports.

Engines:
Mk1/2: 1147cc, 4-cyl in-line, ohv, 63-67bhp;
Mk3/IV: 1296cc, 4-cyl in-line, ohv, 70-63bhp (US: 48bhp);
1500: 1493cc, 4-cyl in-line, ohv, 71bhp (US: 57-53bhp).

Layout: Front engine, rear wheel drive, 4-speed manual gearbox
(with optional overdrive).

Performance:
Mk1/2: Top speed c.90 mph, 0-60mph in c.16sec;
Mk3/IV: Top speed c.95mph, 0-60mph in c.15sec;
1500: Top speed c.100mph, 0-60mph in c.13sec.

Price Today: £+

Above: **A Triumph publicity photo for the Spitfire 4, the launch name
for the car. Retrospectively, it is called the Spitfire Mk1.**

Below: **A Spitfire 4 with the early hardtop design.**

Below: **A Spitfire Mk2 which could be identified by the front grille
having fewer slats than the Mk1.**

The Spitfire, introduced in 1962, became one of Triumph's greatest sports car successes with over three hundred thousand sold. It took its name from the famous RAF fighter aircraft and was originally marketed as the Spitfire 4, though it is retrospectively called the Spitfire Mk1. The car, styled by Michelotti, had been developed from the popular Triumph Herald.

In 1965 came the Spitfire Mk2 with a different camshaft and exhaust manifold, boosting power to 67bhp. An identifying feature is that the front grille had fewer slats. The car was better trimmed than the more spartan Mk1 and overdrive and wire wheels were now available as optional extras.

Modified Spitfires took class wins at Le Mans and there were many other racing successes over the following years.

In 1967 came the Mk3 with a larger 1.3-litre engine. It is easily recognisable due to its raised bumpers (to meet Federal regulations). A big improvement with the Mk3 was that the soft-top roof was now attached to the car and folded back when in the "down" position. Earlier cars had required the whole soft-top assembly to be dismantled and stowed in the boot.

An important landmark came in late 1970 with the introduction of the MkIV, which featured a very attractive and up-to-date Michelotti restyled body. The new model designation "IV" was in Roman numerals to avoid any confusion with the earlier Spitfire 4.

In addition to the new body, the MkIV had a revised facia, which placed the instruments in front of the driver. The rear suspension was also modified, significantly reducing the "jacking up" characteristic of the earlier cars. This could occur if an enthusiastic driver lifted off the throttle when cornering hard and sometimes led to loss of control due to the suddenness of the understeer changing to oversteer. With more "ordinary" driving this characteristic would not have been noticed.

The difference in quoted bhp between the Mk3 and MkIV is apparently due to a change in the method by which horsepower was calculated, so the actual power produced by the two models was probably similar. The MkIV's higher gearing gave better fuel consumption and more relaxed highway cruising. The car now had synchromesh on all forward gears and an alternator replaced the dynamo. Overall the MkIV was quieter and more sophisticated than its predecessors.

The next model, the Spitfire 1500, was introduced in N. America in 1973 and in the home market the following year. This was the final version of this car. Apart from the distinctive "Spitfire 1500" decals on the front bonnet and rear boot lid, and seat facings in an attractive houndstooth fabric, it looked identical to the earlier MkIV. The 1.5-litre engine, which it shared with its old rival, the MG Midget, gave the car some extra power. The engine was a long-stroke derivative of the earlier 1.3-litre engine.

In the last few years of production there were other, mainly minor, improvements to the model and from 1975, US models had large black 5mph impact bumpers.

Optional extras included wire wheels (only on the Mk1 to Mk3 cars) and overdrive (still a desirable feature today). The optional steel hardtop was sometimes left in place by owners, making the car effectively a fixed-head coupé. On the 1500 model, head restraints were available.

Early Spitfires were also available with different states of engine tuning. These kits, from SAH Accessories, were fitted by Triumph dealers.

Specific Checks: First start with the paperwork. Check the commission and engine numbers match the paperwork and then later, to verify the car's authenticity, contact the Heritage Motor Centre Archives at Gaydon (unless the car already has a Heritage Certificate).

Moving on to check the car itself, first look at the chassis, especially the outriggers. Under the bonnet, check the visible chassis rails for signs of accident damage (eg buckling of the longitudinal chassis rails).

The bodywork can rust badly. Particular areas to check on the Spitfire include the battery box area, the large one-piece forward-hinged bonnet (which is expensive to replace), the sills (which are structurally significant as the chassis does not have side rails), the wheelarches, floor pan, spare wheel compartment and the bulkhead. Check also the gap between each door's

Photo Top Right: **The Mk3 had raised bumpers to meet Federal regulations and it featured an improved soft-top roof and the larger 1.3-litre engine. Wire wheels were an optional extra.**
2nd From Top: **The MkIV hardtop was much sharper than the previous hardtop (see previous page) and had distinctive crease lines in the roof. This LHD car has US-spec head restraints and wing side markers.**
Lower Two Photos: **A MkIV with its soft-top roof up and then lowered. Attractive perforated steel wheels were now standard on the Spitfire.**

rear edge and the bodywork. It should be the same from top to bottom. If not, it could mean the whole structure is seriously rusted or has residual accident damage. Note that panel fit can be a problem when rebuilding a car after a full body-off restoration.

A characteristic of the separate chassis and large one-piece bonnet is that the car is naturally prone to body rattles, but these should not be excessive.

The 1500 engine suffers from tappet noise and runs hot. An oil cooler can help. Although the engine is not noted for its longevity in the Midget, it seems to last better in the Spitfire, but this also depends on how it is treated.

These 1500 engines can sometimes destroy their crankshaft thrust washers – to check this, push the crankshaft bottom fanbelt pulley rearward as hard as you can, then ask someone to depress the clutch pedal. If you see and maybe even hear the pulley move forwards, the engine may need major repairs.

Another check is with the engine idling, press the clutch and listen for a low rumbling noise – this could be from a worn bottom end.

Gear levers on pre-1500 gearboxes that "sizzle" are quite common, but it is not usually a serious problem. The differential should not whine.

The front suspension trunnions need regular lubrication to avoid failure. The rear also has trunnions. Note that on the MkIV and 1500 cars, the noticeable negative camber of the rear wheels is normal.

Modifications found on cars today include a wider radiator (which is apparently better than fitting an electric fan) and a swing-spring conversion kit to remedy the tuck-in problem of pre-MkIV cars. Finally, some cars have acquired the 2-litre engine from the Triumph GT6.

There is good spares availability and support for the Spitfire range.

Prices Today: The 1500 was the largest selling model during the Spitfire's 18-year production run, accounting for nearly a third of all Spitfires made. Three-quarters of all Spitfires produced were exported.

With Spitfire prices, condition is the really all-important factor and note that overdrive is always a desirable option to look for.

Photo Top Right: **Externally, the Spitfire 1500 looked identical to the earlier MkIV, apart from the decals on the bonnet and boot lid.**
2nd From Top: **The very functional hardtop made the Spitfire 1500 good for use throughout winter. The hardtops were in body colour.**
3rd From Top: **A Spitfire 1500 with soft-top roof down and stowed.**
Lower Right: **The cockpit of a Spitfire 1500 in 1974. The car was comfortable and relatively well equipped. The walnut veneer facia gave a touch of luxury.**

Dates: 1966-73

Numbers Built: Mk1: See text. Mk2: c.12,060
Mk3: c.13,040

Body/Chassis: Steel body on separate steel chassis,
2-seater rear-hatch fixed-head coupé.

Engine: 1998cc, 6-cyl in-line, ohv, 95bhp (104bhp from 1968);
(US: 95-79bhp).

Layout: Front engine, rear wheel drive, 4-speed manual gearbox
(with optional overdrive).

Performance: Mk1: Top speed c.105mph, 0-60mph in c.12sec;
Mk2/Mk3: Top speed c.110mph, 0-60mph in c.10sec.

Price Today: £+ (See text).

Above: **A Triumph GT6 Mk1 with optional wire wheels.**

Below: **A Triumph GT6 Mk1. Note the small rear bumpers, later raised on the Mk2 (see Mk2 photo at foot and overpage).**

Below: **A Triumph GT6 Mk2. Note the heated rear window elements that, unusually, run vertically. The Mk2 also has distinctive extractor vents visible on the rear three-quarter panels.**

The Triumph GT6 was launched at the 1966 London Motor Show. It was a successful blend of Triumph Spitfire styling and Triumph Vitesse underpinnings. The Spitfire was elegantly adapted by Michelotti to incorporate a fastback with opening rear-hatch. Except for the bonnet bulge, the GT6 looked similar to the Spitfire from the front, and they both had the same waistline. However, the smooth six-cylinder 2-litre engine and fixed-head fastback of the GT6 gave it a quite different character to the Spitfire.

As to how many Mk1 cars were made, many sources quote 15,851 cars, but the chassis numbers appear to run from KC1 to KC13752.

In 1968 the Mk2 was introduced, the US model being called the GT6 Plus. The Mk2 had many improvements, such as a revised rear suspension, reducing the tendency for the car's rear to jack up if lifting off the throttle when cornering hard. The engine now had a new cylinder head and camshaft, which increased power by 9bhp (US models had different carburettors, emission controls and produced only 95bhp). The interior was also improved with a revised facia, new seats and better ventilation. The Mk2 is easily distinguished by its raised bumpers, bonnet side louvres and extractor vents on the rear three-quarter panels.

In 1970 came the Mk3 with major restyling and removal of the previous external seams on top of the front wings. The rear of the car adopted the standard Triumph tail, also seen on the Spitfire and Stag.

The last of the GT6 cars were given a face-lift in 1973 which included new fabric upholstery, servo-assisted brakes, new instruments, Sundym tinted glass, optional head-restraints and yet another revised rear suspension. This suspension was the simpler "swing-spring" system with solid drive shafts. These cars were the best of the GT6 range.

The author's own GT6 Mk3 was one of his favourite sports cars. It cruised effortlessly, had a comfortable interior and its rear-hatch was very practical. The GT6 was a pleasure to drive, the engine making a lovely happy burbling sound. Continued....

Typical optional extras you might find include overdrive (most common on the Mk3 cars) and wire wheels (not common in the UK, and more usually seen on early US-spec cars).

Specific Checks: First start with the paperwork. Check the commission and engine numbers match the paperwork and then later, to verify the car's authenticity, contact the Heritage Motor Centre Archives at Gaydon (unless the car already has a Heritage Certificate).

Moving on to check the car itself, first look at the chassis, especially the outriggers, also the main chassis rails around the differential where water settles and the chassis rots through from the inside. Under the bonnet, check the visible chassis rails for signs of accident damage (eg buckling of the longitudinal chassis rails).

The bodywork can rust badly. Particular areas to check on the GT6 include the battery box area, the large one-piece forward-hinged bonnet (which is expensive to replace), the front edge of the roof, the sills (which are structurally significant as the chassis does not have any side rails), the wheelarches, floor pan, spare wheel compartment and the bulkhead. Check also the gap between each door's rear edge and the bodywork. It should be the same from top to bottom. If not, it could mean the whole structure is seriously rusted or has residual accident damage.

A characteristic of the separate chassis and large one-piece bonnet is the car is naturally prone to body rattles, but these should not be excessive.

The engine is a good solid unit though it does leak oil and has the same crankshaft thrust washer problem as the 6-cylinder TRs (refer to those entries for details). If the differential whines, it may be worn. The gearbox is the weak link so check it particularly carefully – it should not be noisy or "crunch" when changing gear.

The front suspension trunnions need regular lubrication or may fail. On Mk2 and early Mk3 cars, also check the rubber is not peeling on the large rubber Rotoflex couplings on the rear drive shafts. In addition, the transverse leaf spring begins to sag as time marches on and worn rear suspension bushes can affect handling over bumps.

Over half of all GT6 production went to North America.

There is good spares availability and support for the Triumph GT6 range.

Prices Today: All three Marks have their particular devotees, and pre-1973 cars have a special appeal due to their free road tax status, but as usual, condition is the critical factor in a valuation.

Photo Top Right: **The Mk2 had raised bumpers to meet Federal safety regulations. The Rostyle steel wheel trims were standard. The wheel nuts are dummies!**
2nd From Top: **This Mk3 has non-standard, but period, alloy wheels.**
3rd From Top: **A Mk3 with the attractive, standard perforated steel wheels.**
Lower Right: **The comfortable cockpit of a Mk3.**

Dates: 1970-77

Number Built: 25,939

Body/Chassis: Steel unitary, 2+2 seater open sports.

Engine: 2997cc, V8, ohc, 145bhp.

Layout: Front engine, rear wheel drive, 4-speed manual (some with overdrive) or 3-speed automatic gearbox.

Performance: Top speed c.117mph, 0-60mph in under 10sec.

Price Today: ££+

Above: **A Triumph Stag with Rostyle steel wheel trims (complete with dummy wheel nuts).**
Below: **The T-shaped roll-over safety bar can be seen, with its front attached to the windscreen top. Note the optional wire wheels.**

This Michelotti-styled luxury sports car was one of the most desirable of its time (and still is today) despite having a poor early reputation for reliability. The car came well equipped and it had a permanent T-shaped roll-over safety bar. The name "Stag" was originally its factory pre-production code name but was liked by the Triumph dealers and was eventually adopted as its final production name.

In 1972, overdrive became standard and the engine overheating problems were addressed by fitting a new radiator and a sealed cooling system. These cars were identified by a chrome moulding fitted to the sill panels.

The MkII, launched in 1973, sorted out other issues. The power-assisted steering had been criticised initially for having too little "feel", so Triumph fitted a smaller steering wheel and reduced the power assistance. The engine had new domed pistons and a reshaped combustion chamber. Inside the car there were restyled instruments, which now had their gauge needles pointing upwards rather than downwards. MkII cars were given black sills, a black tail panel and side stripes.

The sill covers changed again in 1976 to brushed aluminium and by this time alloy wheels and tinted glass were standard. The rear panel was back to body colour, rather than black. The last major change was a new model of Borg-Warner automatic gearbox. Automatic transmission was fitted to almost two thirds of Stags.

The main problem with the Stag, particularly at the beginning, was its new engine. It sometimes overheated, its timing chains stretched (leading to valves striking pistons) and the alloy cylinder heads had a tendency to corrode, warp and blow their cylinder head gaskets. But today these problems have either been solved or their prevention is better understood, and the Triumph V8 has gained some belated but deserved respect. A properly rebuilt and maintained engine should be reasonably reliable.

Above: **The Stag with its soft-top roof in place.**
Below: **The luxurious cockpit of the Triumph Stag.**

Of the nearly 26,000 cars made, just over a quarter (6,780) were exported. Exports to North America were only made during 1971-73.

Typical optional extras included overdrive (which was standard from 1972), wire wheels, air-conditioning (to 1975) and a hefty steel removable hardtop which incorporated a heated rear window. Also, head-restraints were available from 1973. Continued....

Specific Checks: Start with the paperwork and check the numbers on the car match. Then later to verify the car's authenticity, contact the Heritage Motor Centre Archives at Gaydon (unless there is already a Heritage Certificate).

Next inspect the body. In addition to the usual checks, open the doors to examine the windscreen pillars and door posts for rust (as they are difficult to repair). The door bottoms tend to rust both inside and out. The rear wing to sills joint is another difficult area to repair. Look inside the soft-top's storage well for rust around the damper mountings. The sill covers may conceal rust.

The engine's foibles have already been mentioned. Timing chain stretch may reveal itself by a slight rattle at idle speed when starting from cold but lasting only a few seconds – this is a warning that timing chain replacement is probably urgent.

Engine overheating can still be a problem. It might simply be a silted up radiator, though it could be head corrosion blocking waterways (often caused by using insufficient antifreeze with its corrosion inhibitor). A thorough road test should reveal whether or not the engine is running at the correct temperature.

The manual gearbox is usually reliable and it should not whine or grumble unduly, though the synchromesh on the intermediate gears can be weak. The auto box is also strong but check that it kicks down correctly and does not change up a gear with a jerk.

Check the soft-top operation as it is easy to damage the soft-top roof frames if the folding process is not done correctly. While in this area, check also the door locks as they can fail and, as with all open cars, check for rainwater ingress causing damage to trim. If carpets are wet or look as if they are water damaged, try to check the condition of the flooring below them as rust is likely.

A modification is to replace the engine with a Rover 3.5-litre V8 unit, a Ford 3-litre V6 or a Triumph straight-six (all of which can reduce the car's value).

Prices Today: The Stag Owners' Club estimates that c.9,500 cars survive. Authenticity and condition are key to a Stag's value. Cars with manual gearboxes are slightly more valuable than those with automatic gearboxes.

Below: **The immaculate engine bay with its Triumph V8 in HDY 628N (shown on the previous page).**

Above: **This car was the first pre-production Stag, hand built alongside the TR6 line in late 1969.**
Below: **A hardtop in place. This Stag has the attractive alloy wheels which are also fitted to the two cars shown below it.**

Above: **A nice Triumph publicity photo for the Stag.**
Below: **A Stag with its body coloured hardtop.**

Dates:	1958-67	**Number Built:** c.800 (See text).

Body/Chassis: GRP body on tubular steel chassis, 2-seater FHC.

Engines: Mark I: Coventry Climax, Ford or MGA (See text);
Mark II: Mostly MGA 1588cc, 4-cyl in-line, ohv, 80bhp;
Mark IIA: Mostly MGA 1622cc, 4-cyl in-line, ohv, 86bhp;
Mark III: Initially MGA 1622cc, then MGB 1798cc, 95bhp;
1800S/Mark IV: MGB 1798cc, 4-cyl in-line, ohv, 95bhp.

Layout: Front engine, rear wheel drive, 3 or 4-speed manual gearbox.

Performance: Mark IIA: Top speed c.100mph, 0-60mph in c.12sec;
1800S: Top speed c.110mph, 0-60mph in c.11sec.

Price Today: £+ (See text).

Above: **One of three TVR Granturas built for the 1962 Le Mans race.**

The initials "TVR" are from TreVoR Wilkinson, who set up the original company in 1947. In 1958 they launched their first full-scale production car, the Grantura. This was offered with a wide variety of engines, including the Ford 100E 1172cc side-valve (35bhp unit if standard, 56bhp if supercharged) with a 3-speed gearbox, also the Ford 105E 997cc, ohv, 39bhp unit, the MGA 1500 72bhp unit and the exciting (and more numerous) Coventry Climax FWE 1216cc, sohc, 83bhp engine.

The hard suspension was based on the VW Beetle's trailing link independent suspension with torsion bars used at both the front and rear of the TVR. Drum brakes and centre lock wire wheels were standard. Probably about 100 Mark I cars were made, but no pre-1966 production records survive today.

The Mark II (from 1960) had a lightly reworked rear with small fins added. By now the MGA engine (1500, later 1600) was becoming almost standard. A Ford 105E or Coventry Climax engine were options. The blister over the front wheelarches on earlier cars was now matched with a blister over the rear wheelarches. The following year saw the launch of the Grantura Mark IIA, with front disc brakes as standard. From late 1961, another engine option was the Ford 109E 1340cc unit. A Mark IIA with a tuned Coventry Climax engine was the first TVR to be independently tested at over 100mph (by *Autocar* magazine). About 400 Mark II and IIA cars were made.

The much improved Mark III appeared in early 1962. By this time, Trevor Wilkinson had left TVR. The Mark III Grantura had its front restyled (with the grille raised and the sidelights and flashers moved) plus a completely new and improved chassis. Although still tubular, it was more sophisticated, more rigid (highly triangulated) and it dispensed with the earlier VW-derived suspension. Instead it had double wishbones and coil springs front and rear, giving a softer ride with better handling. Rack and pinion steering was now standard. The wheelbase was also increased by 1.5in. The engine and gearbox were now standardised to the MGA units, but production of the MGA ceased in 1962 so by 1963 the MGB engine and gearbox (with optional overdrive) was used instead. A few Mark III cars had Ford or Coventry Climax engines. A total of c.90 Mark III cars were made.

In 1964 came the Grantura 1800S, now with only the MGB engine. The car had the new "Manx tail" (see photo in the TVR Vixen's entry) and a very large rear window, both of which were to become features of later TVRs. Finally, the rear lights were changed to the circular Ford Cortina MkI units. About 130 1800S cars were made.

In 1965, TVR was taken over by Arthur Lilley and his son, Martin. They steered TVR successfully right up to the early 1980s, when they sold the business.

In 1966 came the Mark IV. It was an improved 1800S and 78 were produced before it was replaced by the new Vixen in 1967. Most Granturas were exported.

Specific Checks: Chassis corrosion and badly done accident repairs are key items to look for. A quick check to find out if the chassis is straight is to insert your hand between the rear of the front wheel and the wheelarch. The gap should be the same on both sides of the car. Also, the car should run straight. The bodies were bonded to the chassis, which makes repairs more difficult. Check the underside of the car for damage caused by grounding.

For specific checks on the MG engines, refer to the entries for the MGA and MGB earlier in this book.

Many of these early TVR cars will have been modified in some way, either visually or mechanically, and many will have been raced.

Prices Today: The TVR Car Club estimates that perhaps 15-40% of these cars survive world-wide. Top condition and especially any racing history can multiple the price.

Below: **Period shot of a MkII at Lime Rock circuit in Connecticut, US.**

Dates: 1963-73 (See text).   **Numbers Built:** See text.

Body/Chassis: GRP body on tubular steel chassis, 2-seater FHC.

Engines: Griffith: Ford 4727cc (289cu in), V8, ohv (bhp - See text);
Tuscan V8: Ford 4727cc (289cu in), V8, ohv (bhp - See text);
Tuscan V6: Ford 2994cc, V6, ohv, 128bhp (DIN)/136bhp (net);
2500: Triumph 2498cc, 6-cyl in-line, ohv, 106bhp.

Layout: Front engine, rear wheel drive, 4-speed manual gearbox.

Performance: Griffith/Tuscan (271bhp): c.150mph, 0-60 in c.6sec;
Tuscan V6: Top speed c.125mph, 0-60mph in c.8sec;
2500: Top speed c.110mph, 0-60mph in c.9-10sec.

Prices Today: V8: £££   V6/2500: ££

Above: **A TVR Griffith 400 (1965), seen in 2006.**

Jack Griffith, an American motor trader, put a Ford 4.7-litre V8 into his Grantura Mark III and decided he could sell examples of this road burner. The new model, called the Griffith 200, required a bonnet bulge, strengthened chassis, modified suspension and brake servo. The car was launched in 1963 (in the US) and the engine was available in two states of tune with a quoted 195bhp or 271bhp gross. In fact, the power outputs were more like 150bhp and 220bhp net, but this was still a lot of power in a relatively small and light vehicle. The cars were shipped to the US without engine or gearbox and these were then fitted by Jack Griffith.

In the UK, the car was first shown at the 1965 Racing Car Show in London. After an unknown but relatively small number of Griffith 200 cars were made, in 1964 came the better-developed Griffith 400. This was less prone to overheating and it also had the Manx tail. In total, possibly as many as 300 cars were made to 1967, though there were only about 20 or so made for the home market.

With the Lilleys' takeover of TVR, in 1967 the car was renamed the Tuscan. It was given better trim and the engine's tendency to overheat was again tackled. With the "195bhp" engine it was called the Tuscan V8 and with the higher tuned "271bhp" engine it was called the Tuscan V8 SE (Special Equipment) and came with better trim. The Tuscan V8 SE LWB (Long Wheelbase) had the wheelbase increased by 4.5in to 90in. The extra length allowed for more space for the occupants and wider doors, a shortcoming of earlier TVRs. There were also light styling changes to the bonnet and rear. A total of 73 Tuscan V8s were built to 1970, including 21 "wide-body" cars, which were 4in wider than normal.

Almost all these cars were exported, but in 1969 TVR launched the Tuscan V6 with a Ford 3-litre "Essex" engine and aimed more at the UK market. The car looked like the then current Vixen except for the badges, twin exhausts and wider (alloy) wheels. It also had the Tuscan V8's brakes, servo, differential and final drive. From 1969 to 1971, 101 Tuscan V6 cars were built (7 were exported).

The Ford 3-litre engine did not meet US regulations, and so in 1970 TVR launched the 2500. This used the Federalised version of the Triumph TR6 engine with twin Stromberg carbs rather than fuel injection. The new TVR 2500 also used the TR6 gearbox with optional overdrive. The car was available in the UK as well as being exported.

Production overlapped with the new M-Series chassis and M-Series cars so in 1972-73, 96 cars were made with the new chassis but original bodyshell before the introduction of the 2500M version. 385 examples of the TVR 2500 were sold, mostly to the US.

Specific Checks: Chassis corrosion and badly done accident repairs are key items to look for. A quick check to find out if the chassis is straight is to insert your hand between the rear of the front wheel and the wheelarch. The gap should be the same on both sides of the car. Also, the car should run straight. Until 1968, the bodies were bonded to the chassis, making repairs more difficult. After that date the bodies were bolted to the chassis.

The Ford V6 and V8 engines, in particular, are understressed in this application unless the cars have been raced, which is quite common. The Ford and Triumph engines are all relatively reliable and predictable but the Triumph engines can destroy their crankshaft thrust washers – refer to the Triumph TR6 entry in this book.

Overheating can be a problem, especially on the highly tuned engines, so check temperatures after a good test drive. Be particularly careful if a car has a faulty cooling fan as damage may have already been done.

Inspect the front and rear suspension and the drive train, particularly on the more powerful variants. Check also the underside for damage caused by grounding.

Many of these TVRs will have been modified, either visually or mechanically, and raced.

Prices Today: The TVR Car Club estimates that perhaps 25-50% of the V8s and 40-70% of the V6s survive worldwide. The V8s are worth about triple that of the V6 or the 2500, and LWB or wide-body examples can be about 50% more. Top condition, provenance and any racing history can increase the price considerably.

Above: **A rare Tuscan V8 "wide-body" model at Earls Court in 1970.**

| Dates: | 1967-73 | Numbers Built: | Vixen: 746 | 1300:15 |

Dates: 1967-73   **Numbers Built:** Vixen: 746   1300:15

Body/Chassis: GRP body on tubular steel chassis, 2-seater FHC.

Engines: Ford 1599cc, 4-cyl in-line, ohv, 86-88bhp;
1300: Triumph 1296cc, 4-cyl in-line, ohv, 63bhp.

Layout: Front engine, rear wheel drive, 4-speed manual gearbox.

Performance: Vixen: Top speed c.110mph, 0-60mph in c.10sec.

Price Today: £+

Above: **A Vixen S2. A sunroof is desirable as the interior can get hot.**

Launched in 1967, the Vixen was produced in four series, the majority being S2 and S3 cars. The Vixen S1 was virtually identical to its predecessor, the Grantura Mark IV, except that the engine and gearbox were changed from MGB to Ford Cortina GT (though a dozen early Vixens had MGB engines). The car also had an air intake in the bonnet to feed air to the Weber carburettor. In total, 117 Vixen S1 cars were made.

In 1968 came the S2 with a new, longer, chassis with the GRP body bolted rather than bonded to it. The extra length (4.5in) allowed for wider doors and more space for the occupants. The S2 had many other improvements, such as better brakes (from the Triumph TR5), a quieter final drive (now from Triumph), standard brake servo and rocker switches. TVR's cast alloy wheels became available as an option. The S1's circular Cortina MkI rear lights were replaced by rectangular, wraparound, Cortina MkII lights and the bonnet was changed, with the air intake removed and a long bulge added. From 1969, two small recessed air intakes were created in the bonnet. 438 Vixen S2 cars were made.

The S3 (from 1970) had only minor differences such as the front wing vents were changed to grilles (taken from a Ford saloon). The engine was now the Ford Capri GT unit, rated at 86bhp (DIN)/93bhp (net). 168 of the Vixen S3 cars were made. The 23 Vixen S4 cars (built from 1972) featured the new stronger chassis shortly to be used on the M-Series cars.

The 1300 was a short-lived and commercially unsuccessful model with only 15 made. It used a Triumph Spitfire engine and gearbox but cost only marginally less than the identical but more powerful Vixen S3. The last 6 cars had the new M-Series chassis and the final 1300 made also had an M-Series bodyshell. Most 1300 owners have since fitted larger engines.

Specific Checks: First, check for chassis corrosion, key areas being the front and rear outriggers and sill tubes. With the owner's permission, jack up the car and remove each wheel, one at a time, to check behind. While there, check to see if the suspension grease points have been greased recently. Look for cracks in the suspension components (especially mountings). If the front tyres show uneven wear across their width, this might indicate wear in the front suspension.

You also need to check for poor accident repairs. A quick check to find out if the chassis is straight is to insert your hand between the rear of the front wheel and the wheelarch. The gap should be the same on both sides of the car. Also, the car should run straight.

The build quality of TVRs was improving all the time and their GRP and paint finish was to a high standard, but stress cracks can occur and are unsightly. Panel fit should be good unless doors have dropped.

Rear springs can sag and if the car is fully laden, it can ground on bumps, so check for underside damage.

Rainwater leaks can damage carpets and seats. Leaks can originate from many sources, including door and window seals, and through the engine bay. If the rear window seal is causing leaks, check the fuel tank below as it could be rusty. The rear window was initially made of perspex, then later of glass.

Check all electrics very carefully as they can be problematic, as with any GRP car, due to the lack of earths. The original wiring was done with black wire and coloured identity tags but these can get lost or damaged, leading to problems tracing circuits.

Prices Today: Finding a good, original example can be challenging, which can have a bearing on price.

Above: **A Vixen S2 with typical TVR "Manx" tail and large rear screen.**
Below: **A Vixen S3 with front wing grille.**

Dates: 1971-79 (See text).

Numbers Built: 2500M: 947 1600M: 148 3000M: 654
Turbo: 63 Taimar: 395 Convertible: 258

Body/Chassis: GRP body on tubular steel chassis, 2-seater
fixed-head or rear-hatch coupé or open sports.

Engines: 2500M: Triumph 2498cc, 6-cyl in-line, ohv, 104-106bhp;
1600M: Ford 1599cc, 4-cyl in-line, ohv, 84-86bhp;
3000M: Ford 2994cc, V6, ohv, 135-142bhp (US: 136bhp);
Turbo: Ford 2994cc, V6, ohv, 230bhp.

Layout: Front engine, rear wheel drive, 4-speed manual gearbox
(some with overdrive).

Performance: 2500M: Top speed c.110mph, 0-60mph in c.9-10sec;
1600M: Top speed 105+mph, 0-60mph in c.10-11sec;
3000M: Top speed c.125mph, 0-60mph in c.8sec;
Turbo: Top speed over 140mph, 0-60mph in c.6sec.

Prices Today: FHC: £+ 3000S: ££ Turbo: Contact Club.

Above: **The TVR 2500M. The first of this good-looking series.**

The first M-Series car, the 2500M, was unveiled at the 1971 London Motor Show with production starting in 1972. The "M" was for "Martin" after Martin Lilley, TVR's Managing Director. The new cars had much longer, sleeker, bodies than earlier TVRs. A key feature was the stiffer chassis that gave a better ride and handling. The spare wheel was mounted at the very front which increased the boot space greatly. All M-Series cars shared the same chassis design and they looked identical apart from the Convertible and the rear hatch of the Taimar.

2500M: The 2500M was aimed mainly at the US market so had a Federal-spec TR6 engine with twin Stromberg carbs rather than fuel injection (hence less power). It also used a Triumph gearbox and differential. From 1973 it was for export only and production ceased in 1977 with the ending of the supply of TR6 engines.

1600M: Intended to replace the TVR Vixen, in 1972 came the 1600M with the Ford "Kent" engine and excellent gearbox. The 1600M was the economy model of the range and was a competent sports car, but sales were never strong and it had a break in production between mid-1973 and spring 1975, and finally ceased in 1977.

3000M: The 3000M with its Ford "Essex" V6 was the best selling version of this series in the UK and 654 were made between 1972 and 1979. The car was progressively improved during its production, including a revised interior and improved ventilation in 1973. Overdrive became an option in 1975. Along with the other M-Series cars, the front wing side vents were removed from 1975 and in 1976 the bonnet was slightly reshaped at the front end to improve engine cooling. The facia and tail lights were changed (again). For the US market, its Ford 3-litre was specially de-toxed to meet Federal regulations.

Turbos: TVR launched their first Turbo in 1975 (with production cars available from the following year). This was TVR's first turbocharged car and it had thundering performance. Broadspeed blueprinted the 3-litre engine,

reduced the compression ratio, balanced and turbocharged the engines, then later they set up each car on their rolling road. Around 100-125 man-hours were spent just doing the work on the engine, so not surprisingly these cars cost typically about 50% more than the non-Turbo models. Of the 63 TVR Turbos made, there were 20 Coupés, 30 Taimars and 13 Convertibles, the cars being emblazoned proudly with *Turbo* in large letters along each side. It was the first British turbocharged production car and TVR also claimed the Convertible Turbo was the first turbocharged open sports car in the world. The Turbo cars were not exported to the US.

Taimar: Access to the boot space in all TVRs had been a problem as there was no boot lid and access became even more difficult with higher seat backs. The solution was the practical Taimar (from 1976) which had an unobtrusive rear-hatch, but was otherwise identical to the 3000M. The hatch was secured by an electric latch, the release button being cleverly hidden in the driver's door jamb. But a problem with some Taimars is exhaust fumes entering the cockpit via the hatch.

Convertible: The last of the M-Series was TVR's first open top car, the Convertible (also called the 3000S), built in 1978-79. It used the Ford 3-litre engine on the same M-Series chassis but had a body that was different from its windscreen rearwards, including sliding glass sidescreens and a fully detachable soft-top roof. Due to a lower windscreen base, the facia was also different and this resulted in the main instruments being sited in the centre of the facia rather than in front of the driver. Note the TVR S convertible, launched in 1986, was a completely different car.

Below: **Scene at TVR in December 1978, photographed by the author.**

Options included a sunroof, vinyl roof, tinted glass, reclining seats, leather trim, heated rear window (essential) and overdrive (from 1975). Electric windows were to special order. TVR's alloy wheels were standard but Wolfrace wheels were extra. The limited edition (and rare) 3000ML (1973-74) came with a vinyl roof, opening sunroof and a luxury interior including walnut dash. The even rarer Martin 3000M (10 made) celebrated 10 years of TVR under Martin Lilley. These cars had Wolfrace wheels, a high specification and were brown with a distinctive band along the sides and the word "Martin".

US-spec cars had "intrusion barriers" in the doors, federalised engines and side reflectors.

Specific Checks: First, check for chassis corrosion. The key areas are the front and rear outriggers, the sill tubes and on the top of the square section chassis tubes at the rear of the chassis where they are bolted onto the body. With the owner's permission, jack up the car and remove each wheel in turn, to check the chassis behind. Look also for poorly repaired accident damage – a quick check is to insert your hand between the rear of the front wheel and the wheelarch. The gap should be the same on both sides. The car should run straight. Imprecise handling could also be caused by wear in the front suspension. The GRP bodies were well made, but they can get stress cracks especially around the headlights and on the bonnet above the rear catches.

Other points worth checking include the front and rear suspension and the drive train, particularly on the more powerful variants. Check under the engine and gearbox for damage caused by grounding. On this series the handbrake tends not to be very effective.

The Ford and Triumph engines are relatively reliable but the Triumph engine can destroy its crankshaft thrust washer – for details, refer to the Triumph TR6 entry.

Turbocharging in road cars was still in its infancy in the 1970s, so inspect any Turbo car's engine and turbocharger with particular care.

Rainwater leaks, especially found in early cars, can damage carpets and seats. Check all the electrics as they can be problematic. Note that some of these cars will have been driven hard or even track raced.

Prices Today: The TVR Car Club estimates that perhaps 40-70% of the 3000M and Taimars survive and probably a higher percentage of Convertibles and Turbos. The Turbos are the most valuable cars.

Above: **A 1600M with the optional vinyl roof and sunroof.**
Below: **A similar looking car, but this is a 3000M.**

Above: **Convertible with non-standard roll bar.** Below: **1600M cockpit.**

Below: **The Taimar was a 3000M with a rear hatch.**

Dates: 1980-90 (See text).

Numbers Built:

	Coupé	Plus 2	Convertible
Tasmin/280i:	258	47	862
Tasmin 200:	16	Nil	45
350i:	52	6	897

Body/Chassis: GRP body on tubular steel chassis, 2-seater (or 2+2 seater) rear-hatch coupé or 2-seater open sports .

Engines: Ford 2792cc, V6, ohv, fuel injection, 160bhp (DIN);
Ford 1993cc, 4-cyl in-line, ohc, 101bhp (DIN);
Rover 3528cc, V8, ohv, fuel injection, 190-197bhp (DIN).

Layout: Front engine, rear wheel drive, 4-speed (optional 5-speed; standard on 350i) manual or 3-speed automatic gearbox.

Performance:

Tasmin/280i: Top speed c.130mph, 0-60mph in under 9sec;
Tasmin 200: Top speed c.115mph, 0-60mph in c.10sec;
350i: Top speed c.135mph, 0-60mph in c.6-7sec.

Prices Today: Tasmin/280i: £ 350i: £+

Above: **The handsome TVR Tasmin Convertible.**

The Tasmin was launched in 1980, the first of a series that was to become known affectionately as the TVR "wedges". Almost everything about the Tasmin was new – the handsome and eye-catching body, the improved chassis, and engines that were new to TVR. The good-looking car was designed by Oliver Winterbottom (who had also styled the Lotus Elite and Eclat) with chassis design by Ian Jones (also ex-Lotus).

For the first time with TVR, a 2+2 seater and automatic transmission became available (though the latter is rare, with only 14 cars so fitted). There were also disc brakes all round (inboard at the rear), the headlamps were "pop-up" and the spare wheel was moved from the very front of the car (as in the M-Series) to the very rear. The independent suspension was all new too, with a Ford-derived front end and a custom TVR rear end.

The development of the car had taken a great deal of time and money but it was a good investment as the series was the mainstay of TVR production during the 1980s and over 2,600 "wedges" of all types were made.

The launch engine for the Tasmin was the Ford "Cologne" V6 with fuel injection. The gearbox was an all-synchromesh Ford unit (overdrive was not available) and the car used a Salisbury final drive.

To begin with there was only the 2-seater Coupé, but this was joined later in 1980 by the Convertible and the 2+2 seater Coupé. The Convertible had electric windows, rather than the previous M-Series Convertible's sidescreens. The 2+2, although it looked similar to the 2-seater Coupé, had in fact a quite different body with a shorter nose, different bonnet (without louvres), longer tail, altered roofline and prominent, flared, side skirts and a bigger chin spoiler up front. Perhaps surprisingly, the car was not a great seller, with only 47 sold and so production of that version ended in late 1985.

In spring 1981 came the Series 2 Coupé, which was a 2-seater but used the bodyshell of the 2+2 car. The Convertible continued unchanged. Later that year, TVR launched the Tasmin 200, which was a Tasmin 2-seater Coupé or Convertible with the Ford "Pinto" 2-litre engine. The car also had a lower trim specification (for example, some had manual windows) to get its launch price under £10,000, but it was not a commercial success and was phased out in 1984 with only 61 cars sold. The 2-litre engine was not offered for the 2+2 car.

In 1982, the Ford 5-speed manual gearbox, the Ford 3-speed automatic transmission, air-conditioning, and power steering all became options on the Tasmins. That same year, at the British Motor Show, TVR showed a turbo version of the Tasmin, but only two were ever made.

The following year, 1983, saw the important step of TVR returning to the US market, selling mainly the Convertible but also the Coupé. This move had required TVR to get the V6 engine certified – the process reduced the power output to 145bhp and the car's weight increased by c.300lb. The effort paid off, with hundreds of cars going to North America over the next few years.

In 1982, Martin Lilley sold TVR to Peter Wheeler and Stewart Halstead became Managing Director.

In 1983 TVR made the important decision to use the Rover 3.5-litre V8 in the car. Another decision saw the "Tasmin" name quietly phased out, the cars becoming simply the TVR 280i and TVR 350i.

Below: **The Tasmin Convertible's neat soft-top roof is easy to use.**

In 1984 TVR offered an optional 3905cc bored-out version of the Rover engine, producing a quoted 275bhp and that TVR was called the 390SE Convertible.

During 1985-86 there came the Series 2 Convertibles with more rounded lines, new bumpers and changed front spoilers. Through the 1980s there followed ever-larger Rover-engined models, but these are outside the period covered by this book. There were also many improvements, particularly to the US-spec cars, but production of the 280i Coupé ended in 1987, the 280i Convertible ended in 1988 and the 350i cars in 1990.

Specific Checks: The critical item is the chassis as a badly corroded or accident damaged chassis will require a body-off repair that might cost more than the car is worth. Ideally get the car up on ramps or a garage lift to check its underside. Corroded outriggers are common in these TVRs but in all the early cars they can be replaced without the need for a body-off repair.

Check also the front suspension brackets for signs of distortion or cracking due to impact. Check both front and rear suspension for corrosion. If the car does not run straight this might indicate a distorted chassis.

The glassfibre bodies were beautifully made and painted but might have suffered from impact damage. Stress cracks can occur anyway which, although only cosmetic, can spoil the look of the car.

The V6 and V8 engines are good and normally reliable if serviced correctly, but check for overheating. Some cars have an extra electric cooling fan to help ease this situation, but it is probably better to ensure that all parts of the cooling system are in tiptop condition.

The inboard rear brakes can be neglected and this may be the case if the handbrake seems faulty.

The Tasmin family had lots of electrically powered items. Check all electrical equipment carefully, especially the driver's door window lifter and the pop-up headlamps (the units are not regarded as faulty if they do not rise together, but note replacement motors are expensive). Faulty electrical kit is often due to corroded earths. Pre-1983/4 cars used identity tags instead of colour-coded wiring, which can make circuit tracing a problem if tags are lost or damaged.

Rainwater leaks are not uncommon with both coupés and convertibles – check the seats and carpets for water damage, and the boots of convertibles.

The windscreens are specific to these cars so check carefully for stone damage, scratches or delamination (seen as white marks within the glass).

Prices Today: The TVR Car Club has a detailed record of all of these early "wedges" and the Club estimates that 40-60% have survived (perhaps fewer early Tasmin/280i cars and more of the 350i Coupés). In terms of value, as a general rule, the convertibles cost slightly more than the coupés and the 350i cars are worth perhaps about one third to one half more than the V6 models, with the Tasmin 200 worth the least, but value depends much on condition. A high mileage but well cared for car will be worth more than a low mileage neglected example. Overall, these cars, especially the early models, are probably currently undervalued.

Above & Below: **The rare 350i Plus 2 (1983). Only six were made.**

Above: **The 350i Coupé.**   Below: **The Tasmin Convertible (1982).**

INTRODUCTION

This section covers an interesting and diverse range of sports cars, some very rare, which have been selected for inclusion in this book for completeness.

The largest group in this section are cars from selected smaller manufacturers whose omission, we believe, would be an error. Although normally excluded, a few kit cars (and body conversions) appear, usually because of a close connection with a sports car that is already listed. Also included are models which were made by a major manufacturer but which were only made in small numbers. There are also a few models that some readers may not consider as "real" sports cars while other readers would disagree with that view.

Finally there are a couple of sports cars which were launched later than the normal date limits for this book, so are not strictly "classics", but are included to prevent any confusion as they have the same names as their illustrious forebears.

At the end of this section is a short Photo Miscellany illustrating other interesting sports cars.

ASTON MARTIN DB3 & DB3S

Dates: 1951-56

Nos. Built: 10 & 30

Price Today: HiValue

Left: **A DB3S seen at Wiscombe Park Hill Climb, 1979.**

Body/Chassis: Aluminium body on steel chassis, 2-seater sports-racer.
Engines: 2580cc, 6-cyl, dohc, 140+bhp (DB3S: 2922cc, 180-240bhp).
Layout: Front engine, RWD, 5-speed (DB3S: 4-speed) manual gearbox.
Performance: 180bhp DB3S: c.140mph, 0-60mph in c.6-7sec.

THIS book normally excludes sports-racers but the DB3 and DB3S are included to complete the DB number sequence.

These cars were often modified during their lives, so this is a much simplified description. In 1950 Aston Martin took on the well-known Austrian engineer, Robert Eberan von Eberhorst, to help design a car specifically to win international races. The result was the DB3 with its new all-tubular chassis, IFS and de Dion rear. It first raced in 1951. 10 cars were made. Race successes were marred by crashes and mechanical problems.

In 1953 came the much revised, lighter and compact DB3S, conceived by Willie Watson, styled by Frank Feeley and with input from von Eberhorst. The new car was more competitive. 2493cc, 2992cc engines and disc brakes were also tried. Despite crashes, there were many race successes, including class wins (and overall 2nds) at Le Mans. 30 DB3S cars were made.

ARKLEY SS

Dates: Since 1970

Number Built: NK

Price Today: Contact Club

Body/Chassis: GRP & steel unitary, 2-seater open sports.
Engines: As per Austin-Healey Sprite/MG Midget.
Layout: Front engine, RWD, 4-speed manual gearbox.
Performance: As per Sprite/Midget (slightly quicker).

THE attractive Arkley SS is a straightforward (and relatively cheap) body conversion kit for the Sprite/Midget and was the brainchild of John Britten, a successful racing driver. The Arkley conversion kit is still available today from Peter May Engineering (www.petermayengineering.com).

The conversion entails removing some panels at the front and rear of the car, but leaving the floorpan, centre-body, doors and windscreen untouched. Then a one-piece forward-hinged GRP front is fitted. At the rear another GRP section is bonded on which also supports the externally mounted spare wheel. Access to this new boot space is from inside the car.

The bodykit completely alters the car's looks and most onlookers do not realise the underpinnings are simply a Sprite or Midget, but its lighter weight gives it better performance.

BERKELEY SPORTS

Dates: 1956-60

No. Built: c.2,100

Price Today: £

Left: **Note the door front slopes. Later cars were stronger and had vertical door leading edges.**

Body/Chassis: GRP/alloy monocoque, 2-seat (rare 2+2) open sports.
Engines: Anzani 322cc, 2-cyl, 15bhp; Excelsior 328cc, 2-cyl, 18bhp;
Excelsior 492cc, 3-cyl, 30bhp. (All 2-stroke engines).
Layout: Front transverse engine, FWD, 3/4-speed manual gearbox.
Performance: 322/328cc: c.60mph; 492cc: c.80+mph.

THE Berkeleys were designed by Laurie Bond. These pretty and petite sports cars (only 10ft 3in long) had coil spring independent suspension, and used small air-cooled motorbike engines driving the front wheels via a chain drive. The engine and gearbox were mounted ahead of the front wheels.

The Type SA322 cars had a 3-speed column change and c.164 of these cars were made. From early 1957 came the SE328 and by mid-year it had a 4-speed floor change. About 1,250 of these 328cc cars were made before the SE492 (492cc) came in late 1957 (c.650 made). There was also the larger Foursome 2+2 (under 20 sold) and the 1960 B65 (with 328cc engine, c.10 sold). There were racing successes, especially with the SE492.

Over half were exported. About 200 cars survive world-wide.

BERKELEY B95 & B105

Dates: 1959-60
Number Built: c.200
Price Today: £

Body/Chassis: GRP/alloy monocoque, 2-seater open sports.
Engine: Royal Enfield 692cc, 2-cyl, ohv, 40 or 50bhp.
Layout: Front transverse engine, FWD, 4-speed manual gearbox.
Performance: See text.

IN search of higher performance, Berkeley launched the B95 and B105 in 1959. Unlike the other Berkeleys, these cars used 4-stroke engines (but still air-cooled). The B95 used the Royal Enfield Meteor engine with 40bhp, while the similar looking B105 used the tuned Constellation version producing 50bhp. The front of the car had to be restyled to fit the taller engines.

Weighing only c.7cwt (c.350kg), performance was brisk. The model numbers reflected the claimed top speeds of 95 and 105mph, but 90 and 100mph were more realistic. The B105 could also reach 60mph in about 16sec. Some cars were raced.

Berkeley also announced the larger "Q" 2+2 seater and "QB" with more luggage room but probably only a handful were made.

Most B95 and B105 cars remained in the UK. The Berkeley Enthusiasts' Club estimates that about 50 survive world-wide.

BERKELEY T60

Dates: 1959-60
Number Built: c.1,800
Price Today: £

Body/Chassis: GRP/metal monocoque, 2-seat (& 2+2) open sports.
Engine: Excelsior 328cc, 2-cyl, 2-stroke, 18bhp.
Layout: Front transverse engine, FWD, 4-speed manual gearbox.
Performance: Top speed c.60mph, 0-50mph in c.30sec.

THE T60 3-wheeler was for the UK market. Its structure included some steel. It had a 16in longer wheelbase (at 7ft 2in) and sold well, partly because it could be driven on a motorbike licence. As with all Berkeleys, it was available with a soft or hard top.

The last cars made had revised suspension subframe layouts to address structural problems.

In late 1960, a 2+2 seater, the T60/4, was launched, with revised rear bodywork, but only c.50 were made.

Over the years many cars have been modified with other motorbike engines, while others have used a Mini engine complete with gearbox and front subframe (flared wheelarches identify these Mini-powered T60s). In the 1990s, a few more T60s and Mini-based "Bandinis" were built.

The club estimates that about 200 T60 cars survive.

BOND BUG

Dates: 1970-74
Number Built: c.2,268
Price Today: £

Body/Chassis: GRP body on steel chassis, 2-seater FHC.
Engines: Reliant 701cc, 4-cyl in-line, ohv, 29bhp (700ES: 31bhp); From 1973: 748cc, 4-cyl in-line, ohv, 32bhp.
Layout: Front engine, RWD, 4-speed manual gearbox.
Performance: Top speed c.75-80mph, 0-50mph in c.13-15sec.

THE Bond Bug was in fact made mainly by Reliant, who had taken over the Bond company. The car's futuristic and eye-catching design was by Tom Karen of Ogle Design. Road testers praised its stability and the word "fun" was used frequently when describing the car.

The car was only available in a tangerine colour with a black interior. As it had 3 wheels and weighed under 8cwt (c.400kg) it could be driven in the UK on a full motorbike licence.

The car was available in three trim states: the 700, 700E and 700ES. The 700 was very basic, and seemingly only one car was made; the 700E had side screens, heater and canopy telescopic damper (but no spare wheel) and the 700ES had everything!

From 1971, the gearbox had synchromesh on all forward gears. In 1972, the steering column was shortened to permit a safer dished steering wheel. In 1973, the 750E and 750ES replaced the 700 models. These had a larger engine (all-alloy as before), and 142 cars were made before production ended.

In the late 1980s the Webster Motor Co. made a few 4-wheeled Bugs, which were good-looking.

The Bug Club estimates that there may be 700 or more Bond Bugs left today, some of which have had the more powerful 850cc Reliant Robin engine fitted.

When checking a Bond Bug, the key item to check is the body/chassis unit. The GRP body is fastened to the chassis with pop rivets, which can corrode or work loose and the chassis itself rusts. Lift the seats to check the body/chassis mounting points. Also check for bulging of the GRP near the canopy hinges, damper strut mounts and in the boot (due to corrosion of local steel reinforcement plates sandwiched in the GRP body). Look underneath to check the chassis and the steering box mounting. Also check the four rear suspension trailing arms for rust.

The engine (which is quite noisy), gearbox and rear-axle are all relatively reliable. The brakes are from the Mini.

Left: **Entry is by raising the large canopy, which also gives access to the engine. The car's sidescreens can be removed and then stowed in the 3cuft boot.**

BUCKLER

Dates: 1949-62?

Total Number Built: c.400 (all types)

Prices Today: Contact Club

Left: **A MkV.**

Right: **A DD2.**

Body/Chassis: GRP or alloy body on steel chassis, 2-seat open sports.
Engines: Mainly Ford 1172cc, side-valve, but many other types too.
Layout: Front engine, RWD, 3/4-speed manual gearbox.

DEREK Butler was highly innovative and apparently was the first to sell spaceframed sports cars. He also pioneered purchase tax-free car kits, was an early user of GRP, and built close-ratio gearboxes and karts. The MkV was their first main production car (there were no MkI-IV). There was also the slab sided Ninety (1954-62), the later DD1, DD2 and others. All cars were road/racers. The Buckler Car Register knows of about 100 survivors.

FAIRTHORPE (Technical Exponents) TX

Dates: 1966-79?

Number Built: 86

Prices Today: £

Left: **A TX-SS.**

Body/Chassis: GRP body on steel chassis, 2-seat FHC (Tripper: Open).
Engines: Various Triumph engines, usually 2L or 2.5L, 6-cyl (See text).
Layout: Front engine, RWD, 4-speed manual gearbox.
Performance: Faster than equivalent engined Triumph sports car.

THE TX series were the last production cars from Fairthorpe and were the creation of Torix Bennett, who had patented an ingenious transverse-rod IRS and displayed this on the one-off TX 1 roadster at the 1965 London Motor Show. This was followed by the TX-GT coupé, which used a Triumph GT6 engine, gearbox, tailgate and modified chassis, but only 7 were made. In 1968 came the TX-S (usually with the GT6 engine) and TX-SS (with TR6 engine and a large bonnet bulge). The cars had larger rear three-quarter windows and a fixed rear screen (from an MGB GT). Only 10 of the TX-S/TX-SS were made (the last in 1976) but not all had the Torix rear suspension.

The TX-Tripper was launched at the 1971 Racing Car Show. It had a beach buggy style GRP body bolted onto a Triumph Spitfire or GT6 chassis and 68 were sold from 1971 to c.1979.

DAVRIAN

Dates: 1967-83

Number Built: c.320

Price Today: £

Left: **A Mk5.**

Body/Chassis: GRP monocoque, 2-seater, mainly FHC.
Engines: Mainly Imp Sport 875cc, 4-cyl, sohc, 51bhp or 998cc, 65bhp.
Layout: Rear engine, RWD, 4-speed manual gearbox.
Performance: 998cc: Over 100mph, 0-60mph in under 10sec.

THE Davrians were created by Adrian Evans, initially in London, then later in Wales. Most Davrians were Imp-based, using the Imp engine/transaxle (rear-mounted, as usual) with Imp front and rear suspension and brakes. Pop-up headlamps were usually fitted. The GRP monocoque was unusually stiff due to large foam-filled sills, a rigid floor and sturdy bulkheads.

Early cars were all built as open cars with optional hardtop or soft-top (and open top cars were still available up to about 1973). The design evolved, and after c.39 cars had been built came the Mk4, in 1969, with a front-mounted radiator. The new model also had a front-hinged (or detachable) front to facilitate maintenance. The attractive Mk5 from 1970 had a completely removable rear to give access to the engine, which was supported by a new steel A-frame. The Mk6/6a, from 1973, added some refinements, including opening rear quarter lights and the Mk6a had headlamps which retracted flat (so the lamps were facing upwards). Some earlier Davrians also had this feature.

Whereas earlier Davrians were mainly road cars that could be used for competition, the Mk7 from late 1974 was more for competition work. The Mk7 had a longer wheelbase and wider track. The standard bonnet had a deep recess to aid airflow through the radiator. The twin wing fuel fillers were gone so refuelling now required the bonnet to be opened to gain access. A roll cage was built-in as standard and access to the door handles were now via neat recesses at the back of the doors. A key feature of the Mk7 was that it could take a variety of engines to suit different competition classes. The Mk7a, from 1978, had rectangular headlamps and/or full width grille. The final Mk8, from 1978, had fixed rectangular headlamps, more squared styling and about half were Imp powered, the remainder being mainly Ford. The final model, the Dragon, was the most developed, and used a transverse, mid-mounted Ford engine, but only 12 were made.

Despite many racing successes, the company ceased trading in 1983. One successor, the Corry Cultra was short-lived. However, in 1985, production of a true successor, the Darrian, was started by Team Duffee Engineering in Wales.

Left: **A very rare Mk7 Demon. The Demon was a mid-engined version, usually with Mini power. Note the humped rear deck. Only a few Demons were made.**

GORDON-KEEBLE GK1 & IT

Dates: 1964-66

Number Built: 99+1

Price Today: £££££

> **Body/Chassis:** GRP body on steel chassis, 4-seater sports saloon.
> **Engine:** Chevrolet 5355cc (327cubic inch), V8, ohv, 300bhp (gross).
> **Layout:** Front engine, RWD, 4-speed manual gearbox.
> **Performance:** Top speed c.140mph, 0-60mph in c.7sec.

THIS handsome car with its classic styling by Giugiaro (then working at Bertone) appeared in prototype form at the Geneva Motor Show in 1960, badged as the Gordon GT. The chassis design by Jim Keeble comprised a complex spaceframe chassis built mainly of 1-inch square tubing. It featured coil spring suspension, a de Dion rear axle and disc brakes all round with twin brake servos (the front and rear had separate hydraulic circuits). The car had an all-steel body and a 4.6-litre Chevrolet Corvette V8 engine. *Autocar* magazine said it was "the most electrifying vehicle it had ever tested", but it was not until 1964 that the car eventually went into production, in slightly modified form. It was renamed the Gordon-Keeble GK1 and now had a glassfibre body with a larger, 327cubic inch, Chevrolet engine.

Over the years many owners have made modifications to the cars, specifically to improve the steering, and some have upgraded the brakes (which were good even when standard) and re-trimmed in leather (vinyl was the original trim). A few cars have had automatic gearboxes fitted.

These were well built cars but check for corrosion of the jacking points (which should have end plugs fitted), also check the suspension and differential mountings. If major corrosion is suspected, this would require the aluminium under-shield to be removed. The engine is long-lived if treated properly but look for healthy oil pressure, no overheating and no blue smoke when revving a warm engine. The gearbox is also sturdy with synchromesh on all forward gears. Check also the exhaust which is sometimes low slung and a grounding may damage the exhaust manifolds. The electrics can give problems, but this is usually due to poor earthing or corroded contacts.

Although Gordon-Keeble was not a major manufacturer, their car caused a stir and became well known, but the original company failed. New owners renamed it the IT (for "International Touring"), but that company also failed. 99 cars were made plus a further car created from spare parts several years later.

The Gordon-Keeble Owners' Club knows all the 90+ "Keebles" that have survived. Top prices are for cars that have already had the important mechanical modifications.

Left: **Knock-on wheels were a standard fit. The car's bonnet badge features a tortoise which is amusing as the Keeble is certainly not slow!**

INNOCENTI SPIDER & COUPE

Dates: 1960-68

Numbers Built:
Spider: c.6,860
Coupé: c.790

Price Today: Contact Club

> **Body/Chassis:** Steel unitary, 2-seater open sports & FHC.
> **Engines:** Austin-Healey Sprite 948-1098cc, 4-cyl in-line, ohv, 43-59bhp.
> **Layout:** Front Engine, RWD, 4-speed manual gearbox.
> **Performance:** Similar to Sprite/Midget.

THE good-looking Spider 950 (styled by Ghia) was Italian, but is included here for interest as it was based on the Austin-Healey Sprite in a collaborative venture with BMC, who made the Sprite. The Spider used the Sprite's floorpan, engine, transmission, suspension, brakes and steering but in a better equipped car.

From 1963, the Sprite's 1098cc engine was used and the car became the Innocenti S. Production of the open car ended in 1965, though a Coupé version, the Innocenti C, was introduced in 1966 and continued until 1968 (still with the 1098cc engine). Approx. 790 Coupés were made. Despite the connection between Innocenti and BMC, the latter did not import the cars (which remained LHD only). Sales were slow as the cost was high. Today there are probably less than a dozen cars in the UK and to purchase one (anywhere) that has not succumbed to rust, is a challenge.

LENHAM

Dates: 1963-90s?

Number Built: NK

Price Today: Contact Club

See also photo on page 13.

> **Body/Chassis:** GRP & steel unitary, 2-seater FHC.
> **Engines:** As per Austin-Healey Sprite/MG Midget.
> **Layout:** Front engine, RWD, 4-speed manual gearbox.
> **Performance:** As per Sprite/Midget (slightly quicker).

THE Lenham Motor Company was well known in the 1960s and 1970s for their hardtops made for many British sports cars. The company was also known for its attractive Sprite/Midget body conversion kit (as shown above). Lenham claimed their conversion increased the car's top speed by up to 9mph due to better aerodynamics, and the lighter body (by c.100lb/45kg) gave the car better acceleration. Interestingly, Lenham also initially made the Arkley kit (see page 156) under contract.

The Lenham conversion entailed removing most of the donor car's tail and bonding on a new GRP one-piece roof/rear. A special "Superfast" forward-hinged front completed the new look. There was the "Le Mans Coupé", the "GT" (which did not have rear side windows) and the GTO DHC (only 2 made). Lenham also made a GT conversion for the Triumph Spitfire.

LEA-FRANCIS 14HP SPORTS

Dates: 1947-49

Number Built: 109-111

Price Today: £££

Body/Chassis: Alloy panels on steel frame mounted on steel chassis, 2-seater open sports.
Engine: 1767cc, 4-cyl in-line, ohv, 77-87bhp.
Layout: Front engine, RWD, 4-speed manual gearbox.
Performance: Top speed c.90mph, 0-60mph in c.19sec.

THE Lea-Francis company had been producing cars since well before WW2. In 1946 they launched their first postwar models and in 1947 came the 14HP Sports (the "14HP" was not the actual power of its engine but a figure calculated solely on engine size, and relating to tax). The handsome streamlined styling was advanced for its time, though it still had rear-hinged doors. There was a useful amount of storage space behind the seats, especially when the soft-top roof was up.

The 1.8-litre engine, designed by Hugh Rose, was notable for having its overhead valves set at 90 degrees to each other and operated by very short pushrods from two camshafts, one on each side of the cylinder block and located in a high position. The engine in the Sports produced more power than the saloon's by using a high-lift camshaft, a higher compression ratio and twin SU carbs. The prototype and one other car had a 12HP 1.5-litre engine, but these were soon changed for larger units.

The chassis was conventional with semi-elliptic leaf springs at the front and rear, though at the end of the model's production run the last three cars were fitted with independent front suspension. The drum brakes were operated mechanically.

In addition to the 14HP Sports cars, a further 18 chassis were made, 14 of which became Connaught sports-racers (these had independent front suspension like the last three 14HP Sports).

The 14HP Sports had some rally successes such as being one of only 36 cars (out of 121 starters) to finish the gruelling 1950 Alpine Rally.

When inspecting a "LeaF" (as enthusiasts call these cars), first check the paperwork then contact the Lea-Francis Owners' Club as it has records of all the cars and knows most of them. The "LeaFs" were sturdy and well built, the main area of deterioration being the steel rear floor which can corrode.

The Club estimates that more than half the 14HP Sports still exist. An excellent survival rate.

Left: **14HP Sports. The rear wheel "spats" are easily removable. The bumper-mounted indicators are non-standard.**

LEA-FRANCIS 2½-LITRE SPORTS

Dates: 1949-53

Number Built: 85

Price Today: £££

Body/Chassis: Alloy panels on steel frame mounted on steel chassis, 2/4-seater open sports.
Engine: 2496cc, 4-cyl in-line, ohv, 95-100bhp.
Layout: Front engine, RWD, 4-speed manual gearbox.
Performance: Top speed c.95-100mph, 0-50mph in c.8-9sec.

AT the London Motor Show in late 1949, Lea-Francis announced a new sports model, the 2½-Litre Sports, to replace the earlier 14HP Sports. The 2½-Litre Sports used a new engine (again by Hugh Rose) which retained the characteristic high positioning of the camshafts, and had four individual rocker boxes.

The new car had much in common with the 14HP Sports but there were several important improvements in the bodywork including a 3-inch increase in cockpit width, new front-hinged doors, and wind-up windows instead of sidescreens. Some owners have since changed the door glass to lighter perspex. In addition, a rear seat for occasional use was fitted as standard.

The 2½-Litre Sports used the same chassis as the earlier 14HP Sports but the brakes were now hydro-mech, ie hydraulic at the front and mechanically operated at the rear (though this became all hydraulic in 1952). Additionally, the chassis now had independent front suspension with torsion bars.

As with the 14HP Sports, when inspecting a car, first check the paperwork then contact the Lea-Francis Owners' Club as it has records of all the cars and knows most of them. The "LeaFs" were sturdy and well built, the main area of deterioration being the steel rear floor which can corrode. Check that the Armstrong Siddeley gearbox works without excessive noise in all gears (ask if it has been replaced or reconditioned). Though many owners find this gearbox perfectly satisfactory, some have fitted an alternative.

The 2½-Litre Sports never achieved the success it perhaps deserved due to its price, being hand-built in small numbers.

In 1960, Lea-Francis launched a completely different sports car, called the Lynx. It had a 2.5-litre Ford Zephyr engine but only 3 were made (apparently all have survived).

The Club estimates that around half the 2½-Litre Sports still exist. An excellent survival rate. The 2½-Litre Sports is valued slightly more than the 14HP Sports.

Left: **The 2½-Litre Sports. There are no running boards, whereas there were on the earlier 14HP. The indicators on this particular car are non-standard.**

LOTUS ELAN (Type M100)

Dates: 1989-95

Number Built: c.4,650

Price Today: ££

Body/Chassis: GRP body on steel chassis, 2-seater open sports.
Engines: Isuzu 1588cc, 4-cyl, dohc, fuel injection, 130bhp (Turbo: 165bhp).
Layout: Front transverse engine, FWD, 5-speed manual gearbox.
Performance: Turbo: Top speed c.135mph, 0-60mph in c.6-7sec.

THE Elan was launched in 1989 (US: 1991) and due to General Motors owning both Lotus and Isuzu, the latter's new 1.6L, 16-valve, twin cam engine was adopted. It was mounted transversely in the front, giving a significant front weight bias. The attractive Elan was styled by Peter Stevens. It had disc brakes all round and power-assisted steering. The coil spring independent suspension was finely developed to provide excellent handling. There were two engines: the normal Turbo version (in the Elan SE) and the non-Turbo (only c.130 cars made). The Elan was a highly competent modern sports car.

Production stopped in 1992, then restarted in 1994 as the Elan S2 to use up the stock of Isuzu engines. The S2 had minor improvements and c.800 were made.

Postscript: Kia purchased the rights, installed their own engine, and sold the car in the Far East until c.1999.

MINI JEM

Dates: 1966-76

Number Built: c.350

Price Today: £

Left: **The author's Mk2 in the early 1970s.**

Body/Chassis: GRP monocoque on steel subframes, 2-seater FHC.
Engines: Mini 848-1275cc, 4-cyl in-line, ohv, 33+bhp.
Layout: Front transverse engine, FWD, 4-speed manual gearbox.
Performance: Faster than equivalent engined Mini.

THE pretty Mini Jem had a loose connection with the Mini Marcos. The Mini Jem was sold only as a kit car, ie as a body unit to which the buyer had to add all the usually second-hand mechanical and electrical parts, including Mini front and rear subframes. Cars were factory trimmed from the Mk2.

The Mk2 had no external door handles – a door window was unlocked and lowered to permit the interior handle to be used. Side windows were glass but the large flat rear screen was usually perspex. The Mk3 had an optional rear hatch.

The design had the benefit of wind tunnel testing and the car was rock steady at speed in cross winds. It also had good handling and could be easily drifted around corners.

The kit was made by various manufacturers, plus 10 made in Australia. Later there were c.35 Kingfisher Sprint derivatives.

MORGAN PLUS 4 PLUS

Dates: 1963-67

Number Built: 26

Price Today: Contact Club

Body/Chassis: GRP body on steel chassis, 2-seater FHC.
Engine: Triumph 2138cc, 4-cyl in-line, ohv, 105bhp.
Layout: Front engine, RWD, 4-speed manual gearbox.
Performance: Top speed c.110mph, 0-60mph in c.12sec.

IN an attempt to market a more modern Morgan, the company launched the Plus 4 Plus in 1963 at the London Motor Show. The streamlined and stylish car was radical (for Morgan) as it used a GRP body and was a FHC, unlike all their previous cars. Only the grille and badges indicated the car was a Morgan, but mechanically the car was virtually a standard Plus 4 (though the chassis had extensions at the front and there was a new bulkhead to improve rigidity and provide body mounting points).

The Plus 4 Plus was a good car but was expensive and sales were less than expected. With hindsight one can see that the market simply wanted more traditional Morgans.

Refer to the Morgan Plus 4 entry for specific checks when inspecting a Plus 4 Plus.

The Morgan Sports Car Club knows of 23 survivors of these rare and collectable cars.

PEERLESS GT

Dates: 1957-59?

Number Built: c.300

Price Today: ££

Body/Chassis: GRP body on steel chassis, 2+2 seater FHC.
Engine: Triumph 1991cc, 4-cyl in-line, ohv, 100bhp.
Layout: Front engine, RWD, 4-speed manual (optional overdrive).
Performance: Top speed over 110mph, 0-60mph in c.10sec.

THE Peerless used a multi-tubular semi-spaceframe chassis (much triangulated for strength) with a GRP body of nice proportions. The project was supported by Triumph who supplied the Triumph TR3 engine and running gear, but the Peerless had a de Dion rear suspension. John Gordon, later behind the Gordon-Keeble car, was involved in the project.

A Peerless GT completed the 1958 Le Mans in a commendable 16th place, averaging 84mph.

In 1959 the Phase II appeared with revised front, no "P" insignia in the grille and recessed headlights. The new GRP bodyshell was lighter and easier to fabricate (with fewer sub-mouldings), and was not bonded/riveted to the chassis as before. About 50 Phase II cars were made before the company ceased trading, but the design resurfaced as the Warwick GT (see page 165).

PIPER GTT & P2

Dates: 1967-74
Number Built: c.80?
Price Today: ££/£££

Left: **An early P2.**

Body/Chassis: GRP body on tubular steel chassis, 2-seater FHC.
Engine: Ford 1599cc, 4-cyl in-line, ohv, (Piper tuned 100bhp).
Layout: Front engine, RWD, 4-speed manual gearbox.
Performance: Top speed c.110-120mph, 0-60mph in c.9sec.

THE stunning Piper GTT's styling was by Tony Hilder. 40 cars were made before the Piper P2 (ie "Phase 2") version arrived in 1971. The P2 looked similar to the GTT but had twin headlamps rather than single rectangular units, different tail lights, a 6-inch longer and stiffer chassis and improved rear suspension. In 1972 the headlamps became pop-up units.

Equipment usually included tinted glass/perspex, wide alloy wheels and twin alloy fuel tanks (no fuel gauge on early cars!).

The author recalls his own P2 (illustrated) attracted much attention in the mid-1970s, but town driving was tricky due to restricted visibility, especially in rain which caused the fixed side windows to mist up. High speed cruising was relaxed and cornering was impressive (in the dry).

Piper was not a major sports car manufacturer, but is included here for interest (and because the author owned one).

RELIANT SCIMITAR SS1, SST & Sabre

Dates: 1984-95
No. Built: c.1,700
Prices Today: £

Left: **An SS1, with its unusual "lens upward" pop-up headlamps.**

Body/Chassis: Composite body on steel chassis, 2-seater open sports.
Engines: Ford 1.3/1.4/1.6 CVH; Rover K 1.4i; Nissan 1.8Ti; 69-135bhp.
Layout: Front engine, RWD, 4/5-speed manual gearbox.
Performance: 1.6: c.105mph/10sec; Turbo: c.125mph/7sec.

DESIGNED by Michelotti, the SS1's bodywork was technically advanced using different composites (but this causes paint to fade at different rates, and panel gaps to vary). The complex chassis rusted badly, so later cars were galvanised. To improve performance, a Nissan 1.8 Turbo (135bhp) became available in 1988, making the most of the excellent chassis.

The redesigned SS2 did not go into production, but in 1989 came the SST ("T" for designer Bill Towns) which had cleaned-up lines, all-GRP body and conventional pop-up headlamps. The Ford 1.4 "Lean burn" engine replaced the 1.3-litre, but the Nissan Turbo remained available. In 1992 there was a major restyle and rename to Sabre, then Scimitar Sabre, and the 1.4 Rover K-Series replaced the Ford engine. The Reliant Scimitar & Sabre Owners' Club estimates that c.50 SST and c.140 Sabres were produced.

RILEY RMC & RMD

Dates: 1948-51
Nos. Built:
RMC: c.474
RMD: c.498
Prices Today: £££

Left: **An RMC.**

Body/Chassis: Steel panels on ash frame with steel chassis, RMC: 3-seater open sports; RMD: 4-seater DHC.
Engine: 2443cc, 4-cyl in-line, ohv, 100bhp.
Layout: Front engine, RWD, 4-speed manual gearbox.
Performance: Top speed c.95mph, 0-60mph in c.16sec.

IN 1945, Riley launched their new and luxurious RM range, with their classic elegant lines. The RMA, RMB, RME and RMF models were saloons, while the RMC was a roadster and the RMD was a drophead coupé. All these RMs had rear-hinged front-opening doors. Of the nearly 23,000 RMA-RMF cars built (from 1945 to 1953), the RMC & RMD were the least numerous. Production was at the MG factory at Abingdon.

The 2.5-litre long-stroke engine in the RMC and RMD was of prewar design and had two camshafts mounted high in the cylinder block driving the overhead valves via short pushrods. Twin SU carburettors were used. The brakes were hydro-mechanical and there was IFS with twin wishbones, torsion bars and telescopic dampers. There were leaf springs at the rear.

The RMC was aimed mainly at the US market and had 3-abreast seating which required a column gearchange and an offset steering column. The car also had a fold-flat windscreen and, unusually, four overriders on the bumpers. In 1950, a floor gearchange became available. The RMC's bonnet was lower than the other RMs and its body panels were different. The RMD was a 4-seater aimed more at the UK market.

When checking one of these cars it is best to take an RM expert with you. The bodywork and ash frame are potentially the most costly and time-consuming problem areas. It all needs careful inspection, especially the A-post timbers (look into the front wheelarches). Sills are metal-covered wood. The bonnet tops are aluminium and can deform. The mechanical parts are long-lived, reflecting solid Riley engineering, but check the engine does not overheat. The rear leaf springs tend to sag with age.

Splits or bad wear in the leather seats are costly to repair. Overall, spares availability through the clubs is good. The Riley RM Club believe that world-wide, three-quarters of the RMCs and over half the RMDs may have survived – excellent survival rates.

Left: **An RMD.**

ROCHDALE OLYMPIC

Dates: 1960-73

Number Built: c.400?

Price Today: £

Body/Chassis: GRP monocoque, 2-seater FHC.
Engines: Phase I: Riley 1.5L, 4-cyl, 60bhp; Phase II: Ford 1.5L.
Layout: Front engine, RWD, 4-speed manual gearbox.
Performance: Phase I: c.105mph/12sec; Phase II: c.115mph/11sec.

FOLLOWING a number of kits, including the successful 1957 GT (c.1,350 made), Rochdale launched the Olympic in 1960 (the year of the Rome Olympic Games). The car was styled by Richard Parker and this little gem had a technically advanced GRP monocoque with a steel roll-over hoop in the windscreen pillars and a front tubular steel subframe. The Phase I cars (c.250 made) used a Riley engine and gearbox. A new Phase II model appeared at the 1963 Racing Car Show in London. The Phase II was designed for Ford power and used Triumph Spitfire based front suspension with disc brakes. These Phase II cars had lighter bodies, opening rear hatches and larger bonnets. Production of the car wound down in the mid-1960s with the firm diversifying into other GRP products. Few cars were made after 1968 though one was made as late as 1973. About half survive but only c.25 are roadworthy at any one time.

TORNADO TALISMAN

Dates: 1962-64

Number Built: c.186

Price Today: £

Body/Chassis: GRP body on steel chassis, 4-seater sports saloon.
Engine: Ford 1340/1498cc, 4-cyl in-line, ohv, 85/95bhp.
Layout: Front engine, RWD, 4-speed manual gearbox.
Performance: Top speed over 100mph, 0-60mph in c.10sec.

TORNADO Cars was started in 1957 by Bill Woodhouse and Anthony Bullen. Their first model, the Typhoon (see p.167), was a successful kit car and this was followed by the Tempest (c.10 made) and Thunderbolt (1 made). Then, after a factory fire in 1961, the company decided to go up-market. Based on Woodhouse's ideas, coachbuilders Williams & Pritchard created an aluminium prototype and this was shown, as the Talisman, at the 1962 Racing Car Show. It used a Cosworth-tuned Ford 1340cc engine as standard and had front disc brakes and coil spring independent suspension. The Talisman also had a well equipped interior. It was available fully built or in component form (to beat tax), and was quite pricey. Although the company traded into the 1980s, car production ended in 1964. The Tornado Register estimates c.20 of these handsome Talismans survive.

SWALLOW DORETTI

Dates: 1954-55

Number Built: 280-290

Price Today: Contact Club

Body/Chassis: Alloy panels on steel frame mounted on steel chassis, 2-seater open sports.
Engine: Triumph 1991cc, 4-cyl in-line, ohv, 90bhp.
Layout: Front engine, RWD, 4-speed manual (optional overdrive).
Performance: Top speed c.100mph, 0-60mph in c.13sec.

THE Swallow Coachbuilding company were part of the giant Tube Investments organisation and the latter decided they could sell a sports car in the US using spare capacity at Swallow and incorporating Tube Investments' products in its construction. The resulting good-looking car was designed by Frank Rainbow and its name, Doretti, was from "Dorothy" as Dorothy Deen (and her father) were the energetic US distributors for the car.

The Doretti used the Triumph TR2's engine, transmission and suspension which was mated to Swallow's own alloy body on a steel inner skin mounted on a tubular chrome-molybdenum steel chassis. Front suspension was coil and wishbone and the rear suspension was by semi-elliptical springs with radius arms to locate the live rear axle. The engine was located 7in further back than the TR2 which gave a near 50:50 weight distribution. The cars were well finished, with leather interiors.

A prototype was created in record time and shipped on the *Queen Mary* to the US to assess market reaction, which was positive, so the car went into production.

Sales were good, with almost half being exported to the US. However, production was stopped due to pressure from rival car companies who used Tube Investments' products and did not like the competition.

Frank Rainbow also designed a MkII version (called the Sabre) with stiffer frame, larger interior and bigger boot, but only three cars were made.

When checking a Doretti, first check the paperwork and ensure the car's numbers match. Contact the Swallow Doretti Register who know most of the cars.

The inner steelwork and alloy outer panels of the body can be difficult to restore so their condition is important. For mechanical checks, refer to the Triumph TR2 entry in this book.

The Register estimates that there are over 60 cars in the UK, half of them roadworthy. A greater number exist abroad, mainly in the US, though also in Australia and many other countries.

Top: This Doretti has non-standard bumpers and the optional aero-screens fitted.

Left: Note the right hand car has no rear bumper fitted.

TRIDENT CLIPPER, VENTURER & TYCOON

Dates: 1966-76

Number Built: c.70-85

Prices Today:
Clipper: £££
Venturer: ££
Tycoon: ££

Body/Chassis: GRP body on steel chassis, 2+2 seater FHC.
Engines: Clipper: Mainly Ford 289cu in (4.7L), V8, ohv, 271bhp (gross);
Venturer: Ford 2994cc, V6, ohv, 141bhp (net);
Tycoon: Triumph 2498cc, 6-cyl in-line, ohv, fuel injection,150bhp.
Layout: Front engine, RWD, 4-speed manual (some overdrive or auto).
Performance: See text.

THIS handsome car, styled by Trevor Fiore, had a complicated birth involving several car companies, notably TVR, but was finally launched as a Trident convertible (the only one made) at the 1966 Racing Car Show. The definitive Clipper followed, first appearing at the 1967 show. Although Trident never made it to being a major sports car manufacturer, they are included in this book due to their TVR connection and because the marque is well-known even though relatively few cars were made.

Powered by a large US Ford 289 V8 engine, early cars used an Austin-Healey 3000 chassis but with the ending of Big Healey production this was changed in 1969 to a lengthened Triumph TR6 chassis. The Clipper could do 140+mph and had an 0-60 time of 5-6 seconds (c.31-35 cars made). A second model, the Venturer (c.31-41 cars made), was launched in 1969. It had a Ford 3-litre V6 "Essex" engine and was considerably cheaper. It could still do 120+mph and 0-60 in about 8 seconds. A few post-1971 Clippers had Chrysler 5.6L or Ford 5L V8s. Trident also fitted the TR6 fuel injected engine with optional automatic transmission into 5-6 cars, called the Tycoon. All three Trident models looked similar, the external changes being mainly different frontal treatments and different front wing side grilles.

In the UK the cars were available in component form to avoid Purchase Tax. All Tridents were well equipped for the era, including Sundym glass, headrests and electric windows (but no spare wheel). Factory fitted options included air-conditioning, sunroof and overdrive.

The company ceased trading in the early 1970s then resurfaced briefly, the last two cars being made in 1976.

When checking a Trident with the TR6 chassis, look for rust especially under the seat area. The Healey chassis is sturdy. Note that parts availability for Tridents is mostly good.

The Trident Car Club estimates that about 50 cars survive, half of them roadworthy. Clippers are valued about 50% more than the other models.

Left: **On early cars, the large rear window was fixed. From late 1971, it opened on two gas struts. The Trident illustrated left (and in the photo above) is a Venturer.**

TRIUMPH ROADSTER

Dates: 1946-49

Nos. Built:
1800: c.2,500
2000: c.2,000

Prices Today: £££

Left: **Note the dickey seat.**

Body/Chassis: Aluminium panels (steel front wings) on ash frame with separate steel ladder chassis, 3/5-seater DHC.
Engines: 1800: 1776cc, 4-cyl in-line, ohv, 65bhp;
2000: 2088cc, 4-cyl in-line, ohv, 68bhp.
Layout: Front engine, RWD, 4-speed (2000: 3-speed) manual gearbox.
Performance: Top speed over 75mph, 0-60mph in c.30sec.

THE Triumph Roadster had splendid 1930s styling despite having been designed in the mid-1940s by Frank Callaby, Arthur Ballard and Ray Turner, not forgetting the influence of Sir John Black (the Standard Motor Company's boss), who wanted to build a sports car under the recently acquired Triumph name.

Due to postwar material shortages, the car was of traditional construction. It also used the same Standard engine and gearbox as supplied to Jaguar. The Roadster had IFS with a transverse leaf spring, while at the rear there were half elliptic leaf springs and a live axle. The car used hydraulic drum brakes all round.

Performance was adequate and one travelled in style and luxury. The Roadster had rear-hinged doors and a bench seat that could accommodate three people sitting abreast. This necessitated a column gearchange, though some cars have since had a floor change conversion.

The Triumph Roadster was the last UK car to feature a dickey seat (called a "rumble seat" in the US), whereby the rear boot lid split, the top part rose to create a glazed windscreen, while the lower part hinged down to reveal two extra seats. Access to these seats were via a step on the rear bumper. The dickey seat was behind the soft-top roof, hence no weather protection.

The initial Roadster, the 1800, was replaced by the 2000 model in 1948. This had the new 2-litre Vanguard engine with a 3-speed gearbox.

When checking one of these cars, ideally take along someone who is a Roadster expert. The engines and gearboxes are relatively robust. The tubular ladder chassis is strong but the ends at the bumpers and jacking points rust badly. The wood frame can rot, especially the door frames, sills, A-pillars, around the windscreen and boot. The steel front wings and inner wings can rust. Inside, check the condition of the Jaeger instruments (rare) and leather trim (expensive to replace).

The Triumph Roadster Club estimates that approximately 1,000 cars survive world-wide.

Left: **The dickey seat's windscreen can be seen folded down when not in use.**

TRIUMPH ITALIA 2000

Dates: 1958-62
Number Built: c.185?
Price Today: Contact Club

Left: **This restored Italia is minus its chrome bumpers.**

> **Body/Chassis:** Steel body & chassis, 2-seater FHC.
> **Engine:** Triumph 1991cc, 4-cyl in-line, ohv, 100bhp.
> **Layout:** Front engine, RWD, 4-speed manual (optional overdrive).
> **Performance:** Top speed over 105mph, 0-60mph in c.13sec.

THE Italia was created by Triumph's Italian dealer, Salvatore Ruffino, using a TR3 rolling chassis and a very good-looking Michelotti designed body. An alloy body prototype was shown in 1958 but altered slightly for production, which started in 1959. There were some mechanical differences to the TR3, eg an extra leaf in the rear springs due to the heavier body. The cars were virtually hand built by Vignale in Turin (so there are minor differences between cars) and nearly all were LHD.

Triumph lost interest after being taken over by Leyland, so Ruffino renamed it the Italia 2000. The last 30 cars were based on the TR3B. Today there are only a handful of Italias in the UK and probably less than 100 world-wide. If considering one of these desirable cars, note that front and rear screens and most trim (especially chrome items) are not currently available.

WARWICK GT

Dates: 1960-62
Number Built: c.40
Price Today: ££

> **Body/Chassis:** GRP body on steel chassis, 2+2 seater FHC.
> **Engine:** Triumph 1991cc, 4-cyl in-line, ohv, 100bhp.
> **Layout:** Front engine, RWD, 4-speed manual (optional overdrive).
> **Performance:** Top speed over 110mph, 0-60mph in c.10sec.

WHEN the Peerless company failed (see page 161), a new company reworked the Peerless design, giving it a one-piece forward-hinged front, and small, though distinctive, fins at the trailing edge of the roof gutter line. The handsome car retained the Triumph TR3 engine and transmission together with the Peerless GT's de Dion rear, and was renamed the Warwick GT.

Optional extras included leather trim, wire wheels and fabric sunroof, in an attempt to move the car up-market.

A handful of cars had a Buick 3.5-litre V8 engine fitted with a Moss gearbox and these cars were known as the 350GT and they could do 140mph. They were intended for export to the US but in early 1962 the company was wound up.

The final Warwick GTs were assembled by another company, D. A. Mallard Ltd, who had purchased the last components.

TURNER

Dates: 1955-66
Number Built: c.670
Prices Today: Climax: Contact Club Others: ££

Left: **950 Sports. This is a later car with tail fins.**

> **Body/Chassis:** GRP body on steel frame/chassis, 2-seat open sports.
> **Engines:** Austin & Coventry Climax, then Ford (See text).
> **Layout:** Front engine, RWD, 4-speed manual gearbox.
> **Performance:** 950/MkI: Top speed 80+mph, 0-60mph in c.18sec;
> Climax: Top speed 100+mph, 0-60mph in c.12sec.

THIS range of sports cars was created by Jack Turner. After making a few specials, he launched his first production model, the A30/803 Sports in 1955. It used the Austin A30's 803cc engine, gearbox, rear axle, front suspension and hydromechanical brakes, with Turner's rear suspension of trailing arms and torsion bars. The chassis consisted of two 3in steel tube side members with cross tubes. Bolted to the chassis was an all steel inner body consisting of front and rear bulkheads, floor, wheelarches and door frames. Perhaps c.40 of these cars were made to 1957. Then a new model, the 950 Sports, was launched with the Austin A35's larger 948cc engine and full hydraulic brakes. The early 950 Sports looked the same as the previous model but later ones had tail fins. A handful had Coventry Climax engines. Wire wheels and front disc brakes were options. About 225 of the 950 Sports were made, and most were exported.

In 1959 came the MkI (an unofficial title). This had a revised and nice looking GRP body bolted to the earlier steel inner body/ chassis, with the same 948cc engine and c.160 were made. In 1961 came the much improved MkII (149 made) with narrower doors, roomier cockpit and a different bonnet. The MkII was the start of a change from Austin to Ford engines, but c.60 of the MkI/II cars had Coventry Climax engines and c.40 had Alexander tuning of the Austin engine, with a crossflow head.

The MkIII (83 made) from 1963, had mostly Ford 1500GT engines and a large air intake in the bonnet.

All these Turner cars were light with good handling and were highly successful on the race track.

During 1961, Jack Turner unveiled the Turner GT coupé which he had designed. It was Ford 1500cc powered and had a GRP body bonded to a steel floor and fabricated steel frame, but only 10 cars were made, plus one Alexander Turner GT. The company ceased trading in 1966 mainly due to the ill health of Jack Turner.

The Turner Register estimates that nearly half of the cars made survive today and over a third of these are in the US.

Left: **A Turner MkI with a Climax engine. About 160 MkI cars are thought to have been made, but no factory records exist from before mid-1960.**

Dates: 1949-54

Number Built: c.89?

Price Today: ££+

AC BUCKLAND TOURER
4/5-seater open tourer. 1991cc, 6-cyl engine. AC delivered rolling chassis to Buckland who added their own attractive body. MkI had straight door tops, more usual MkII had cutaway doors. About 45 cars survive.

Dates: 1953-55

Number Built: See text.

Prices Today:
FHC: ££+
DHC: £££+

ALVIS TC21/100
4-door sports saloon or 2-door DHC. 2993cc, 6-cyl engine. Often known as the "Grey Lady" and capable of a sprightly 100mph. Of the 727 TC21 cars made, not all made (or upgraded) to TC21/100 specification.

Dates: 1950-53

Number Built: c.4011

Price Today: ££

AUSTIN A40 SPORTS
Alloy body (steel bonnet) on chassis, 4-seater convertible. 1200cc, 50bhp. Interesting design by Eric Neale of Jensen, who built them for Austin. Top speed c.80mph; 0-60mph in c.25sec. Under 20 survive in the UK.

Dates: 1961-63

Number Built: c.90?

Price Today: £££

BRISTOL 407
4-seater luxury sports saloon. Chrysler 5130cc, V8, 250bhp claimed. Automatic. First of the Bristol cars with big North American V8 power and capable of 125mph. Looks similar to the 406 but with twin exhausts, twin electric cooling fans and many other subtle changes.

Dates: 1963-76

Number Built: ~500?

Price Today: £££

BRISTOL 408-411
4-seater luxury sports saloons. Chrysler 5130-6556cc, V8. All automatics. Model shown is 410 but others look broadly similar, with different side trims and 411 has different grille. The 411 is the most common model, with five Series (1968-76) and 6+ litre engines (140mph capability).

Dates: 1975-93

Number Built: NK

Price Today: Contact Club

BRISTOL 412/BEAUFIGHTER
4-seater convertible. Chrysler 6556-5899cc, V8. Automatic. New Zagato attractive clean-cut styling. Rear soft-top could be replaced with hardtop. The Beaufighter (above), made 1980-93, was turbocharged. It could do 150mph and reach 60mph in under 6 seconds. Rare.

Dates: 1976-82

Number Built: NK

Price Today: £££

BRISTOL 603
4-seater sports saloon. Chrysler 5900cc (Economy 5211cc until 1978), V8. Automatic. Better ground-clearance, slimmer pillars, more luxury.

Dates: 1982-94

Number Built: NK

Price Today: Contact Club

BRISTOL BRITANNIA/BRIGAND
4-seater sports saloon. Chrysler 5900cc, V8. Automatic. The Brigand was similar to the Britannia, but was turbocharged. Rare.

Dates: 1950-57

Number Built: <230

Price Today: Contact Club

DELLOW
Founded by Ken Delingpole and Ron Lowe, Dellow made these successful sports/trials 2-seaters, mostly with Ford 1172cc side-valve engines. Made in six Marks (mostly MkI/II). MkI shown here.

Dates: 1948-53

Number Built: 34

Price Today: Contact Club

FRAZER NASH LE MANS REPLICA
2-seater sports-racer. Bristol 1971cc, 6-cyl engine. Named after achieving 3rd place in 1949 Le Mans. MkII from 1952 had new parallel-tube frame. Note there are replicas of these desirable Replicas. Very expensive.

Dates: 1951-54

Number Built: 28

Price Today: Contact Club

HEALEY G SERIES
2-seat (bench) open sports. Alvis 2993cc, 6-cyl, 106bhp engine (though 3 cars have other engines). Intended as UK market version of the similar US-only Nash-Healey (which used larger Nash engines). Rare.

Dates: 1939-56

Number Built: 112

Price Today: Contact Club

HRG 1500
Founded in 1935 by Halford, Robins and Godfrey. The traditional 1500 with modified Singer 4-cyl ohc engine followed the earlier Meadows 4ED engine cars. There was also an 1100 (49 made to 1950). Desirable.

Dates: 1949-57

Number Built: 88

Price Today: Contact Club

JENSEN INTERCEPTOR
4-seater cabriolet, sports saloon and rare stylish sedanca. Austin 3993cc, 6-cyl, 130bhp engine. Car designed by Eric Neale. Capable of c.100mph.

Dates: 1983-92

Numbers Built:
Coupé: 170
Spyder: 119

Prices Today: ££/£££

MARCOS MANTULA & MANTULA SPYDER
2-seater coupé, and from 1985 in spyder form too. Rover 3528-3947cc, V8 engine. A lightly updated version of their attractive 1960s steel-chassis model (refer to page 94). A timeless and popular design.

Dates: 1958-62

Number Built: >300?

Price Today: £+

TORNADO TYPHOON
Good-looking 2 or 2+2-seater open sports, FHC or estate ("Sportsbrake"). Ford 933-1172cc side-valve engines. Kit cars. About 20 survive.

Dates: 1960-62

Number Built: c.10

Price Today: ££

TORNADO TEMPEST
2 or 2+2-seater open sports, FHC or estate ("Sportsbrake"). Ford 105E 997cc engine. Same body as Typhoon but different chassis. Sold complete in kit form. c.4 survive world-wide. Car shown has unique fastback.

167

INTRODUCTION

The purpose of this Guide is to help you get an indication of the general condition of a specific car, by checking it in a methodical manner. Informative tips will help guide you along the way. But there are limitations as to what any checklist can achieve as the only way to find out the exact condition of a vehicle would be to dismantle much of it!

Please note this Guide does not claim to be comprehensive, but it should help you to screen out cars that are best avoided and to narrow down your search to one or two likely cars. You can then bring in an expert to help you make a final choice.

To use this Guide will require some knowledge of what the main parts of a car are called, where they are located and, in general terms, their function. No test equipment is required, but it may help to have protective gloves, overalls, camera, torch, magnet and an old rug to lie on. Refer to the *Specific Checks* in this book for the model concerned. It will take at least 2 hours to go through the checklist, so you may choose to do it in two sessions; just stop if you realise a car is not for you. Do all the tests yourself, ie do not rely on the seller to do them for you!

IMPORTANT CAUTIONS

This Guide may not reveal any damage or fault that has been intentionally concealed, nor may it reveal the fitting of incorrect or substandard components. Also it may not show up any intermittent or incipient fault. You may also be unable to discover the condition of hidden chassis or body sections.

The Car Owner's Manual should be consulted for information specific to that type of car.

Before purchase, a professional engineer (with knowledge on that model) should check the vehicle.

Please note no responsibility for loss occasioned to any person acting or refraining from action as a result of material in this Guide can be accepted by the author or publisher.

CAR PARTICULARS (Complete this page on initial visit; following pages on subsequent visits).

Seller's Name:	Phone:
Seller's Email:	Mobile:
Seller's Address:	

Car Make/Model:	Year Registered:	Registration No.:
Body Identification No.:		Engine Size: cc
Chassis No. (if relevant):		Recorded Mileage:
Engine No.:		Vehicle Colour:
Tax Disc Expiry Date:	Historic (Tax Exempt)? Yes/No	MOT Expiry Date:

Extras (eg sunroof):

Recent Service History Summary:

Restoration Log Summary:

List major parts repaired/replaced recently:

Warranty (if any):	Asking Price: £

Notes:

Photos: With permission, take a full set (ie front and rear three-quarter views, both sides, engine bay, boot & interior).

Note 1: The author welcomes feedback and suggestions regarding this Checklist so that it can be improved in future editions. Please email or write to him.
Note 2: This Checklist can be purchased separately from Hingston Publishing. See our website (www.hingston-publishing.co.uk) for details.

PAPERWORK CHECKS	Tick Off	Your Notes
1 Check the seller's name and address is the same as that shown on the Registration Certificate.		
2 Check all the particulars on the Registration Certificate match the car (including the registration plates).		
3 Check the particulars on the windscreen tax disc match the car.		
4 Check the MoT details match the car.		
5 Check the details on a Heritage Certificate match the car (where a certificate is available).		

EXTERNAL CHECKS

General Bodywork Condition

6 Check paintwork (in daylight). Is it free from dents, stone chips, scratches or fading? Assess overall paint finish from Poor-to-Excellent. See Tip 1.

7 Check body for rust. Typical external rust areas are around headlights, under front bumper, back of front wings, rear wings, wheelarches, door bottoms and panel seams. (Further checks made later). See Tip 2.

8 Check sills for rust. Tap hard to see how solid they sound. Use magnet to detect filler. If sills are new, check they are not simply tacked or screwed on. Be wary of metal oversill trims that can hide rusty sills.

9 Check panel fit, especially gap between door and B-post on one side of car equals gap on other side. Do a similar check where rear of bonnet meets body. Unequal gaps may indicate accident or poor restoration. Note that the original fit may not have been good! See Tip 3.

10 Check for accident damage. For steel or aluminium bodywork, bend down and with your eye near the front wing, look along each side of the car. Are there any ripples in the bodywork? This is usually accident damage. For glassfibre bodies, see Tip 4.

11 Check for paint overspray on window rubbers, lights, bumpers, tyres or exhaust pipe. This may indicate accident or corrosion repair or a poor restoration.

12 Check the car sits evenly on level ground (as viewed from the front or rear). If not, it's not a good sign! It could be sagging springs or a serious structural issue.

External Trim (See Tip 5)

13 Check exterior mirror(s) and lights. Is water caught inside the lens of any light? Are any lenses cracked?

Tip 1. Paintwork. If this looks patchy or one panel is a slightly different shade, it usually indicates a partial respray - ask why? Hairline cracks might indicate poor preparation under the paint. A key question: Is a full respray needed (as that can be expensive)?

Tip 2. Corrosion. All cars with a steel body or chassis will suffer from corrosion, which can eventually become dangerous or expensive to repair. On a less serious level, advancing corrosion can look unsightly. The amount of corrosion should relate to the car's age. Less corrosion than expected indicates the car has been looked after, restored, maybe had rust concealed, or perhaps it has been imported from a drier climate. Note that where aluminium panels meet steel it can aggravate corrosion.

Tip 3. Body Panels. Note that rust, other marks or dents and paint finish variations may help confirm the originality of individual body panels.

Tip 4. Glassfibre Bodies. Many suffer from surface crazing which can be from minor bumps. This can be unsightly even if not structural. Removal requires grinding away the damage and replacing with glassfibre before respray - this takes skill. A very recent respray may conceal minor defects which will soon resurface.

Tip 5. Trim. These items can often be surprisingly expensive to repair or replace. Spare parts may not even be available.

EXTERNAL CHECKS (continued)	Tick Off	Your Notes

14 Check both number plates are correct, legal, fitted securely, clearly legible and not damaged.

15 Check the petrol cap opens/closes. Is it lockable?

16 Check the radio aerial extends/retracts. Leave it up.

17 Check soft-top (if applicable). With soft-top up, check fit and inspect fabric for tears and torn stitching. Check clarity of rear windows. Look inside for water marks. Check the soft-top folds down and goes up easily. Leave soft-top up for road test.

18 Check sunroof (if applicable). Ensure it opens and closes fully. Look around headlining for water marks.

Tyres, Wheels, Hubs & Shock-absorbers

19 Check each tyre and wheel in turn. (Note: The spare wheel is checked later at Check 29). If originality is important, are the wheels correct? See Tips 6, 7 & 8.

20 Check the shock-absorbers by pressing down each corner of the car in turn. On release the body should return to its rest position. Additional oscillations may indicate worn shock-absorbers.

Doors & Windows

21 Check all locks work (from inside too). Spare keys?

22 Check each door for ease of opening and closing, operation of interior courtesy light(s) and door stays. Especially on open top cars, doors that do not open/ close easily may indicate a collapsing chassis (or simply worn door hinges, if door drops when opened. Look for rust stains on A-posts due to rusty hinges).

23 Check each window opens & closes easily and fully.

24 Check windscreen is free from stone chips and cracks. Look also for delaminating (white marks). Replacement screens can be expensive.

Boot or Rear-hatch

25 Check lock works and boot/rear-hatch opens and closes easily. Check the boot lid prop/stay works.

26 Check boot light works (if fitted).

27 Check boot carpet condition. If wet it indicates a leak. Lift the carpet to check for corrosion underneath.

28 Check the car has a jack & wheelbrace. Toolkit too?

29 Check condition of spare wheel and tyre. Check for rust or water in the spare wheel well (if applicable).

Tip 6. Tyres. Check all tyres are the same type, are correctly inflated and are suitable for the car's wheels and performance. Then inspect each tyre for: tread depth around its circumference and across its width (the wear should be even); side-wall scuffs (from rubbing kerbs); cuts; missing tyre valve caps; bulges in sidewalls (may indicate possible dangerous internal damage – detect by running hand around the sidewall on both sides, as far as possible).
Caution: *Some of these faults are dangerous and illegal.*
If the car has been standing for some time, tyres can get flat spots causing vibration when driving.
Caution: *Tyre rubber degrades with time and can become unsafe.*

Tip 7. Wheels. Check the wheel rims for damage caused by kerbing or clumsy tyre fitting. Ensure all trim present. With alloy wheels be careful about corrosion and presence of cracks.
Caution: *Old alloy wheels have been known to break up when driving.*
If wire wheels are fitted, check each spoke for corrosion, breakage and tension.

Tip 8. Hubs. If possible, and with the owner's permission, jack up each wheel, one at a time.
Caution: *If jacking up a car, ensure it is on firm level ground and chock one wheel (front and behind). Never go under the car and never put your hand between the wheel and arch or ground where it might be trapped if the car fell off the jack.* Once a wheel is off the ground, try spinning it by hand. It should rotate easily (unless it has a drive shaft attached). A gravelly noise may indicate worn wheel bearings. Put hands near the top and bottom and try to rock the wheel, then do the same with your hands at each side of the wheel. No play should be perceptible. Removing a wheel may also permit inspection of brake discs, pads and splines, where applicable (see also Check 71). With splines, check for cleanliness and freedom from damage and wear.

INTERNAL CHECKS	Tick Off	Your Notes

Seats & Seat belts

30 Check each seat by examining it for wear, sagging, cuts and cleanliness. Look under each seat.

31 Sit on each seat. Check the front seats can move back /forward, recline and raise/lower (as applicable).

32 Check if proper (safety) head-restraints are fitted.

33 Check cleanliness and operation of all seat belts. Ensure belts are untwisted, mountings secure and the webbing is free from chaffing. If no seat belts are fitted, is the car legal (and is that safe?).

Vehicle Interior

34 Check condition of steering wheel. Is it original?

35 Check facia, dashboard top and instruments for cleanliness and that everything appears to be intact, undamaged, correct and secure. See Tips 9 & 10.

36 Check condition of all interior trim, including door trim and headlining, for wear, stains and tears.

37 Check operation of sun-visors (where fitted) and inspect the rear-view mirror for clarity and fixing.

38 Check glove compartment opens/closes properly. Check lock (if fitted) - important with soft-top cars.

39 Check under facia for dangling wires. See Tip 11.

40 Check the carpets for wear and cleanliness. If the carpet is wet or stained, where is the leak? Are there removable mats?

41 Check for floor-pan corrosion by lifting the carpet edges carefully (if possible). May need seller's OK.

42 Check pedal rubbers are not too worn (is the wear commensurate with the claimed condition?)

ENGINE COMPARTMENT CHECKS

43 Caution: First read Tip 12, then open bonnet. Check inner wings/bulkhead for corrosion (look under master cylinders and heater). Is bonnet prop/stay OK?

44 Check for tidiness and cleanliness. See Tip 13.

45 Check, if possible, visible condition of engine mounts.

46 Check for radiator and water pump leaks (look for green encrustation and possibly water). Check water hoses by squeezing and looking for cracking. The water hose connections should be secure and dry.

Tip 9. Interior Cleanliness. This is not only desirable, but can reveal how the car has been treated by previous owner(s). For instance, smokers may have stained the headlining or if pets have been in the car, they may have left hairs or scratched/chewed the trim.

Tip 10. Soft-Top Cars. Not surprisingly, the interiors of these cars can suffer from the elements. Wooden dashboards can de-laminate, soft trim deteriorates and carpets get wet and disintegrate. Check everything in an open cockpit very carefully.

Tip 11. Botched Electrics. Finding botched electrics is a common problem and dangling wires, non-original insulating tape and non-matching wiring are tell-tale signs. Botched electrics can lead to many problems and can be surprisingly difficult and time consuming to sort out. ***Caution:*** *Botched wiring can lead to a fire.*

Tip 12. Engine Compartment. When you first open the bonnet, don't touch anything. ***Caution:*** *Parts of a recently run engine such as the cooling system, exhaust manifold and exhaust can scald. Do not touch. Also keep clear of any electric cooling fan which may operate on some cars even with the engine switched off. Also avoid skin contact with the top of the battery due to likely presence of corrosive acid.*

Tip 13. Engine Compartment. The engine compartment should appear tidy (a good sign), eg any wiring should be neat. If the engine has been steam-cleaned it should look splendid, but all oil and water leaks will have been washed off and you must check again after the test drive. Some sellers apply a type of black paint to rubber hoses, ignition leads etc which might look good but obscures their real condition. Where the engine is covered in normal road dirt, be suspicious of an area such as the rocker cover which is cleaner, indicating work has been done there recently. Ask what work?

ENGINE COMPARTMENT CHECKS (continued)	Tick Off	Your Notes
47 Check coolant level (but do not remove the pressure cap unless the engine is cold). Try to assess the antifreeze concentration. See Tips 14 & 15.		
48 Check fan belt condition and other drive belts. Look for cracks on inside surface of belt. Belts shouldn't be too tight or too slack (refer to car's handbook).		
49 Check oil level. Also check there is no water contamination (droplets or a whitish emulsion) on dip stick or underside of oil filler cap, which may indicate a blown head gasket or cracked cylinder block.		
50 Check for oil leaks. Depending on type of engine, some small oil leaks may be usual but they will not normally result in oil patches on the road - look on the ground where the car is usually parked.		
51 Check brake & clutch fluid levels. Inspect hydraulic pipes in the engine bay for integrity. Check also for bodywork corrosion around the brake & clutch fluid reservoirs, since spilt hydraulic fluid can strip paint.		
52 Caution: First read important Tip 16. Check battery mounted securely and terminals clean.		
53 Check power steering fluid level (if applicable).		
54 Check condition of camshaft drive belts (if visible).		
55 Check for any fuel leaks by smell and fuel weeping from cracks in fuel lines or marks on carburettor sides. Caution: Fuel leaks can cause fires. **Now close the bonnet.**		

SYSTEM CHECKS

Steering

56 Check steering lock (where fitted) by turning the steering wheel until it locks. Insert key, turn (but don't start engine) and ensure the lock releases.		
57 Check play in steering by holding the steering wheel and looking at the front wheel. A very small wiggle of the steering wheel should cause the front wheel to move slightly. (Note: this check is mainly applicable to cars with rack and pinion steering).		
58 Check the steering column is secure by attempting to waggle it. It shouldn't move.		

Starting the Engine (First read Tips 17 & 18)

59 Check first the oil pressure and ignition warning lights work by switching on the ignition (but DON'T START the engine yet). If a light doesn't work, its bulb may have been removed to conceal a fault.		

Tip 14. Antifreeze. The antifreeze concentration in the engine coolant is crucial, particularly for engines with alloy heads or alloy blocks. This is due to the corrosion inhibitor included in antifreeze. Failure to use the correct amount of antifreeze can cause serious damage to an engine.

Tip 15. Engine Fluids. When checking engine fluids (ie coolant, oil and brakes) ensure that they are not only up to the correct levels but also that they look clean and smell fresh.

Tip 16. Battery Cautions. Battery acid is very dangerous. Avoid contact. Protect your eyes and skin.

Tip 17. Engine Start-Up. When you first start the engine you need to check several items almost simultaneously. First, the oil-pressure warning light should extinguish almost immediately and at the same time the oil-pressure gauge (if fitted) should swing up to its correct figure (see car's handbook). Second, the ignition warning light should extinguish immediately. Third, if the engine is cold, listen for a brief "knocking" or "rattling" sound on start-up which may indicate a worn engine. Be wary if the seller has warmed up the engine prior to your inspection.
Note: Difficulties in starting may be a BAD SIGN!

SYSTEM CHECKS (continued)	Tick Off	Your Notes
60 Check if choke required then start the engine. The starter motor should operate quietly, turn quickly and the engine should start first or second time.		
61 Check exhaust (Tips 18 & 19). Leave engine ON.		
Electrical Tests (First Read Tip 20)		
62 Check instruments for correct function and readings.		
63 Check horn, indicators and hazard flashers (where fitted). Ideally get someone to help you.		
64 Check headlights, headlight flasher, panel lights, front & rear lights and number plate lights.		
65 Check washers and wipers (at all wiper speeds) and check the blades don't wipe over the windscreen edge.		
66 Check heated rear window (if fitted) by switching on, then after a minute or so breathe gently on the elements inside the car to see if the moisture clears.		
67 Check demister/heater blower. A clattery fan may be caused by glass pieces from a broken windscreen trapped inside the ducts (often quite difficult to rectify).		
68 Check radio (if fitted) and listen for interference from the engine (with bonnet closed and wipers on). Glassfibre bodied cars can be problematic.		
69 Check the car's electrical system with an electrical load test - see Tip 21. At the end, switch OFF the engine.		
Brakes		
70 Check brake feel. Push brake pedal hard to floor. It should not move too far or feel "spongy". If it hardens after several pushes, the brakes may need "bleeding".		
71 Check condition of disc brakes (where fitted and visible through the wheel spokes). They should be shiny and smooth, not ridged, worn or cracked. Rust on the disc rim is common and usually not a problem.		
72 Check visible rigid and flexible brake pipe condition.		
UNDERSIDE CHECKS		
73 Caution: First read important Tip 22. Check for leaks under engine/gearbox. (Engine oil is normally dark whereas gearbox oil is normally clearer*).		
74 Check for rust, repairs or accident damage. Knock the main chassis members (or the box sections of a unitary car). If visible, check the fuel tank underside is not rusty (they also rust on top). See also Tip 23.		

*Consult car handbook for type of gearbox oil.

Tip 18. Exhaust Smoke. When you start the engine for the first time, look in the rear view mirror or get an assistant to observe the exhaust when you blip the throttle gently a few times. You may see steam (quite normal, especially in cold weather) but dark blue smoke could indicate a worn engine. With petrol engines, black smoke may indicate faulty carb adjustment (or a fuel injection problem).

Tip 19. Exhaust System. Listen for a noisy exhaust when you blip the accelerator (often caused by holes or missing silencer baffles) or an exhaust that "chuffs" on releasing the accelerator (usually due to leaks in the system or impending exhaust system failure).

Tip 20. GRP Cars. These often have earthing problems, usually caused by corroded earth connections. To test, switch each item on and off several times.

Tip 21. Electrical Load Test. Switch on the headlights, heated rear window, heater blower and any extra lights to provide a load on the electric system. Then with the engine turning at about 1000-1500 rpm (a fast idle if no rev counter is fitted), the ignition warning light should be out and the indicators should flash at their normal rate. If the warning light glimmers or the indicators flash slowly, there may be a fault in the generator or in the car's wiring, or the generator drive belt (fan belt) may be slack. An alternator (where fitted) should cope with a load test better.

Tip 22. Underside Safety. A good view of a car's underside requires proper ramps. If these are unavailable, instead lie beside the car on an old rug and view the underside with the aid of a torch. ***Caution:*** *Do not be tempted to go under a car when it is supported solely on a jack, as it may collapse or the car can run off the jack, crushing you underneath the car. This will seriously spoil your day!*

Tip 23. Underside Condition. Look for mud or fresh underseal which may be hiding corrosion or accident repairs. Look also for signs of new welding (scorch marks) or a crease in any box section (a sign of possible accident damage).

173

UNDERSIDE CHECKS (continued)	Tick Off	Your Notes
75 Check (as far as is practical) the suspension units, mountings and steering for wear, play and integrity.		
76 Check exhaust system for corrosion or damage. If COOL, waggle the silencer tail pipe to check the hangers - the tail pipe shouldn't move too much.		

THE TEST DRIVE

77 Caution: First read important Tip 24. Check you are fully insured and that the car is road legal, then START the engine and set off.		
78 Check the speedo works and its needle does not jerk.		
79 Check for general comfort and noise. See Tip 25.		
80 Check for suspension problems by listening for body rattles and suspension noises, especially when going over bumps at low speed. (Note: Scuttle shake can be a problem with many open-top models).		
81 Check temperature gauge (if fitted) is rising correctly. Also check the heater after the engine has run for 10 minutes. The air should be warm/hot. See Tip 26.		

Brakes

82 Caution: First read important Tip 27. Check brakes cautiously. If OK, try braking more firmly. The brakes should not pull car to one side or "snatch" and there should be no premature wheel lock up. IF BRAKES ARE NOT OK, END THE TEST DRIVE.		
83 Check brakes are not binding by depressing clutch at 5mph and, without braking, the car should continue to glide forward. See also Tip 28.		

Engine & Transmission

84 Caution: First read important Tip 29. Check engine performance by an acceleration run.		
85 Check for unusual noises and vibrations by driving at speed (assuming speed limits and conditions permit).		
86 Check clutch not worn or out of adjustment by ensuring the pedal releases correctly.		
87 Check handbrake by stopping on an incline. This will also test for clutch slip and judder when you start off - see Tip 30.		
88 Check gearbox/transmission by slipping the gearlever into neutral at about 40mph, then release the clutch pedal and listen for any unusual noises from the gearbox/transmission.		

Tip 24. Test Drive Caution: *Make sure you are fully insured to drive the car, and it is road legal. This is important! The test drive needs at least 10 miles of winding, bumpy roads and high-speed highway. To begin with just get used to the feel of the car.*

Tip 25. Soft-top Cars. Start with the roof up as you will hear mechanical noises better. But after Check 93, stop and lower the top so you can experience the car with the roof down.

Tip 26. Heater. If the heater does not give warm air within c.10min, this may be because the thermostat is faulty or has been removed to conceal an overheating problem.

Tip 27. Brake Test Caution: *Only try this test on a wide, straight road with no other road users or pedestrians around. Warn your passengers and check the rear view mirror before braking! If the road is slippery, don't do this test.*

Tip 28. Brakes. Brakes can seize on cars left unused. Squeaks while you drive might be the brakes (confirmed if a gentle dab on the brake pedal stops the noise). Squeals on braking are not unusual but may indicate the need for a mechanic to check. Shudders on braking may be more serious.

Tip 29. The Acceleration Run Caution: *If speed limits permit, the road is dry, clear of pedestrians and other road users and the brakes have tested satisfactorily, you might consider an acceleration run from 0 to 50mph to check the engine power output. A slow time could be due to an out-of-tune engine, binding brakes, a slipping clutch or other problems. Don't burn tyre rubber on takeoff and don't over-rev the engine.*

Tip 30. Clutch Slip or Judder. Stop the car on an upward slope with handbrake on. Engage 1st gear and release clutch slowly - the engine should stall. If it fades, the clutch may be slipping. Alternatively, accelerate up a hill in 3rd gear. If the revs rise without speed increase, suspect clutch slip. Clutch slip may also show up when accelerating. Clutch slip or judder is usually expensive to rectify.

THE TEST DRIVE (continued)	Tick Off	Your Notes

89 Check all gears (& reverse) select easily. Note 1st and reverse gears may "whine" but a "tinkling" sound might indicate a broken gear-tooth. Difficult changes may be due to worn synchromesh (where applicable). (Note: Some models need their gearbox oil to warm up before you get smooth changes). See also Tip 31.

With an automatic gearbox, ABS brakes, cruise control or overdrive - see Tip 32.

Steering Check & Final Tests

90 Check the wheels are balanced correctly. A strong vibration of the steering wheel at over 30-40mph may be due to unbalanced wheels. Ideally get the seller to rectify this problem as the fault could be more serious.

91 Check the steering wheel is correctly aligned (ie it looks straight when the car is on a straight road which has no camber). If not, ask why?

92 Check the car doesn't steer to one side. See Tip 33.

93 Check the radio etc, especially on favourite channels.

If applicable, now lower the soft-top roof.

94 Check for wind noise from an ill-fitting door or a side window, while travelling at speed.

95 Check the general handling and feel of the vehicle (eg rolling on corners). At low speed, check that on full lock the wheels do not catch the bodywork.

During the final 5 minutes of the test drive, apply the brakes as sparingly as safely possible to keep them cool. On parking, leave the engine running.

POST-DRIVE CHECKS

96 Check engine temp. and oil pressure - see Tip 34.

97 Check the exhaust for clues as to engine wear. Look behind and blip the accelerator. No heavy blue (oily) smoke should come from the exhaust.

98 Check for binding brakes or worn wheel bearings by testing the temperature of each tyre and hub with your hand. See Tip 35.

99 Check for anything unusual under the bonnet. Is there a smell of fuel? Listen for odd noises. The engine should idle evenly. Look for oil or water leaks. Close the bonnet.

100 Check the hot engine restarts easily by switching it off, waiting for a few minutes then trying to restart it again. Finally, switch OFF the engine and get out.
End of test. Well done!

Tip 31. Gearbox/Transmission. Try quick gear changes to test the synchromesh. With each gear, accelerate hard and take your foot off the accelerator suddenly. The gearlever should not jump out of gear. A dull, irregular knocking might indicate worn engine big-ends and a "clonk" from the rear might indicate wear in the rear axle, prop-shaft or universal joints.

Tip 32. Auto Box etc. Refer to the car's handbook for correct operation. Faults can be expensive, so check fully. With auto gearboxes, check gear changes are smooth, not snatchy and the kickdown is smooth. Try all gear positions manually. With a non-functioning overdrive, it might simply be a faulty solenoid.

Tip 33. Steering Check. On a straight, clear, uncambered road with nobody around, briefly release the steering wheel. Car should continue straight. Note that any camber will tend to steer the vehicle to that side.

Tip 34. Post-Drive Checks. The checks may show up a variety of expensive engine faults. The engine temperature should be normal (or just above normal on a hot day or after sitting in slow-moving traffic) and the oil pressure (on idle) should be as per the car's handbook. High water temperature may indicate a blown head gasket, faulty water pump or blocked radiator. Also, on raising the bonnet with the engine still running, there should be no steam and the engine should not smell hot. Low oil pressure is usually due to a worn engine. If no oil pressure gauge fitted, the low oil pressure warning light should not illuminate on a medium idle speed. If gauges are fitted but do not work, they may have been disconnected to conceal poor readings.

Tip 35. Wheels & Tyres. These should be cool-to-warm. If hot at the end of the test drive (and the brakes were not used heavily in the last 5 minutes), it may indicate binding brakes or worn wheel bearings. Note: with some cars the wheels can get hot from hot air from the engine compartment.

Introduction: The clubs are listed here alphabetically, by marque, then club. Some of the larger clubs employ staff and have offices manned during normal working hours, while other clubs are operated by volunteers from home. Hence the information given in this listing varies from club to club, reflecting (in most cases) what they asked us to print. Some clubs requested that only their email/website was published (so apologies to any reader without internet access).

Here is the usual disclaimer: Inclusion in this listing does not imply any recommendation or approval.

AC

AC Owners' Club
Contact: Eric Gates
8 Nether Way, Upper Poppleton, York YO26 6JQ
Tel: 01904 793563
Email: ericacoc@tiscali.co.uk
Website: www.racecar.co.uk/acoc

ALLARD

Allard Owners' Club
Captain: J. Tiller
Dart Vale, Laughton Road, Ringmer,
Lewes, E Sussex BN8 5NH
Tel: 01273 812568
Email: allard@dartvale.net
Website: www.allardownersclub.org

ALVIS

Alvis Owner Club
General Secretary: Nadine Fox
Graber House, 4 Field Lane, Normaby-by-Spital,
Market Rasen, Lincs LN8 2HB
Tel: 01673 878148
Email: gensec@alvisoc.org
Website: www.alvisoc.org

ARKLEY

Refer to **Midget & Sprite Club.**

ASTON MARTIN

Aston Martin Owners' Club
Club Secretary, Drayton St Leonard,
Wallingford, Oxfordshire OX10 7BG
Tel: 01865 400400
Fax: 01865 400200
Email: secretary@amoc.org
Website: www.amoc.org

AUSTIN

Austin Counties Car Club
Contact: Tony Eades
Sunnyside, 74 Blenheim Drive, Bredon,
Tewkesbury, Gloucestershire GL20 7QQ
Tel: 01684 773104
Website: www.AustinCounties.org.uk

AUSTIN-HEALEY

Austin-Healey Club
Contact: Colleen Holmes
4 Saxby Street, Leicester, Leicestershire LE2 0ND
Tel: 0116 254 411
Email: membership@austin-healey-club.com
Website: www.austin-healey-club.com

Healey Drivers' Club
Tel: 01392 276887
Email: billcummings@talktalk.net
Website: www.healeydriversclub.co.uk

Midget and Sprite Club
Secretary: Terry Horler
63 Littledean, Yate, Bristol BS37 8UQ
Tel: 01454 881770
Website: www.mgcars.org.uk/midgetspriteclub

BERKELEY

Berkeley Enthusiasts' Club
Contact: Mike Rounsville-Smith
41 Gorsewood Road, St Johns,
Woking, Surrey GU21 8UZ
Tel: 01483 475330
Email: becmembership@yahoo.co.uk
Website: www.berkeleyclub.co.uk

BOND

Bond Owners' Club
Tel/Fax: 0121 784 4626
Website: www.bondownersclub.co.uk
Note: The website has a link to the Triumph Sports Six Club, which includes Bonds as a Triumph derivative.

The Bug Club
Contact: Leslie Gore
Tel: 01293 426954
Email: lesliebondbug@blueyonder.co.uk

BRISTOL

Bristol Owners' Club
Membership Secretary: Ruth Atkinson
Tel: 01730 823921
Email: mem.sec@boc.net
Website: www.boc.net

BUCKLER

Buckler Cars Register
Chairman: Chris Johns
Forge Cottage, 9 Charlecote, Warwick, CV35 9EW
Tel: 01926 642555
Website: www.bucklercars.com

CATERHAM

Refer to **Lotus Seven Club.**

CLAN

Clan Owners' Club
Contact: James Spencer
32 Beaulieu Close, Banbury, Oxon OX16 4FQ
Tel: 01295 255539
Email: secretary@clanownersclub.com
Website: www.clanownersclub.com

DAIMLER

Daimler & Lanchester Owners' Club
Contact: Lionel Morris
108 Montpelier Avenue, Blackpool, Lancs FY2 9EH
Tel: 01253 352076
Email: V8boy1@aol.com
Website: www.dloc.org.uk

Daimler SP250 Owners' Club
Contact: Graham Frost
15 Broom Mead, Bexley Heath, Kent DA6 7NZ
Tel: 01322 522958

DAVRIAN

New Davrian Register
Co-ordinator: John Rawlins
4 Browns Lane, Uckfield, East Sussex TN22 1RS
Tel: 01825 763638
Email: NEW_DAV_REG@compuserve.com

DELLOW

Dellow Register
Secretary: David Haley
2 King Alfred Close, Pewsey, Wiltshire SN9 5AY
Website: www.dellowregister.co.uk

DeLOREAN

DeLorean Owners' Club
Contact: Dave Howarth
17 Merlewood Drive, Astley, Tyldesley,
Manchester M29 7PG
Website: www.deloreans.co.uk

ELVA

Elva Owners' Club
Contact: Roger Dunbar
Emails: elvadunbar@btinternet.com
        roger.dunbar@elva.com
Websites: www.elva.com or www.elvacourier.com

FAIRTHORPE

(Including ASHLEY, EB, FALCON, HISTORIC SPECIALS,
ROCHDALE, TORNADO and TURNER)
Fairthorpe Sports Car Club
Contact: Tony Hill
9 Lynhurst Crescent, Hillingdon, Middlesex UB10 9EF
Tel: 01895 256799
Email: anna.tony.fscc@tesco.net
Website: www.fairthorpescc.com

FRAZER NASH

Frazer Nash Car Club
Post-war Registrar: James Trigwell
Email: trigwell@ntlworld.com
Website: www.frazernash.co.uk

GILBERN

Gilbern Owners' Club
Membership Secretary: Stephen Arnold
6 Church Green Cottages, Great Wymondley,
Hitchin, Herts SG4 7HA
Tel: 01438 354710
Email: stephen.arnold@gilbernoc.co.uk
Website: www.gilbernoc.co.uk

GINETTA

Ginetta Owners' Club
Membership Secretary: Duncan Campbell
23 Thornton Avenue, Ashby, Scunthorpe DN16 2BA
Tel: 01724 352801
Email: membership@ginetta.org
Website: www.ginetta.org

GORDON-KEEBLE

Gordon-Keeble Owners' Club
Contact: David Yeomans
26 Burford Park Road,
Kings Norton, Birmingham B38 8PB
Tel: 0121 459 9587
Email: gkoc@yeomans26.freeserve.co.uk
Website: www.gordonkeeble.org.uk

HEALEY

Association of Healey Owners (AOHO)
Secretary: Roger Crouch
Slades Paddock, East Coker,
Nr Yeovil, Somerset BA22 9JY
Tel: 01935 863061
Email: roger_crouch@btinternet.com
Website: www.healeyowners.co.uk

Healey Drivers' Club
Tel: 01392 276887
Email: billcummings@talktalk.net
Website: www.healeydriversclub.co.uk

HILLMAN IMP & DERIVATIVES

The Imp Club
Email: membership@theimpclub.co.uk
Website: www.theimpclub.co.uk

HISTORIC SPECIALS

Historic Specials Register
Refer to Fairthorpe entry.

HRG

The HRG Association
Hon Sec: Peter Mitchell
Tel: 01243 582055
Email: hrgsec@pcmitchell.com

INNOCENTI

Refer to **Midget & Sprite Club.**

JAGUAR

Jaguar Drivers' Club Ltd
Jaguar House, 18 Stuart Street, Luton,
Bedfordshire LU1 2SL
Tel: 01582 419332
Fax: 01582 455412
Email: jaguar_drivers_club@lineone.net
Website: www.jaguardriver.co.uk

Jaguar Enthusiasts' Club Ltd
General Manager: Graham Searle
JEC, Abbeywood Office Park, Emma Chris Way,
Filton, Bristol BS34 7JU
Tel: 01179 698186
Fax: 01179 791863
Email: jechq@btopenworld.com
Website: www.jec.org.uk

Jaguar E-Type Club
PO Box 2, Tenbury Wells, Worcestershire WR15 8XX
Tel: 01584 781588
Email: info@e-typeclub.com
Website: www.e-typeclub.com

Jaguar XK Club
PO Box 2, Tenbury Wells, Worcestershire WR15 8XX
Tel: 01584 781588
Email: info@xkclub.com
Website: www.xkclub.com

JENSEN

Jensen Owners' Club
Membership Secretary: Keith Andrews
2 Westgate, Fullshaw Park, Wilmslow, Cheshire SK9 1QQ
Tel: 01625 525699
Email: join@joc.org.uk
Website: www.joc.org.uk

JOWETT

Jowett Car Club Ltd
Contact: Mary Young
15 Second Avenue, Chelmsford, Essex CM1 4ET
Tel: 01245 256944
Website: www.jowett.org

Jupiter Owners' Auto Club
Membership Secretary: Mrs J Kennedy
Rivermead, Red Rail, Hoarwithy, Hereford HR2 6QS
Tel: 01432 840347
Email: davehkennedy@wyenet.co.uk
Website: www.jowettjupiter.co.uk

LEA-FRANCIS

Lea-Francis Owners' Club
Contact: Robin Sawers
French's, Long Wittenham, Abingdon, Oxon OX14 4QQ
Tel: 01865 407515 (General)
Tel: 01933 226806 (Membership)
Email: secretary@lfoc.org
Website: www.lfoc.org

LENHAM

Refer to **Midget & Sprite Club.**

LOTUS

Club Elite Mk14 Ltd
Secretary: David Pawson
c/o James's Place, Pound Bank, Far Forest,
Kidderminster, Worcs. DY14 9DG
Tel: 01299 266790 or 07774 226952
Email: davidpawson@emtelle.com

Club Lotus
58 Malthouse Court, Dereham, Norfolk, NR20 4UA
Tel: 01362 691144 or 01362 694459
Fax: 01362 695522
Email: alan@clublotus.co.uk
Website: www.clublotus.co.uk

Historic Lotus Register
Chairman: Mike Marsden
Email: mikemarsden@waitrose.com
Secretary: John Watson
Email: JWW@OneTel.com
Website: www.historiclotusregister.co.uk

Lotus Drivers' Club
PO Box 638, Worcester, WR6 6WY
Website: www.lotusdriversclub.org

Lotus Seven Club
Tel: 07000 572582 (L7CLUB)
Emails: chairman@lotus7club.com
        gensec@lotus7club.com
        memsec@lotus7club.com
Website: www.lotussevenclub.com

MARCOS

Club Marcos International
Contact: Isobel Chivers
26 Blackberry Close, Chippenham, Wilts SN14 6RG
Tel: 01249 464795
Email: info@clubmarcos.net
Website: www.clubmarcos.org.uk

Marcos Owners' Club
Chairman: Roger Young
14 Node Hill, Studley, Warwickshire B80 7RR
Tel: 01527 854407
Membership: Phil Mugford
Ebony, Gorsewood Road, Hartley, Kent DA3 7DH
Email: phil.mugford@btinternet.com
Website: www.marcos-oc.com

Mini Marcos Owners' Club (including Mini Jem)
Membership: Melanie Garland
General enquiries: Roger Garland
28 Meadow Road, Claines, Worcester WR3 7PP
Tel: 01905 458533
Email: info@minimarcos.org.uk
Website: www.minimarcos.org.uk

MG

MG Car Club
Kimber House, PO Box 251, Abingdon, Oxon OX14 1FF
Tel: 01235 555552
Fax: 01235 533755
Email: mgcc@mgcc.co.uk
Website: www.mgcc.co.uk

MG Octagon Car Club
Unit 1-3, Parchfields Enterprise Park, Parchfields Farm,
Colton Road, Rugeley, Staffs WS15 3HB
Tel: 01889 574666
Fax: 01889 574555
Email: info@mgoctagoncarclub.com
Website: www.mgoctagoncarclub.com

MG Owners' Club
Octagon House, 1 Over Road,
Swavesey, Cambridgeshire CB24 4QZ
Tel: 01954 231125
Fax: 01954 232106
Email: mginfo@mgownersclub.co.uk
Website: www.mgownersclub.co.uk

Midget and Sprite Club
Secretary: Terry Horler
63 Littledean, Yate, Bristol BS37 8U
Tel: 01454 881770
Website: www.mgcars.org.uk/midgetspriteclub

V8 Register – Refer to MG Car Club.

MINI JEM

Refer to **Mini Marcos Owners' Club.**

MORGAN

Morgan Sports Car Club
Membership Secretary
7 Woodland Grove, Dudley, W. Midlands DY3 2XB
Email: membership@mscc.uk.com
Website: www.mscc.uk.com

PANTHER

Panther Car Club
Membership Secretary
Email: membership@panthercarclub.com
Website: www.panthercarclub.com

Panther Enthusiasts' Club
Contact: George Newell
Tel: 01252 540217
Email: George@Pantherclub.co.uk
Website: www.pantherclub.co.uk

PEERLESS & WARWICK

Peerless and Warwick Owners' Register
Registrar: Nigel Cluley
Tel: 07803 201600
Website: www.peerless-gt.co.uk

PIPER

The Piper Sports & Racing Car Club
Contact: Barry Miller
The Piper Club, PO Box 55, Bourne PE10 9FX
Email: contact@thepiperclub.org.uk
Website: www.thepiperclub.org.uk

RELIANT

Reliant Sabre & Scimitar Owners' Club
Email: chairman@rssoc.co.uk
Website: www.scimitarweb.com

RILEY

The Riley RM Club
Enrolment Secretary: Mrs Jacque Morris
Y Fachell, Ruthin Road, Gwernymynydd, Mold, CH7 5LQ
Tel: 01352 700427
Website: www.rileyrmclub.org.uk

ROCHDALE

Rochdale Owners' Club
Chairman: Roger Coupe
Tel: 01606 889384
Secretary: Roger Drinkwater
Tel: 01380 871332
Email: roger@sallesdebains.wanadoo.co.uk
Website: www.rochdale-owners-club.co.uk

SINGER

Association of Singer Car Owners
Secretary: Barry Paine
3 The Close, School Lane, Little Melton, Norfolk NR9 3AE
Tel: 01603 810598
Email: SecretaryASCO@aol.com
Roadster Contact: Bill Haverly
Email: spullen3@aol.com
Website: www.asco.org.uk

Singer Owners' Club
Secretary: Martyn Wray
11 Ermine Rise, Great Casterton,
Stamford, Lincs PE9 4AJ
Tel: 01780 762740
Email: martyn@singeroc.free-online.co.uk
Website: www.singerownersclub.co.uk

SUNBEAM

Sunbeam Alpine Owners' Club
Membership Secretary: Simon Edwards
Tel: 01376 342025
Website: www.sunbeamalpineownersclub.co.uk

SUNBEAM (Continued)

Sunbeam Talbot Alpine Register (STAR)
Chairman: John Badger
Email: john_badger@btinternet.com
Website: www.stardust.uk.com

Sunbeam Tiger Owners' Club
Membership Secretary: Brian Postle
Beechwood, 8 Villa Real Estate,
Consett, Co. Durham DH8 6BJ
Tel: 01207 508296
Email: stoc@sunbeamtiger.co.uk
Website: www.sunbeamtiger.co.uk

SWALLOW

Swallow Doretti Register
Email: info@doretti.co.uk
Website: www.doretti.co.uk

TORNADO

Tornado Register
(Also refer to Fairthorpe entry).
Registrar: Dave Malins
31 Blandford Ave., Luton, Beds. LU2 7AY
Tel: 01582 495351
Email: TornadoRegistrar@aol.com
Website: www.astruc.s.easynet.co.uk/tornado_register

TRIDENT

Trident Car Club
23 Matlock Crescent, Sutton, Surrey SM3 9SS
Tel: 020 8644 9029
Email: trident.carclub@virgin.net
Website: www.tridentcarclub.fsnet.co.uk

TRIUMPH

Club Triumph
Membership Secretaries: John and Bridget Snook
Tel: 01425 274193
Email: enquiries@club.triumph.org.uk
Website: www.club.triumph.org.uk

Stag Owners' Club
Membership Secretaries: Marilyn and Peter Robinson
The Old Rectory, Aslacton, Norfolk NR15 2JN
Tel: 01379 677735
Fax: 01379 677363
Email: membership@stag.uk.net
Website: www.stag.org.uk

The Grinnall Register
(Converted TR7/8)
1 Kipling Close, Thatcham, Berks RG18 3AY
Email: Registrar@grinnall-register.co.uk
Website: www.grinnall-register.fotopic.net

TR Drivers' Club
Chairman: Kevin Morton
Tel: 01562 825000
Email: trdriver@btinternet.com
Website: www.trdrivers.com

TR Register (TR Owners' Club Ltd)
General Manager: Chris Cunnington
Unit 1B, Hawksworth, Southmead Industrial Park,
Didcot, Oxon OX11 7HR
Tel: 01235 818866
Fax: 01235 818867
Email: office@tr-register.co.uk
Website: www.tr-register.co.uk

Triumph Roadster Club
Contact: Robert Fitsall
11 The Park, Carshalton, Surrey SM5 3BY
Tel: 020 8669 3965
Email: info@triumphroadster.org.uk
Website: www.triumphroadster.org.uk

Triumph Sports Six Club
General Manager: Nigel Clark
Sunderland Court, Main Street, Lubenham,
Market Harborough, Leicestershire LE16 9TF
Tel: 01858 434424
Fax: 01858 431936
Email: info@tssc.org.uk
Website: www.tssc.org.uk

Triumph Stag Enthusiasts
President: Andy Hedley
Email: andy.hedley@btinternet.com
Website: www.brmmbrmm.com/trstagenth

Triumph Stag Register
Chairman: Mike Wattam
12 Holly Lodge, Lindsey Road, Poole, Dorset BH13 6BQ
Tel: 01202 761051
Website: www.tristagreg.org

TURNER

The Turner Register
(Also refer to Fairthorpe entry).
Contact: Russell Filby
5 Claremont Gardens, Nailsea,
North Somerset BS48 2HY
Tel: 01275 791569
Email: turnersportscars@blueyonder.co.uk
Website: www.turnersportscars.co.uk

TVR

TVR Car Club Ltd
Suite 5, Nova House, Audley Avenue,
Enterprise Park, Newport, Shropshire TF10 7DW
Tel: 01952 822126
Fax: 01952 822127
Email: office@tvrcc.com
Website: www.tvrcc.com

WARWICK

Refer to **Peerless and Warwick Owners' Register**.

Aston Martin Heritage Trust
Drayton St Leonard, Wallingford,
Oxfordshire OX10 7BG
Tel: 01865 400414
Fax: 01865 400200
Email: secretary@amheritrust.org
Website: www.amheritrust.org

British Motor Industry Heritage Trust
Heritage Motor Centre, Banbury Road, Gaydon,
Warwickshire CV35 0BJ
Tel: 01926 645085 (Archives: 01926 645076)
Email: hmcarch@heritage-motor-centre.co.uk
Website: www.heritage-motor-centre.co.uk

Jaguar Daimler Heritage Trust Archives
Browns Lane, Allesley, Coventry CV5 9DR
Tel: 02476 202141
Email: jagtrust@jaguar.com
Website: www.jdht.com

Rootes Archive Centre Trust
New Devonshire House, Westcott Venture Park,
Aylesbury, Bucks HP18 0XB
Website: www.rootesarchivecentre.com

National Motor Museum Trust
Beaulieu Enterprises Ltd, John Montagu Building,
Beaulieu, Brockenhurst, Hampshire SO42 7ZN
Tel: 01590 614650
Fax: 01590 612655
Email: nmmt@beaulieu.co.uk
Website: www.beaulieu.co.uk/motormuseum

DVLA (Driver and Vehicle Licensing Agency)
Longview Road, Swansea SA6 7JL
Tel: 01792 782341
Website: www.dvla.gov.uk

Below: **The spirit of sports car motoring (MG Midget on the Mynydd Eppynt ranges, Wales).**

All photos are referenced by page number and position letter.

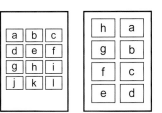

Cover & Page 1   **Inside Pages**   **Rear Cover**

Key:
AMHT: Aston Martin Heritage Trust.
BMIHT: British Motor Industry Heritage Trust.
BOC/BMIHT: Supplied by the Bond Owners' Club,
           reproduced with kind permission of BMIHT.
JR: Jerry Ree at www.magpiemicros.co.uk
PG: Philip Gundy.
PH: Peter Hingston (the Author).
PH/BMIHT: Peter Hingston (photos now in the BMIHT archives).
RM: Richard Monk of the MG Owners' Club.

Covers:
Front: (a,c,d,f-k,) PH; (b,e,l) PG.
Rear: (a-d,h) PH; (e,f) PG; (g) Photo by Michel Zumbrum (copyright Andre Wallimann); (i) Colin Valentine.

Title Page (Page 1): (a,c-i,k) PH; (b) PG; (j) Paul Sinnott; (l) BMIHT.

Inside Pages:
Page 7 Graham Murrell. **Page 8**(a,e) PH; (c) PG. **Page 9**(d) PH; (f) British Leyland. **Page 11** PH. **Page 12** PH. **Page 13** PH. **Page 16**(a-d) PH. **Page 17**(a,b,e) PH. **Page 18**(a,d) PH. **Page 19**(a,d) Ford Motor Co.; (b,c,e) PH. **Page 20**(a,b) PH; (g) Linzi Smart; (h) Graham Murrell. **Page 21**(a-d) PH. **Page 22**(a-c) PH; (d) Jim Tiller. **Page 23**(a-d) and **Page 24**(a,c) reproduced by permission of Earley Engineering Ltd, Alvis Specialists of Abergavenny, UK. **Page 24**(b) PG; (d) PH. **Page 25**(a,c,) AMHT; (d) PH. **Page 26**(a,b) PH; (d) AMHT. **Page 27**(a,b,c,e) AMHT; (d) PH. **Page 28**(a,b) PH; (d) AMHT. **Page 29**(a,b,d) AMHT. **Page 30**(a,b) AMHT; (d) PG. **Page 31**(a,b,d) PH. **Page 32**(a,d) BMIHT; (b) PH. **Page 33**(a) PH; (b,c,e) AMHT; (d) BMIHT. **Page 34**(a) BMIHT; (d) PH. **Page 35**(a) PH; (b-d) BMIHT; (e) AMHT. **Page 36**(a) BMIHT; (d) PH. **Page 37**(a-d) PH. **Page 38**(a-d) PH; (e) PG. **Page 39**(a,d) PH. **Page 40**(a,b,d) BMIHT. **Page 41**(a,c) BMIHT; (b) Stuart Watson; (d) PH. **Page 42**(a) BOC/BMIHT; (b-d) PH. **Page 43**(a,b) PH; (c,d) BOC/BMIHT. **Page 44**(a,c,d) BOC/BMIHT; (b) PH. **Page 45**(a,c,e) PH; (b,d) BOC/BMIHT. **Page 46**(a-c) Ashley James; (d) PH. **Page 47**(a-c) PH; (d) Bristol Owners' Club. **Page 48**(a,b,d) PH; (c) Bristol Owners' Club. **Page 49**(a,d) PH. **Page 50**(a) Caterham Cars; (c,d) Nigel Riches. **Page 51**(a-c) PH; (d) Clan Owners' Club. **Page 52**(a) David Nancekievill; (b,d) Chris Dalton. **Page 53**(a-c) PH; (d) David Nancekievill; (e) Chris Dalton. **Page 54**(a,d) PH. **Page 55**(a,b) PH; (d) Jim Henderson AMPA. **Page 56**(a,b) Charles Armstrong-Wilson; (g,h) Fred Talmadge. **Page 57**(a,c,d) PH. **Page 58**(a,b) PH; (d) Gilbern Owners' Club. **Page 59**(a-d) PH. **Page 60**(a,c,d) PH. **Page 61**(a,c,d) PH. **Page 62**(a,b,g,h) PH. **Page 63**(a,d) BMIHT. **Page 64**(a,c,d,e) PH; (b) BMIHT. **Page 65**(a) BMIHT; (b,d) PH; (c) PG. **Page 66**(a-e) PH. **Page 67**(a,d) PG; (b,c,e) PH. **Page 68**(a) BMIHT; (b) Roger Whalley; (c,d) PH. **Page 69**(a,b) BMIHT; (c,e) Roger Whalley; (d) Norman Hicks. **Page 70**(a,c) Nic Cooper Photographer; (d) Jensen Owners' Club. **Page 71**(a,d) Nic Cooper Photographer; (b,c) PH. **Page 72**(a,d) PH; (b) Nic Cooper Photographer. **Page 73**(a,b) PH; (c,d) Nic Cooper Photographer. **Page 74**(a-d) Nic Cooper Photographer. **Page 75**(a,b) PH; (c,d) Nic Cooper Photographer. **Page 76**(a) PH; (b-e) Nic Cooper Photographer. **Page 77**(a,d) PG; (c) PH. **Page 78**(a,c) PH; (d) A.E.Burch via Historic Lotus Register. **Page 79**(a) Ferret Fotographics; (d) PG. **Page 80**(a,b,d) PH; (c) Ferret Fotographics; (e) PG. **Page 81**(a,c) PH; (d) Ferret Fotographics. **Page 82**(a,b,d) PH. **Page 83**(a-d) PH. **Page 84**(a,b,d) PH. **Page 85**(a,b,d) PH; (c) PG; (e) Martin Ricketts. **Page 86**(a,b,d) PH. **Page 87**(a-d) PH; (e) Lotus Cars. **Page 88**(a) Mike Stripe; (b,d) PH. **Page 89**(a,b,d) Mike Stripe; (c) PH. **Page 90**(a) Lotus Cars; (b,c) Malcolm Cowle; (d) PG. **Page 91**(a-c) PH; (d) Kate Ramsden; (e) Malcolm Cowle. **Page 92**(a,c,d) PH; (b) Ferret Fotographics. **Page 93**(a) Ferret Fotographics; (b,c) PH; (d) Lotus Cars. **Page 94**(a-d) PH. **Page 95**(a,h) Ferret Fotographics; (b,g) PH. **Page 96**(a) PH; (b,c) RM; (d) Stewart Penfound. **Page 97**(a,d,e) RM; (b) PH. **Page 98**(a) MG Car Club; (b) BMIHT; (d) RM. **Page 99**(a-c) PH; (d) BMIHT. **Page 100**(a,b) RM; (d) BMIHT. **Page 101**(a,b) BMIHT; (d) PH. **Page 102**(a) PH; (b) BMIHT; (c,d) PH/BMIHT. **Page 103**(a) Brian Pamment; (b) PH; (d) BMIHT. **Page 104**(a,b) PH; (d) RM. **Page 105**(a,b) BMIHT; (d) PH/BMIHT. **Page 106**(a) PH/BMIHT; (b,c) PH; (d) BMIHT; (e) RM. **Page 107**(a,d) RM. **Page 108**(a,b) BMIHT; (c) Barrie Sharples; (d) PG. **Page 109**(a) RM; (d) PH. **Page 110**(a,d) PH; (b,c) BMIHT. **Page 111**(a) PG; (d) PH. **Page 112**(a,b) PG; (c,d) PH. **Page 113**(a-e) PH. **Page 114**(a) Ferret Fotographics; (d) PH. **Page 115**(a-e) PH. **Page 116**(a) Panther Car Club; (c,d) PH. **Page 117**(a) Panther Car Club; (c,d) PH. **Page 118**(a,c,d) PH. **Page 119**(a-d) JR. **Page 120**(a,c,d) JR. **Page 121**(a) PH; (d) JR. **Page 122**(a-d) JR; (e) PH. **Page 123**(a,c,d) JR. **Page 124**(a,b) PH; (g,h) PG. **Page 125**(a) PG; (d) PH. **Page 126**(a) Derek Hewitson; (b,c,e) PH; (d) Simon Edwards. **Page 127**(a) Sunbeam Tiger Owners' Club; (b,c) PH; (d) Graham Vickery (Sunbeam Tiger Owners' Club). **Page 128**(a,b) PH; (c) National Motor Museum/MPL; (d) Graham Vickery (Sunbeam Tiger Owners' Club). **Page 129**(a,b) PH; (d) BMIHT. **Page 130**(a,d) PH; (b,c) BMIHT. **Page 131**(a,d) PH; (b) BMIHT. **Page 132**(a,b,d) PH; (c) BMIHT. **Page 133**(a,b,d) PH. **Page 134**(a,d) BMIHT; (b,c) PH. **Page 135**(a,b,d) PH. **Page 136**(a) PH; (b-d) BMIHT. **Page 137**(a) BMIHT; (b) Derek Graham (TR Register); (d) PH. **Page 138**(a,b,d) PH; (c) BMIHT. **Page 139**(a-c) PH; (d) Phil Horsley (Grinnall Register). **Page 140**(a-d) PH. **Page 141**(a,c,d) BMIHT. **Page 142**(a,b,d) BMIHT. **Page 143**(a) PG; (b) BMIHT; (c,d) PH. **Page 144**(a-d) BMIHT. **Page 145**(a,b) PH; (d) BMIHT. **Page 146**(a-c) PH; (d) BMIHT. **Page 147**(a-c) PH; (d) BMIHT. **Page 148**(a,c) BMIHT; (b,d,e) PH. **Page 149**(a) Ralph Dodds (TVR Car Club); (d) Ferret Fotographics. **Page 150**(a) PH; (d) Ferret Fotographics. **Page 151**(a) PG; (c,d) PH. **Page 152**(a,d) PH. **Page 153**(a,d) Joan Marsh; (b,c,e) PH. **Page 154**(a,d) PH. **Page 155**(a,b,d) Ralph Dodds (TVR Car Club); (c) PH. **Page 156**(a,f) PH; (c) Berkeley Enthusiasts' Club. **Page 157**(a) Dave Bosworth; (d,h) PH; (f) Berkeley Enthusiasts' Club. **Page 158**(a,g,h) PH; (d) Davrian Developments Ltd; (f) Charles Armstrong-Wilson. **Page 159**(a) PH; (c) David Matthews of World Wide Austin-Healeys; (e) Paul Marshall; (h) Charles Giles. **Page 160**(a,d,e,h) PH. **Page 161**(a) Ferret Fotographics; (c,f,h) PH. **Page 162**(a) BMIHT; (d) Gwyn Morris; (f,h) PH. **Page 163**(a,d,f,h) PH. **Page 164**(a,d) PG; (e,h) David Rowlinson. **Page 165**(a) Russell Filby (Turner Register); (d,f,h) PH. **Page 166**(a-d) PH; (e) Bristol Owners' Club; (f) PG; (g) David Culshaw; (h) Mike Smith. **Page 167**(a) Nic Cooper Photographer; (b,d) PH; (c) Roberto Vespa; (e) Peter Mitchell; (f) Peter Galea, from David Culshaw; (g) James Trigwell; (h) Dellow Register. **Page 181** PG. **Page 183**(b) PG; (c,h) PH. **Page 184** Nic Cooper Photographer.

About the Author, Peter Hingston

The XR-GT. This one-off design by the author was built with the assistance of Neale Woolfall, Peter Bevan and the late Terry Harker. Seen here for the first time in public at a car show near Edinburgh in 1996.

The author first became interested in sports cars while studying GRP during his engineering course at university (where all he could afford was a Heinkel bubble car). Later, on joining the RAF he found many like-minded sports car enthusiasts. He owned a succession of sports cars and began to earn a reputation as a source of information such that airmen from other bases would phone him for advice on buying a sports car. In 1978 he wrote and published a small booklet, "Guide to Buying A Used Sports Car". It was a modest effort but written enthusiastically and it was well received. A quarter of a century later, he decided it was time to write a sequel and hence this new book.

After leaving the RAF, Peter Hingston spent a short time in the motor trade and was an early contributor to the UK's first magazine devoted entirely to specialist sports cars (titled *Alternative Cars*). Some of his photos have also been published in other car magazines and he was one of the last officially sanctioned photographers to be let loose at the MG car plant at Abingdon before it closed. He has recently donated those photos to the British Motor Industry Heritage Trust.

The author has had a great deal of pleasure from owning six sports cars (a Mini Jem, Piper P2, Triumph GT6 Mk3, Clan Crusader, MG Midget MkIII and a Triumph TR7). His current project car is a one-off with retro styling that he designed in the mid 1990s, based on a Ford XR2.

Today, Peter Hingston is well known as an author of books on small business, having sold over 500,000 of his books, in many languages, world-wide.

About Philip Gundy

Philip sitting in his Lotus 7 replica, which he built from a kit in 1988-89.

Philip's MGB Roadster which he restored in 2004-06.

Since the late 1960s Philip Gundy has been an avid enthusiast of all things relating to cars and motorsport. This has included restoring and owning a Morris 1000, building a Lotus 7 replica kit car and restoring an MGB Roadster. His MGB restoration was done during 2004-2006 and involved taking it back to bare metal then rebuilding it with care, making a number of improvements to the brakes, suspension and electrical system. Philip's trade as a precision toolmaker has been invaluable in the preparation and restoration of his cars. His day job has involved machining aerospace parts (including items for Concorde).

He has been an active member in several car clubs, organising events and taking part in circuit racing and rallying.

Over many years, Philip has collected a large archive of interesting literature on classic and sports cars, which he made available to the author. Fortuitously they met several years ago (at a classic car event) when this book was in its early stages. Thus Philip was in time to make a significant and invaluable contribution to the creation, research and compilation of this book.

Rear Cover photos (left to right): Panther Lima S2, Swallow Doretti, Sunbeam Alpine SIII; Triumph Stag, Singer SM Roadster (4AD), Triumph Roadster; Lea-Francis 2½-Litre Sports, Bond Equipe GT, Ginetta G15.

Early Jensen Interceptor by Nic Cooper Photographer.